THE SOFT CAGE

ALSO BY CHRISTIAN PARENTI

LOCKDOWN AMERICA:
POLICE AND PRISONS IN THE AGE OF CRISIS

THE SOFT CAGE

SURVEILLANCE IN AMERICA

FROM SLAVERY TO THE WAR ON TERROR

CHRISTIAN PARENTI

A Member of the Perseus Books Group

Published by Basic Books,
A Member of the Perseus Books Group

Designed by Reginald R. Thompson

Library of Congress Cataloging-in-Publication Data

Parenti, Christian.
The soft cage : surveillance in America from slavery to the war on terror / Christian Parenti.
p. cm.
Includes bibliographical references.
ISBN 0-465-05485-4
1. Social control—United States—History. 2. Electronic surveillance—Social aspects—United States. 3. Political culture—United States. 4. Privacy, Right of--United States. 5. War on Terrorism, 2001 I. Title.

HN57.P35 2003
303.3'3'0973—dc21
2003013330

For my aunt Jeanne Mahon
and
my friends

Everywhere the state acquires more and more direct control over the humblest members of the community and a more exclusive power of governing each of them in his smallest concerns. This gradual weakening of the individual in relation to society at large may be traced to a thousand things.

—Alexis de Tocqueville, 1835

CONTENTS

CONTENTS

ACKNOWLEDGMENTS

Many thanks to Rachael Rakes and Dave Kracke, who helped research early sections of this book. Thanks also to Steve Hiatt, who helped make the book readable. I appreciate the hard work of many people at Basic Books, some of whom I will probably never even meet. For crucial, just-in-time editorial comments, my appreciation goes out to Christopher D. Cook and Theodore Hamm. My comrade Heather Rogers also took a scalpel to the manuscript when needed and helped me at every stage; without her this project would have long ago bogged down in the thickets of frustration that inevitably plague a seriously dyslexic author.

More generally, thanks to Sheila Tully, John Marshall, Williams Cole, Liza Featherstone, Doug Henwood, Josh Mason, Colin Robinson, Garrett Scott, Peter Plate, Eric Drooker, Jose Palafox, Jeff Derksen, Rose Braz, Scott Fleming, Cindi Katz, Omar Dahbour, David Reid, my mother Susan and my father Michael, and numerous others who gave me sources, ideas, and advice. I could not have written this book without generous support from the Soros Foundation/Open Society Institute's Center on Crime and Communities. Both the Blue Mountain Center and Mesa Refuge gave me time, space, and clean air to work and play in. Also a very deep thanks to Neil Smith for his friendship and for giving me an intellectual home at the CUNY Graduate School's Center for Place, Culture, and Politics when I moved to New York. I am very indebted to Adolph Reed Jr., Ron Takaki, and Mike Davis, all of whom have inspired and educated me and who wrote letters on my behalf. Betsy Reed and Katrina vanden Heuvel helped me to work out ideas when portions of this book first appeared as articles in the *Nation*. I borrowed the last lines of the book from an interview on garbage with the eloquent and generous Dick Walker. My old friend Jan Chelminski kindly helped with the illustrations. Finally, hats off to all the librarians who—more than just providing services and information—preserve an alternative social logic: in a cultural landscape marked by venality, price tags, and egotism, librarians steward oases of generosity, free sharing, and collaboration.

1

LIFE IN THE GLASS BOX

First thing when I wake up and
Right before I close my eyes at night
I think, sense, feel man like
I'm under some kind of microscope
Satellites over my head, transmitters in my dollas
Hawkin', watchin', scopin', jockin'
Scrutinizin' me, checkin' to see what I'm doin'
Where I be, who I see, how and where and with whom I make my money
What is this?
Excuse me Miss
May I have your phone number and your social security?
Who me? When all I came to do is buy my double or triple A batteries?
Please, I decline

—Jill Scott, "Watching Me"

The future is already here. Over the last three decades the prevalence of routine, everyday surveillance has increased to sci-fi proportions. Thanks to the proliferation of computers, databanks, and networks, once distinct spaces of knowledge—credit records here, medical records there, criminal records elsewhere—now form a single, coherent informational landscape that is easily mapped and controlled by government and business.[1] Everywhere, one leaves a trail of digital information; all daily tasks—working, driving, shopping, tending to health—now create retrievable records.

Consider this: More than 111 million Americans carry mobile phones, each of which creates a rough electronic account of the user's location in time and space. Cell phones communicate with networks of transmission points that monitor and note a phone's location whenever it is on. These records, stored by phone companies, can be subpoenaed when needed or their aggregate patterns can be "data-mined" for commercial uses. And now, in the age of terror and permanent emergency, the federal government has ordered wireless carriers to create systems for tracking mobile phones in real time. As a result, the latest wireless communications devices often contain built-in Global Positioning System (GPS) chips that transmit the gadget's geographic coordinates to twenty-four Pentagon-maintained satellites, tracking users as they move. The resulting records can be archived, aggregated, disaggregated, and correlated with other information to create a broad overview of group behavior or detailed portraits of individual habits. Thus, a convenience, an Information Age accessory, becomes an electronic tag.[2]

But...who cares?

Why worry that Sprint has buried deep in its guts the coordinates of your exact location? For most people the new surveillance has no immediate material impact. So let's cut to an extreme situation, a dystopic somewhere else, and consider the question again.

POLITICS OF THE MUNDANE

In the occupied territories of the West Bank cell phones have already become critical components in the war between Israelis and Palestinians. During the first year of the *Al Aqsa* Intifada, the Israeli Defense Forces assassinated at least six Palestinian militants with rockets or helicopter gunships by first locating the target's cell phone and then directing fire at the coordinates of the phone. In those days most Palestinian mobile phones were jacked into Israel's politically suspect Cellcom network, headed by a former Shin Bet commander, Yakov Perry. After the link between phones and fire from the sky became clear, Palestinians started boycotting the Israeli cellular system and set up Jawwal, a Palestinian/Swedish telecom joint venture.[3]

From this perspective, routine surveillance takes on a new meaning. With a little imagination one can see that no matter how mundane, surveillance is also always tied up with questions of power and political struggle. And not only in the very direct fashion sketched above, but so too at the level of what Raymond Williams called the "structure of feeling"[4]

Routine digital surveillance is now almost ubiquitous and includes the records produced by credit cards, bankcards, Internet accounts, gym memberships, library cards, health insurance records, and workplace identification badges. All these create electronic files and therefore automatically and inadvertently log our movements, schedules, habits, and political beliefs.[5] In most respects dull, the contents of such electronic dossiers become rich veins of informational ore to be excavated from any number of angles by marketers, insurance firms, or police officials. One recent FBI investigation "seized enough computer data to nearly fill the Library of Congress twice."[6]

Even before the terrorist attacks of 9/11 the routine surveillance of everyday activity was expanding rapidly. But that assault, so galvanizing and palpable for a previously impervious population, has been hijacked by the worst elements of the political class, who seek to steer fear and anger toward the destruction of traditional American liberties, including what Justice Louis Brandeis called "the right to be let alone."

In many ways, 9/11 was only fuel to a fire already raging out of control. The state's drive to tag, monitor, and criminalize, and the media's compulsion to summon fear at every turn, are matched or surpassed only by the aggressive proliferation of commercially based identification, registration, and tracking. This privatized regime of observation and discipline is crystallized in the inexorable slide toward a cashless cybersociety in which every transaction is recorded and correlated to a subject's location in time and space. In Europe, microchip-integrated "smart cards"—the next logical step toward electronic money—are fast replacing all other types of credit and debt cards. Unlike most ATM or credit cards used in the US, smart cards not only deposit information but also record and store data—that is, they build and hold their own records. In the UK, the Boots Pharmacy "Advantage Card" has more than 10 million users. The Netherlands, Belgium, and France are awash in smart cards, and 70 million Germans carry them for health insurance identification purposes.[7] And if we are to credit Moore's Law, which holds that computer processing capacity doubles every eighteenth months, the power of smart cards could grow exponentially.

What does this mean? According to one journalist: "Experts predict that, over the next decade, consumers will carry two or three smart cards: a work card with access to the company's canteen, computer network and car park; a leisure card with gym club membership and lunch money; a banking card with details about your mortgage payments and social security status.... The small plastic card in your wallet will probably know a lot more about you and your particular habits than you'd tell your best friend, from the last purchase you made to what you got in your final exams."[8] Add to this the next generation of wireless telecommunications gear—souped-up cell phones, web-enabled Palm Pilots, onboard navigation and GPS gear for automobiles. Then imagine their interface with the countless rules, dictums, and prohibitions of overbearing state and corporate governance and one begins to see the contours of something rather unpleasant, a world that is nominally free but actually subject to a soft tyranny of omniscient and interlocking regimes of control: work rules overlapping with the criminal law; overlapping with official moralism; overlapping with the concerns of the security-conscious home; overlapping with notions of "correct" political policies; and then all of this overlapping with problematic assumptions about who is dangerous and who deserves privilege.

The new surveillance—which professor David Lyon calls "dataveillance"—often ignores the physical body and instead tracks one's informational doppelganger, but this does not mean that more traditional forms of surveillance are in decline.[9] Quite the opposite: visual and biological monitoring complement high-tech computerized observation. For example, Citgo Petroleum Corp. now drug-tests all job applicants at its 14,500 Citgo-brand gas stations, convenience stores, and Quick Lube outlets with a state-of-the-art, instantaneous saliva-based drug test.[10] Similar tests are becoming common elsewhere.

In New Orleans, at Frederick A. Douglass Public High School—named for America's most famous runaway slave, who forged false identities, lied to authorities, brawled with his enemies, and became one of the nation's most ardent and eloquent champions of liberty—students are encouraged to "volunteer" for hair-strand drug tests. Although there have been only a handful of dirty results so far, these chemical inspections, funded by an anonymous donor are wildly popular with the local press. Similar tests are standard practice at private Catholic schools throughout New Orleans.[11] Educators in one part of northern New Jersey have taken this logic a step further by subjecting all athletes to random, mandatory tests for drugs, alcohol, *and* nicotine. Kids with dirty samples are dropped from the teams.[12]

Various types of "biometric" surveillance that identify individuals by measuring the body are also becoming less expensive and more prevalent. Banks in all fifty states now require thumbprints from customers (not too surprising, considering that some banks have been requiring them since the early 1920s). The industry's biggest trade group, the American Bankers Association, defends the practice for obvious reasons: fingerprinting reduces fraud by an average of 60 percent.[13] The Bank United of Texas skips the prints, having gone one better by installing Sensar Incorporated "iris scanners" at its ATMs. Staff and some frequent flyers at New York's Kennedy Airport also submit to iris scans, while Chicago's Department of Aviation makes truck drivers entering O'Hare swipe an ID card and pass their thumbs over a scanner. Public housing projects in Chicago, Baltimore, Wilmington, Delaware, and St. Paul also use "biometric" hand scanners to control the entrance of residents and guests.[14] Some corporations are equipping themselves with desktop computers containing fingerprint scanners to control network access.[15] Even kids in three Pennsylvania school districts are using digital fingerprint identification in "cash-free" lunchroom transactions: no more schoolyard shakedowns, no more chocolate milk binging.[16]

Visual surveillance—the quintessential example being closed-circuit television (CCTV)—is also on the rise. In Manhattan, some 2,400 surveillance cameras keep watch over streets, parks, and doorways. That number is growing all the time as police do their best "to keep up with the demand."[17] In Minneapolis-St. Paul 80 percent of the highways are under constant watch by more than 250 pole-mounted cameras, as are all the key entry and exit points of most major American cities from San Francisco to

New York.[18] Typically, a major airport now deploys up to a thousand hidden and visible closed-circuit television cameras.[19]

All this is child's play compared to the total hegemony of CCTV in the UK, where one million cameras nationwide watch train stations, the foyers of buildings, shops, highways, and the public spaces of every major town center. And CCTV everywhere is set to converge with digitalized biometrics. The technology debuted when Tampa hosted the 2001 Super Bowl. From a crowd of approximately 100,000 sports fans the police computer had nineteen "hits" for people wanted on minor warrants. No arrests were made, in part because the freely loaned equipment and software were seemingly deployed to generate press hype for the system's manufacturer. But some European cities, along with various US government office buildings and more than a hundred casinos, use similar biometric programs for scanning their surveillance footage.[20]

Perhaps the wackiest examples of this paranoid techno-fetishism are the 2.5 million American pets that have been implanted with microchip identification tags. If a lost pet is found, its ID info can be read with a simple handheld scanner that your local pound may or may not have. The same technology—in the form of a microchip bracelet—is already being used to tend Alzheimer's patients and small children.[21] And, yes, a family in Florida recently had themselves implanted with ID chips containing medical and biographical information. They also bought stock in the chip-making firm just before announcing their stunt to an eager, fear-crazed national press corps.[22] The paranoid imagination of yesterday—animals and humans with chips in them—is already passé, or at least kitsch.

Meanwhile, 75,000 Americans live under house arrest, their ankles shackled with high-tech electronic manacles tethering them to distant police computers.[23] The FBI predicts that its wiretapping activities will increase by 300 percent between 2000 and 2010. And the National Security Agency's ECHELON program monitors most international phone calls emanating from the United States, searching them automatically for key words like "semtex" and "president."[24]

The list could go on and on, spiraling up into the thin altitudes of political psychosis without ever leaving the realm of fact. But what are we to make of all this? And why should we care?

The point is not that any one of these examples taken in isolation is so awful, but rather that they all exist in relation to each other and should be considered as such. Each new type of surveillance forms part of an emerging, society-wide system. In other words, everyday surveillance is troubling in the same way as advertising: it is not that this or that ad is so oppressive, but a whole landscape and culture of commercialism most certainly is.

IS PRIVACY ENOUGH?

The tides of popular culture bring signs that Americans have embraced their loss of privacy with patriotic vigor and pop-culture nonchalance. Opinion polls show approval ratings of 60 to 80 percent for expanding CCTV in public spaces, while webcam exhibitionism and mass online voyeurism are hugely popular. In New York alone, thousands of vigilant parents have installed "nanny cams" bought from ParentWatch to keep remote tabs on their little darlings.[25] Simultaneously, we have new forms of surveillance-based television: the show *Big Brother* casts a group of regular non-actors living together in a house that is completely exposed by cameras; their challenge is to create a life worth watching while on occasion hiding from the audience. These surveillance-as-challenge, "reality"-based shows anesthetize us to the new superintendence and in so doing treat it as another natural element, like heat or cold, with which we must live and against which we test our wits.[26] This reification of a political technology is just one barometer of our increasing habituation to the age of surveillance.

Against the cameras, IDs, and swipe cards arises the cry of *privacy*. But too often this is cast as ipso facto valuable. We are rarely told *why* we should care about privacy: its importance is simply asserted. And when its value is explained, privacy is usually cast as an individual "quality of life" issue, as if being spied on is unpleasant in the same way as loud noises, litter, or offensive language. The best example of this logic comes from the eloquent and forward-thinking Louis Brandeis himself.

A life-long progressive and the first Jew to enter the Wasp bastion of the Supreme Court, Brandeis wrote a famous dissenting opinion in the case of *Olmstead v. United States*, which allowed the police to secretly tap telephones. The core of Brandeis's argument is framed in forthrightly individualistic terms:

> The makers of our Constitution undertook to secure conditions favorable to the pursuit of happiness. They recognized the significance of man's spiritual nature, of his feelings, and of his intellect. They knew that only a part of the pain, pleasure and satisfactions of life are to be found in material things. They sought to protect Americans in their beliefs, their thoughts, their emotions and their sensations. They conferred, as against the Government, the right to be let alone—the most comprehensive of rights, and the right most valued by civilized men. To protect that right, every unjustifiable intrusion by the Government upon the privacy of the individual, whatever the means employed, must be deemed a violation of the Fourth Amendment.[27]

One can concur completely with Brandeis and still want something more, an argument that, in conjunction with Brandeis's superb defense of our spiritual nature, feelings, intellect, beliefs, thoughts, emotions and sensations, raises the stakes by making privacy a more social and political issue.

There is a pragmatic political reason for this as well: privacy as a purely individual issue has limited resonance. Many citizens of Tampa welcomed the new CCTV cameras, and most simply didn't care either way. Likewise, very few AOL subscribers protest the company's ready cooperation with law enforcement.[28] The logic of such passivity is simple: if you don't have anything to hide, why be concerned? This commonsense argument is rarely engaged because it is, in fact, quite hard to counter at the level of everyday experience.

The rest of this book, through historical narrative and description, seeks to complicate and repoliticize the question of privacy. Here "the right to be let alone" and the value of personal autonomy are not assumed a priori, nor addressed simply at the level of the individual. Instead, I explore the problem of surveillance through its connections to the larger social issues of inequality, violence, state power, and collective political action.

POWER AND KNOWLEDGE

Brandeis's dissent in *Olmstead* was by no means the last word on surveillance. In fact, the whole debate underwent a massive transformation with the intervention of Michel Foucault beginning in the mid–1960s. The curious and concerned have been examining the pieces from his demolition job ever since. In Foucault's wake we see that routine surveillance is clearly bound up with political repression, but that it *also* has a "generative" function, helping to elicit and construct politically useful forms of knowledge and behavior.

In short, surveillance instills discipline by forcing self-regulation. Constant surveillance brings forth loyal citizens, trained soldiers, obedient patients, productive workers, and docile, useful bodies. External observation recruits us to monitor and police ourselves: we confess, count calories, open our doors to the Census long form, sign our *real* names on hotel registers, pay our taxes, reel off our Social Security numbers and dates of birth. The entire edifice of modern life is built as much upon the primacy of files, record keeping, and everyday surveillance as it is upon nature and labor.[29]

It is also clear that the knowledge produced by formal observation can justify a wide range of interventions from the intrusive but well-meaning to outright persecution and physical punishment. Once identified and understood, the deviant can be helped, redirected, segregated, imprisoned, or destroyed by doctors, psychiatrists, superintendents, social workers, managers, or police agents.

Foucault's epistemologically relativist argument holds that moral and cultural categories like "madness" or "criminality" are not simply "discovered" and accurately named by science so much as they are *built* by the political and scientific practice and discourses. This is not to say that madness is "unreal," but rather that its reality and cultural meaning are always socially constructed. In other words, whatever biology madness involves, it is also always bound up with, and never appears outside of, the matrix of culture and historically specific forms of knowledge. Hearing voices in one society may be seen as religious insight, while in another it becomes reason for institutionalization. Surveillance thus serves as a "generative" force, one that defines who is an insider and who is an outsider.

FROM THE THEATER OF ATROCITY

For Foucault, the politics of surveillance were bound up with the emergence of modern methods of medicine, psychiatry, and statecraft. He sketched this point most famously by contrasting a quintessential image of premodern power, the spectacular ritual of public torture in the *ancien régime*, with the cold precision of modern power in the form of a youth reformatory.

It begins in the first pages of *Discipline and Punish* with a harrowing, archival account of the long, slow death of Robert François Damiens, who had attempted to stab Louis XV in 1757. The court's instructions were detailed: "The flesh will be torn from his breasts, arms, thighs and calves with red hot pincers, his right hand. . . burnt with sulphur, and on those places where the flesh will be torn away, poured molten lead, boiling oil, burning resin, wax and sulphur melted together and then his body drawn and quartered by four horses."[30] According to Foucault: "Power in this instance was essentially a right of seizure: of things, time, bodies, and ultimately life itself; it culminated in the privilege to seize hold of life in order to surpass it."[31] This type of public execution may seem like a fairly definitive expression of state force, but Foucault argued that it was also wasteful, and dangerously inefficient. Public torture and execution relied heavily on the role of the crowd for its ceremonial and symbolic impact. Such events were political theater and "the people" were its audience. But to some extent this public ceremony distributed power to the spectators, who in turn might choose to rewrite the intended script in very disruptive ways. The crowds at public executions sometimes rebelled, attacking the scaffold to free or kill the prisoner, and in other ways acted to negate or usurp the power of the king. To avoid such political meltdowns, execution and punishment became increasingly invisible, professionalized, and restrained.

DISCIPLINE AND SURVEILLANCE

Foucault's account of classical brutality—the display of "sovereign power"—contrasts strongly with an example of "disciplinary power" from the late 1830s, less than a century after the brutal public execution of Damiens. From the gallows we cut to the super-regimented daily timetable from the "House of young prisoners in Paris"—a classic reform school. The schedule begins rigorously: "*Rising*. At the first drum-roll, the prisoner must rise and dress in silence, as the supervisor opens the cell door. At the second drum-roll, they must be dressed and make their beds. At the third, they must line up and proceed to the chapel for morning prayer. There is a five-minute interval between each drum-roll."[32] Here we see power, the ability to control phenomena, appear not as spectacularly vicious theater, but as a meticulously measured regimentation of time, space, and the human body. Furthermore, the operation of power is now hidden within a house of detention rather than displayed for heuristic political effect before an excitable crowd. This progression, away from traditional repression toward "disciplinary power," is about organizing and harnessing the forces of life; thus Foucault writes of "bio-power." And at the center of this type of regulation is routine surveillance. "Discipline produces subjected and practiced, 'docile' bodies. Discipline increases the force of the body (in economic terms of utility) and diminishes these same forces of the body (in political terms of obedience)"[33] People become more useful as they become more obedient.

During this modernization of social control, the ancient art of torture and confession morphed into the modern methods of surveillance, investigation, and interrogation by which judicial, medical, and moral "truth" can be retrieved from the interior workings of the modern subject. From the new practices emerged the modern "soul"—a political object that displaces the body as the central point of power's leverage. Now interior thoughts, emotions, and patterns become "the effect and instrument of a political anatomy: the soul is the prison of the body."[34]

THE PANOPTICON: SURVEILLANCE AS IDEA TYPE

For Foucault the paradigmatic example of this surveillance-based discipline was the panopticon—an architectural phantasm springing from the twisted imagination of Jeremy Bentham, the utilitarian philosopher whose preserved corpse still sits in a cupboard at the University of London. In Bentham's work, the panopticon is a circular prison in which illuminated cells are watched from a central observation tower. In a panopticon, prisoners know they could be watched at all times and are thus forced to "internalize the gaze" of the overseers and police themselves. For Foucault this became "the diagram of a mechanism of power reduced to its ideal form," the perfect cage in which surveillance harnesses the captive to play the role of both ward and warden.

There is one more element in the story. If domination, control, and bureaucratic organization are ubiquitous, then so too are the counterforces of resistance, protest, sabotage, non-cooperation, and liberty. The hidden history of this sort of resistance is perhaps best captured in Peter Linebaugh and Marcus Rediker's *Many-Headed Hydra: Sailors, Slaves, Commoners, and the Hidden History of the Revolutionary Atlantic.*[35] They show how the state and modern methods of control are produced in the forge of constant political struggle. Everyday surveillance in American has a similar history, having developed through the dialectical tension between resistance and regulation.

2

ANTEBELLUM ID: GENEALOGIES OF IDENTIFICATION AND REGISTRATION

> It should be remembered that no slave was allowed to be off the plantation after sunset, without a written pass.
>
> —Allen Parker,
> *Recollections of Slavery Times*

On November 21, 1745, a slave owner from the tobacco country of the Chesapeake littoral ran the following ad in the *Virginia Gazette:*

> RUN AWAY about the first of *June* last from Subscriber, living on *Chickahominy* River, *James City* County. A Negroe Man, Short and well-set, aged between 30 and 40 Years, but looks younger, having no Beard, is smooth-fac'd and has some Scars on his Temples, being the Marks of his Country; talks pretty good *English*; is a cunning, subtile Fellow, and pretends to be a Doctor. It is Likely he has a great Aquaintance, he may

have procur'd a false Pass. Whoever brings him to me at my House aforesaid, shall have two Pistoles Rerward, besides what the law allows.

—Michael Sherman[1]

Published appeals like this one describing "truant" slaves and servants were common in colonial America, particularly in the South where captive Africans and the indentured English and Irish servants made up more than a third of the population. Under slavery, resistance great and small—ranging from rebellion, assault, and escape to theft, sabotage, witchcraft, and malingering—was a constant feature of life. The *Gazette*, cited above, ran an average of 230 runaway notices a year during the eighteenth century, and all of them had one thing in common: they sought to identify people who, as slaves, supposedly had no identity. In other words, the master class was forced to develop not just methods of terror but also a haphazard system of identification and surveillance. The result was in many ways the earliest imprint of modern everyday surveillance.

IDENTITY AND IDENTIFICATION

Surveillance in the old South was shaped by the bizarre contradictions of slavery. On one hand, Africans were officially nonpersons, just commodities to be bought and sold. From the Middle Passage onward slaves were systematically denied their humanity; worked like beasts, and unable to marry, worship, or learn, they were reduced to subhuman status.[2] Slavery had to limit Black cultural and political identity and suppress the African's humanity, individuality, and identity. Thus, it was illegal in many areas for slaves to take a last name—even their master's.[3]

But denying the slaves *identity* made their physical *identification* more complicated. At one level planters sought to merge slaves into a single category of subhuman, passive "Blackness." But since slaves could escape, plot, steal, set fires, travel between plantations without permission, and even kill whites, the master class was compelled to create systems of identification and routine surveillance.[4] The ad hoc and informal nature of this effort made identity a key site of social control from above and political struggle from below.

NOTATIONS AND RECORDS

When Richard Henry Lee, a Revolutionary War general and leader of the Virginia Antifederalists, rode his vast holdings he always carried a small "memorandum book." Its leather cover was "gently rounded, smoothed, and polished by the action of Lee's rear pocket, saddle and the swaying of his horse." In this notebook Lee inscribed reminders, reading notes, accounts, descriptions of his plantings, and the precise enumeration and condition of his livestock. He also made careful notes on the movements of his slaves, two in particular: his "jobber," named Congo, and a light-skinned girl named Grace.[5]

The surveillance infrastructure of colonial America began here, with the simple accounts of the slave master. Inventories listed lands, tools, animals, *and* people. But the patrician's zeal for record keeping went beyond the merely functional; plantation documents are imbued with the same Enlightenment-era reflex to catalogue that motivated diarists, botanists, and travel writers. George Washington kept a diary that he labeled "where & how my time is spent." Slave productivity was central in his musings: "Their work ought to be well examined," wrote the man on the one-dollar bill. Even when facing crises as president, Washington gave detailed attention to the reports of his steward at Mt. Vernon and often dispatched in return orders and complaints about shoddy work. When his sewing crew "made only Six Shirts a Week . . ." the president was displeased and commented on the work habits of individual slaves: "last week Caroline (without being sick) made only five [shirts]." By the 1840s, publishers were producing ledgers designed especially for plantation management, such as "The Cotton Plantation Record and Account Book, No 1. Suitable for a Force of 40 Hands or Under."[6]

But the surveillance system of the plantation was more complex than mere interpersonal observation and general records. At its heart lay three key "information technologies": the written slave pass, organized slave patrols, and wanted posters for runaways.

MOBILITY AS THREAT

For slaves, mobility was a crucial source of power. Along with maintaining familial and romantic ties, the mobility of Black people produced networks of interpersonal connections that served as the circuitry of resistance. Along with the big "crimes" of escape and murdering masters there was the capillary-level resistance of re-expropriation of the master's stores, fencing pilfered goods, trading produce, and fraternizing with Native Americans, poor whites, and the fugitive slaves who lived as social bandits on the edge of the plantation world.

The most common of these sub-rosa activities was stealing: "the slaves' traffic in stolen goods was extensive, relatively well organized, and carried on with virtual impunity."[7] Poor whites were often involved as accomplices and consumers. Between 1710 and 1745 the Richmond county court passed sentences in 426 cases of theft, a disproportionate number involving free and captive African Americans who had usually taken food, liquor, livestock, or cloth.[8] Planters complained bitterly about such theft, but sometimes tolerated it when perpetrated against their rivals. These localized battles over distribution were all part of the moral economy that made bondage survivable. As one veteran of such struggles put it, "When the slaves took anything the masters called it stealing, yet they were stealing the slaves' time year after year."[9]

To expose and break resistance, courts ordered pilfering slaves to be branded with "T" for "thief."[10] This was both a punishment and a rudimentary form of identification. George Washington was so infuriated by the systematic plunder of his vast plantation that he ordered all slave-owned dogs to be hanged on the grounds that the beasts aided slaves "in their night robberies."[11]

Again, mobility was key to both escape and everyday survival: the more Black people traveled the roads and waterways the harder it was to locate the truant or fugitive.[12] The more contacts a slave had, the more resources at her or his disposal. Mobility was the currency of resistance, and the planter class therefore sought to regulate it tightly.

THE PATROLLERS

To control Black peoples' movements Dixie invented the slave patrols, which always worked in conjunction with the slave pass and the wanted notice. Patrollers, or as slaves sometimes called them, "pattie rollers," are a much overlooked tributary of modern American policing. Their chief functions were surveillance and corporal punishment: patrollers rode at night in "beat companies" of three to six men armed and empowered to search homes for runaways, weapons, or supply caches that might indicate escape plans.

Black people abroad at night had to produce passes written by their masters or "freed papers"—proof of their emancipation. All of this aimed to instill a self-policing caution. In some regions patrollers were paid with tax money, but more often their work was itself a form of taxation, or corvée labor, levied upon all white men. In either case the patrollers were frequently offered, or demanded, bounties from the owners of runaway slaves and truants, who had taken off only temporarily. Former slave Francis Fedric described the patrol customs in Virginia as follows:

> On New Year's Day ten white men are chosen, who are called patrols; they are sworn-in at the court-house, and their special duty is to go to the Negro cabins for the purpose of searching them to see whether any slaves are there without a pass or permit from their masters. . . . If any slaves are found without a pass they are brought out, and being made to strip are flogged, the men receiving ten and the women five lashes each.[13]

These "special bodies of armed men" appear in various slave narratives. Allan Parker wrote that mounted squads "were employed at public expense to patrol the roads" and were instructed to whip every Black person "found at large without a written pass." The patrols—armed with whips and guns, mounted and traveling in groups of two or three—were generally described as "poor whites who did the work partly for the money they could get out of the business, and partly on account of the excitement there was in it."[14] But according to the work of Sally Hadden, the leading historian of this subject, the most active patrollers were of the solid, property-owning middle classes.[15]

Austin Steward, who lived from 1793 to 1860 and escaped slavery many times, knew the pattie rollers all too well:

> Slaves are never allowed to leave the plantation to which they belong, without a written pass. Should any one venture to disobey this law, he

> will most likely be caught by the patrol and given thirty-nine lashes. This patrol is always on duty every Sunday, going to each plantation under their supervision, entering every slave cabin, and examining closely the conduct of the slaves; and if they find one slave from another plantation without a pass, he is immediately punished with a severe flogging.[16]

The patrollers and the technology of the pass constituted the frontlines of the plantation dictatorship. But as with today's police, the sadism of the pattie rollers could at times trigger flash rebellions. Steward's 1857 autobiography relayed the tale of a slave dance that ended in a deadly brawl between patrollers and the slaves.

> Vain is the attempt to describe the tumultuous scene which followed. Hand to hand they fought and struggled with each other, amid the terrific explosion of firearms,—oaths and curses, mingled with the prayers of the wounded, and the groans of the dying! Two of the patrol were killed on the spot, and lay drenched in the warm blood that so lately flowed through their veins. Another with his arm broken and otherwise wounded, lay groaning and helpless, beside the fallen slaves, who had sold their lives so dearly. Another of his fellows was found at a short distance, mortally wounded and about to bid adieu to life. In the yard lay the keeper of the horses, a stiffened corpse.[17]

Occasional casualties aside, pattie rollers were a surveillance mechanism of considerable might.

THE SLAVE PASS

A symbiotic relationship existed between the patrol and the slave pass, that embryonic form of the modern ID. No patrollers, no need for passes; no pass, no fulcrum for the lever of patroller power. The pass and the racially defined contours of (white) literacy and (Black) illiteracy upon which it relied, acted as the slaveocracy's information technology and infrastructure of routine surveillance.

In Virginia the first pass laws, created in 1642, targeted poor whites, such as indentured Irish servants attempting to flee their obligations. Any white person leaving the colony required a pass from the colonial governor to ensure that they were not fugitives or debtors. By 1656 Native Americans entering the colony to trade had to carry passes, or "tickets," issued by the colonial authorities. Earlier iterations of these regulations mentioned slaves, but it wasn't until 1680 that an exclusive slave pass law was enacted in Virginia.[18]

As early as 1649, slave owners in Barbados, prompted by an insurrection, required enslaved people to carry passes. And in 1687 South Carolina lawmakers decreed that "it shall not be lawful for any negroe or negroes, or other slave, upon any pretence whatsoever to travel or goe abroad from his or her master or mistresses house in the night time, between sunsetting and the sunrising, or in the day time without a note from his or her master or mistresse or overseer."[19]

But what did slave passes look like? How exactly did they function? We know that they usually consisted of a short handwritten note from the slave owner naming the bondsperson and giving the dates and destination of the carrier's travel. From Missouri we have this example:

> Gentilmen let the Boy Barney pass and repass from the first of june till the 4
>
> To Columbas MO for this date 1852
>
> Samuel Grove.[20]

Interestingly, the pass makes no attempt to *identify* Barney other than to give his name. How were the patrollers to know he was not a runaway? Only the assumption of slave illiteracy and the patroller's personal knowledge of the master's name ensured against fraud. And usually these factors were enough; most slaves lived in sparsely populated areas and many would have been personally known to patrollers. Or in sociological parlance, this pass, like others, is a document marked by gemeinschaft rather than gesellschaft. The pass is an artifact from a social world of face-to-face "community" relations, not one from a more complex, bureaucratized society structured through an elaborate division of labor and anonymous, more standardized forms of "association" between people.

Though oppressive, the pass and patrol system by no means achieved total control. First and foremost we see the openings provided by literacy: the slave who could read and write became the antebellum hacker, the information outlaw, who could crack the code of the planters' security system. Literate African Americans could resist with the very tools of white oppression; they could in effect bend the political technology of literacy back upon itself. No wonder ignorance was enforced by laws prohibiting the education of slaves.

Since the basic form of identification within the pass system was the name, naming too became a site of resistance. Mothers gave their children distinct names so as to keep track of them, via the grapevine, if they were sold off later in life.[21] And truant slaves visiting distant plantations could try to evade patrollers by simply pretending to be a local of the plantation they were visiting. This loophole became an issue among patrollers after the Stono Rebellion of September 1739. In a pattern that was quite common in the Caribbean (from which more than a few masters and slaves had emigrated) about a hundred slaves outside Charleston, South Carolina, rose up and sacked plantations, stole weapons, and killed roughly twenty whites.

The uprising was soon crushed and terrified whites in the legislature proposed that planters provide lists naming all male slaves, thus "every Slave might be called by Name, when the patrols should visit plantations."[22] Here we see slave resistance provoking planter innovation at the level of surveillance and identification.

As the peculiar institution came under increased attack with the end of slavery in Vermont, then Pennsylvania and other northern states, the contours of slavery hardened. Manumission became less frequent and legally more difficult, while the first Fugitive Slave Act in 1793 projected plantation power north on to "free soil." Authorities pressed for the deportation of manumitted African Americans as the social world of the plantation became ever more militarized. Southern governments enacted broad new laws requiring all whites to enforce the pass system against all Blacks; provided for better-equipped, more frequent patrols; and subsidized the policing of bondage with state-funded rewards and payment to patrollers. Within this tightening noose, knowledge and literacy became crucial political issues.

The Plantation Police (1863) by Francis H. Schell

QUILL-PEN HACKERS

Slave autobiographies recount the many tricks used to jam and foil the pass/patrol system. According to former bondsman Henery Clay Bruce, duping patrollers was frequently rather easy, "because they were as a rule illiterate, and of course could not read writing. The slaves knowing this would take a portion of a letter picked up and palm it off on them as a pass when arrested. The captain would take it, look it over wisely, then hand it telling the slave to go."[23]

Along with forging passes or using random pieces of writing, literate slaves could, as Clay explained, doctor existing passes: "Others would secure a pass from their master, get some one who could read writing to erase the day and month, then use it indefinitely, while others would get their young master or mistress to write them a pass whenever they wanted to go out, signing their father's name." Interestingly, Clay saw the master's reasoning behind not issuing passes as linked to the maximum exploitation of labor power: "Masters objected to giving passes often, upon the ground that they wanted the slave to stay at home and take his rest which he could not get if out often after dark."[24] To control doctored passes, "one group of South Carolinians went so far as to request that patrollers be permitted to punish any slave found with an unspecific pass."[25] Again we see a dialectic relationship between slave resistance and planter efforts to create a more standardized surveillance and identification system.

Forged passes were necessary even for slaves who didn't attempt to escape. "I used to write out passes and slip them to her husband that lived on a neighboring plantation, so he could come and see her," recounted one former slave of his regular cooperation with a fellow bondsperson.[26]

But clearly the heart of the matter was escape and in that saga forged passes were always essential. "My plan at this time was to write myself a pass down to New Orleans, and when I got there, to take a ship to New York or Boston," recounted William J. Anderson, a former slave who escaped and returned to get his wife only to be recaptured and to escape several times more.[27] Frederick Douglass, like all literate slaves, became a group asset during his escape:

> The week before our intended start, I wrote a pass for each of our party, giving them permission to visit Baltimore, during the Easter holidays.
>
> The pass ran after this manner:
>
> "This is to certify, that I, the undersigned, have given the bearer, my servant, John, full liberty to go to Baltimore, to spend the Easter holidays."
>
> "W. H.
>
> Near St. Michael's, Talbot county, Maryland."[28]

Collective resistance, such as the great slave rebellions, also relied on doctored and fabricated documents because both planning and executing an uprising required mobility and secrecy and thus relied on the circuitry of the underground economy. In 1800 the famous rebel slave Gabriel Prosser, "and his lieutenants made extensive use of rivers and watermen, bogus passes, whites who sold them supplies, and religious revivals in order to plan the wholesale destruction of the new capital city."[29] The master class was well aware of such subterfuge and mentioned it repeatedly in the advertisements for runaways in Southern newspapers. A typical example: "She is smart and active, and capable of any business, can read and write, and probably may forge a pass."[30] Or these:

> RUN away from the subscriber, a Mulatto girl named Agnes. . . I have reason to think that she may get a false pass, with an intent to pass for a free woman, and to go out of the colony.[31]

> RUN AWAY from the subscriber. . . a servant named SAMUEL HOMES. . . He has been seen with a forged pass, signed NEWTON KEENE, and went by the name of JOHN HARRIS.[32]

White indentured servants, like slaves, were known to hack into the mainframe of literacy. For example: "He was born in Pennsylvania, bred a farmer, pretends to great skill in farriery, speaks in the Scotch-Irish dialect, and in conversation frequently uses the words moreover and likewise; and as he can read and write, will probably forge a pass."[33] Both whites and Blacks shared their skills:

> an indented servant man named WILLIAM GILL, whose dialect will very readily discover him to be an Irishman. . . . It is likely he has had influence enough over some one of his acquaintances to forge a certificate of his being a freeman, and as such may pass wherever he pleases.[34]

Owners in search of escapees called attention to forged passes in part to encourage greater scrutiny of such documents. "He pretends to be a Newlight [protestant revivalist], and reads and writes a little (generally a very small hand), and forges himself passes, by examing which he may be esily discovered."[35]

STOLEN KNOWLEDGE

Because surveillance and literacy were linked, most Southern states had, by the antebellum period, passed laws designed to keep slaves away from books. Four states completely outlawed any teaching of slaves, while most others only prohibited teaching assembled slaves and tried to limit slave reading to biblical lessons on obedience.[36]

Numerous slave narratives and Works Progress Administration interviews with former bondspersons dwell on the importance of reading, but no author approaches the eloquence, clarity, and measured wrath of Frederick Douglass. His well-known odyssey into literacy and freedom began as a boy with the aid of his owner's wife, who at first was immensely proud of his progress. In fact, Mrs. Auld "exultingly" and naively told her husband about her apt pupil "and of her intention to persevere in teaching [him] . . . to read the Bible."

As Douglass recounted: "Master Hugh was astounded beyond measure, and probably for the first time, proceeded to unfold to his wife the true philosophy of the slave system, and the peculiar rules necessary in the . . . management of human chattels." Hugh Auld forbade his wife from giving any further instruction to their slave boy "Freddy," telling her that it was both "unlawful" and "unsafe." He then explained: "If he learns to read the Bible it will forever unfit him to be a slave. He should know nothing but the will of his master, and learn to obey it. As to himself, learning will do him no good, but a great deal of harm, making him disconsolate and unhappy." And quite crucially: "If you teach him how to read, he'll want to know how to write, and this accomplished, he'll be running away with himself."

The young slave paid close attention to "Master Hugh's oracular exposition" for it was, in an amoral way, "the first decidedly anti-slavery lecture" Douglass had ever heard. The impact on the boy was profound: "His iron sentences, cold and harsh, sunk like heavy weights deep into my heart, and stirred up within me a rebellion not soon to be allayed." Hugh's blunt honesty dispelled the "painful mystery" of "the white man's power" to enslave. "'Very well,' thought I. 'Knowledge unfits a child to be a slave. . . .' From that moment I understood the direct pathway from slavery to freedom."[37]

Another former slave described her father's outlaw struggle for literacy as a boy who "stole what little education he had from his master's children." He would listen to his privileged white peers repeating their lessons "and would often steal their books, especially their speller. . . He studied in the field, or in the old log cabin, at night by the light from the old fireplace." By day, he hid the spelling book in his hat "and while he was pretending to be looking in his hat for vermin which were quite plentiful at that time, he was studying the words he was learning."[38] Yet another former bondsman who carried a covert book in his pocket also studied by reading over and over the addresses of the letters he took to and from the local post office.[39]

Clearly, stolen literacy had more than metaphysical connections to freedom: it was a concrete weapon, since forged passes and manumission papers were essential to everyday survival, escape, and rebellion.

ESCALATING TO TIN

In Charleston, South Carolina, in 1783 authorities adopted what they hoped would be a tamper-proof technology, a system of metal slave "tags" or "slave hire badges." Urban slaves who hired themselves out as wage laborers (the wages going to the masters) were required to obtain from the city a brass or tin badge stamped with the slave's occupation, the date, and a number to record payment of the annual slave tax. The numbered badges—some of the first numbered ID's in America—were not only a means of collecting revenue; they also facilitated the political control of Black people *as a class*.[40] The tags' panoptic effect is relayed to us by the fugitive John Andrew Jackson:

> I joined a gang of negroes working on the wharfs, and received a dollar-and-a-quarter per day, without arousing any suspicion. . . . One morning, as I was going to join a gang of negroes working on board a vessel, one of them asked me if I had my badge? Every negro is expected to have a badge with his master's name and address inscribed on it. Every negro unable to produce such badge when asked for, is liable to be put in jail. When I heard that, I was so frightened that I hid myself. . . .[41]

Similar badges existed for free Blacks, but none is still extant. Since these tags were metal, prefabricated, and cross-referenced to city records, they were apparently not easily forged. The badge and pass system received an invigorating organizational boost after a snitch betrayed a planned uprising led by the famous Denmark Vesey in 1822; in reaction to the Vesey plot the surveillance system was even more rigorously administered.

STRUGGLE ON THE TERRAIN OF IDENTITY

Escaping was not quite as simple as "getting to freedom." For over 150 years, from 1619 when the first imprisoned Africans were off-loaded by pirates at Jamestown, to 1777 when Vermont outlawed commerce in human beings, there was no "free soil" to run to. In the colonial era slaves were therefore more likely to head south into Spanish Florida and the armed autonomy of Seminole country. Or, if newly arrived from Africa, they went west into the not yet white-dominated Appalachian Mountains. For the American-born and acculturated slave with a fair degree of skill, the big, more anonymous coastal towns offered the best refuge; there a fugitive could mix into the larger populations of free Blacks and skilled slaves who worked in craft production and transportation and had a degree of mobility and autonomy. In the big towns, the escapee survived much like the undocumented immigrants of today, hated and hunted by white society but also useful to small craftsmen and other employers who hired their labor at submarket wages. As one slave-hunting owner put it in an ad about a runaway, "some Person in Want of Hands might be induced to engage him."[42]

Ads for runaways frequently mentioned rumors of self-liberated bondspeople passing as free: "He ran from his [sic] about 18 months ago and has passed for a free man ever since. . . ." One frustrated planter in search of a runaway wrote, "He has been lately employed by some Gentlemen in Fredricksburg, as a Freeman." Even newly arrived Africans—survivors of the Middle Passage, frequently described as "outlandish," speaking only broken English, bearing the dramatic decorative scars and pierced earlobes of their home cultures—passed as free. One such man was, according to his former owner, "lately employed on an Oyster boat on *James* River."[43]

In such cases the fugitives created whole new identities. This too is reflected in the advertisements: "There is a wench at Mr. Thomas Husk's between the Rappahannock and Potomack [sic] rivers who calls herself Milla, who may probably be the same [slave as advertised]."[44] Sometimes women's efforts to forge new identities and thwart slave catchers, constables, and patrollers went as far as switching genders. "Jenny, a whip scar on her cheek, 23 years old and from Green Spring" was one of several women in Virginia who "dressed in the habit of a man."[45] More often fugitives adopted a bevy of aliases. Such was the case of Essex, who lived "in the swamps and forests on both sides of the Savannah [River], not many miles from the City of Augusta, Georgia." Sleeping by day, hunted for three years, "Essex had a half-score of aliases. The wily, foxy, dog-killing runaway became the most notorious and best-hated negro in the two States."[46]

But escapees who tried to pass as freedmen needed more than a fake pass. Thus, trafficking in forged manumission documents, or "free papers," was also part of the antebellum underground. This trade in documents also appeared in ads for runaways: "It is probable that he has a forged Register of his Age, that will free him in July 1766."[47] Or in the case of a couple named Phil and Winny suspected of having killed their former owner. "They have endeavoured to pass for free Negroes, and have shewn some forged indentures, with certificates thereon of their freedom, the fellow passing by the name of Daniel Watts, and the woman by that of Mimy Howard. They have such variety of cloaths that their dress cannot be described."[48]

But finding originals from which to copy was difficult. One slave narrative—really a broad verbatim piece of slave reportage—quotes escapee Stephen Jordon with this story:

> There was an old free negro that lived near our place; I got him to let me see his free papers. I tell you, child, I took those free papers and copied every word of them. 'Now,' said I, 'I shall run away, and if I am caught I shall show these counterfeit free papers and get off all right.' Sure enough, I took those papers and stowed them away in a secret place in my cabin, together with . . . some old passes, books, and papers.[49]

Here the technology of identification was already more advanced than with the gemeinschaft logic of the pass. Many manumission papers, particularly in the antebellum era, were standardized, printed forms that required a description of the freed person. This marked a profound shift in the bureaucracy of power and its ability to see, define, and construct the "free" or "unfree" subject.

A fairly typical manumission document from Illinois, dated 1844, is a printed form with blank lines on which the bearer's personal information is handwritten. After an official heading, giving the location of the printing and greetings, it reads:

Know Ye, That _John Jones_
A person of Color, about _twenty seven_ years of age, _past five_
feet _ten_ inches high, _mulatto_
complexion. . . [50]

These innovations (the printed forms and the description of individual physical characteristics) are at one level entirely mundane but at another they are crucial political and ideological maneuvers that *redistribute* power from slaves to slave owners and the state. The standardized, difficult-to-forge document moves the project of identity construction from the realm of oral culture, individual assertion, and community practice to the apparatus of the state and the capital-intensive technologies of literacy and printing. The stipulation of personal features also limits the fungibility of such documents. These little informational snares held terrible risks for the unlucky runaway.

Consider the case of Reuben, who in May 1845 fled Virginia, "having obtained some person's free papers, as a protection against any arrest." But on arriving in Washington, D.C., "he was suspected. . . . His papers being examined were declared false, because his height and colour did not agree with the description. The papers issued by the courts of the States are very particular in their description. The poor fellow was taken to prison." Worse yet, Reuben's brutal master "soon received intelligence of the arrest" and came north to bring his chattel to a "slave pen in the city of Richmond, where he was kept for some months training for the auction block. He was finally sold to a slave dealer in the State of Louisiana. Such was the fate of poor Reuben."[51]

Though manumission papers often included height, weight, and complexion, most receipts associated with the sale of slaves contained no identifying information. This left space for slaves to resist by way of identity fraud. But this course also contained dangers. People manumitted "by word of mouth" and treated as free but who lacked papers were sometimes captured and put back into slavery.[52]

So too, escaped slaves resisting slave catchers often engaged in elaborate legal battles over questions of identification. Reverend Alexander Hemsley, an escapee from forced labor in Maryland, was recaptured in New Jersey and had to fight thugs from Dixie in this manner. From eventual freedom in Canada, Hemsley explained how the crew who captured him contained "a boy with whom I had played in my young days. . . . He was there to swear to my identity." But Hemsley feigned ignorance, and "made strange of him and of every thing he said,—I would not know him nor any of his blarney." Eventually the slavers brought the witness's brother from the south, who—"to get money"—swore that they knew Hemsley "to have been the slave of Isaac Baggs."[53] In such situations forged papers helped, but ultimately no Black identity was safe in a white court.

The famous Sojurner Truth likewise had to fight over the identity of her son, who had been illegally sold away from her. The question of finding and identifying the boy rested on a "bad scar on his forehead," from "Fowler's horse hove."[54]

WANTED POSTER AS ID

The lack of fully operational, standardized identification led, as we've seen, to various forms of resistance, from forged passes to faux "free papers" to verbally asserted new identities. In response to successful slave resistance and escapes, planters made *post facto* efforts to identify their absconded captives with elaborate wanted posters that in many ways embodied the main elements of modern IDs, by using increasingly standardized descriptive criteria for identification. For example:

> RANAWAY, from the Subscriber. . . my Negro Man named George. Said Negro is five feet ten inches high, of dark complexion, he plays well on the Violin and several other instruments. He is a shrewd, smart fellow and of a very affable countenance, and is twenty five years of age…

Another part of the same group ad reads:

> A NEGROE MAN SLAVE, NAMED NOAH,
>
> Full 6 feet high; black complexion; full eyes; free spoken and intelligent; will weigh about 180 pounds; 32 years old; had with him 2 or 3 suits of clothes, white hat, short blue blanket coat, a pair of saddle bags, a packet compass, and supposed to have $350 or $400 with him.

For even more physical detail:

Negro man Slave named Bob,

Copper color, high cheek bones, 5 11 inches high, weighs about 150 pounds' 22 years old very white teeth and a space between the center of the upper teeth. Had a blue blanket sack coat with red stripeed linsey lining.[55]

The wanted posters and ads are examples of both antebellum social control and of the technical and organizational inadequacy of that control: biometric identification was applied to runaways after the fact.

WAR AND STANDARDIZATION

The Civil War created among other problems a crisis of identification in the South. Amid the chaos both armies imposed strict pass laws on all people. At times these military passes were handwritten and as simple as the original slave passes. But more often they were printed forms that incorporated the standardized categories of description that had been part of many "free papers" and ads for runaways. For example, a Union-issued pass for soldier Joseph Meekers (who later became a moderately famous landscape painter) is a double-sided, printed form with underlined spaces for appropriate information to be filled in by hand. It reads:

Office of Provost Marshal,

St. Louis, Mo., *Sept. 27th* 1861

Permission is granted to *J R. Meeker* to

Pass beyond the limits of the city and county of St. Louis,

To go to *Illinois*

Issued by *[illegible signature]*

Major U.S.A., Provost Marshal

And on the reverse side…

Description of Person

Name *J R Meeker*

Age *34*
Height *6 ft 11/4*
Color of Eyes *Hazel*
Color of Hair *DK Brown*
Peculiarities *Good Looking* [56]

Confederate passes required age and height, along with eye and hair color. Interestingly, both armies used a jumbled variety of letter fonts; this was in part typical of the typography of the time but intentionally or otherwise made counterfeiting pass forms all the more difficult.

Another important technology of surveillance is the passport. As John Torpey has detailed, passports are one of the earliest continuously used political technologies of state control. The embryonic form of the passport was the traditional letter of safe passage, and these personalized documents date back to ancient times. From the letter of safe passage emerges the ever more standardized passport. For Torpey, the passport and "identification papers of various kinds constitute the bureaucratic equivalent of money: they are the currency of modern state administration."[57] As early as the 1820s, US passports, still in the form of large folded letters, contained elaborate descriptions of the bearer. These included the usual categories of height and hair and eye color, but they also included some rather subjective features. Passport no. 992, issued to John Finney in 1826, listed several elements in its description column that stand out for their pseudo standardization:

Forehead *common*
Eyes *dark*
Nose *common*
Mouth *common*
Chin *roundish* [58]

Other passports describe "low" foreheads "medium" mouths and "florid" complexions.

Military passes and passports, together with the surveillance regime of slavery, are some of the main tributaries that fed into the development of modern technologies of identification and registration. With the end of slavery and then the end of radical reconstruction the development of surveillance technology shifted to the terrain of criminal justice and the control of immigrant labor. At the same time new technologies, such as photography and precise body measurements, became available, allowing a profound deepening of state control, everyday surveillance, and discipline.

3

THE ACCUMULATION OF BODIES, PART I: IDENTIFICATION AND PHOTOGRAPHY

Photography is so essentially the Art of Truth—and the representative of Truth in Art—that it would seem to be the essential means of reproducing all forms and structures of which science seeks for delineation.

— *The Lancet*, 1859

Industrialization in the mid-nineteenth century brought with it rapid urbanization as well as increased poverty, crime, disease, and rebellion. In these forces, the emerging social order of industrial society faced a host of threats. Some of these were direct, such as the riots that ripped through American cities in the 1830s and 1840s; or the pitched gun battles between workers and state militias during the "great upheaval" of 1877–78. Other challenges were seemingly indirect and apolitical, such as lack of sanitation and widespread epidemics of typhoid, diphtheria, and scarlet fever. Riots were epidemic, and epidemics ran riot.[1]

Between 1800 and 1850 New York's population grew almost tenfold, from 60,000 to half a million; then in the next ten years it doubled to one million.[2] Packs of knife-wielding homeless children roamed wild; the streets were frequently blocked with heaps of garbage, ash, and the fetid corpses of draft horses; feral swine spread filth and disease. Similar conditions obtained in the other booming hubs of commerce and industry.

The overarching concept that connected these social and natural threats in the minds of the better classes was "disorder."[3] Chief among disorders was *crime*—theft, arson, sabotage, assault, gambling, sex work, opium smoking, drunkenness, gang warfare, and killing. Here was the nexus of all bad things. In crime, the rule-breaking of the working classes overlapped with the forces of mental degeneration and biological contagion; it was seen as the wellspring of larger evils: a connective tissue binding both disease and rebellion.

Controlling this broad kaleidoscope of urban threats meant controlling the lower classes in general, and this required a new regime of *everyday* social control, operating at the "capillary level" of routine identification and regulation. Anthony Giddens calls this process, a standard feature in the development of modern nation states, "internal pacification."[4] Commenting on this process more generally, Foucault had this to say: "If the economic take-off of the west began with the techniques that made possible the accumulation of capital, it might perhaps be said that the methods for administering the accumulation of men made possible a political take-off. . . . In fact the two processes . . . cannot be separated. . . ."[5]

This "accumulation" of people required first and foremost their identification as individuals and as social types. In the field of criminal justice this was accomplished with three technologies that developed in a concatenated and layered form. They were photography, Bertillonage, and then fingerprinting. From these arts comes the basic structure of modern identification. The story runs as follows: The advent of professional police forces coincided with the proliferation of photography and police use of the new technology to identify prisoners and criminals. Organizing large police photo logs soon required a coherent system of indexing. From this indexing emerged Bertillonage, the first "anthropometric" or biometric form of identifying bodies with measurements. Finally, from this cumbersome system of body measurements emerged the simpler, more reliable practice of "dactyloscopy," or fingerprinting. We begin with photographs.

FROM CHAOS, THE EVERYDAY STATE

In 1829 the first modern constabulary was born: They were the London Metropolitan Police a full-time, uniformed, and paramilitary force. However, in libertine Jacksonian America, the "London Model," although praised by elites, met with stiff resistance from the general populace who feared that a "standing army" of lawmen would threaten civil liberties. Such sentiment and the general disorganization of local government delayed the formation of any such force in the United States for some time. Instead, Americans relied on private police, slave patrols, and traditional night-watch systems. But as social conflict escalated throughout the 1830s and 1840s culminating in wave upon wave of urban riots, the movement to establish professional police forces gained ground.[6]

Perhaps the demand for professional policing and the routine surveillance that went with it is best understood in relation to the "mobbing" or riots of the mid-nineteenth century. More akin to urban combat than mere "civil disturbances," mobbing often took on political and racial overtones. One African American veteran of the scene left this account of the mayhem and barbarism of a Philadelphia race riot in September 1849:

> I was identified with a company of young men, calling themselves the Stringers, and was placed that night as captain of the company. I fired the first shot on the Moyamensing Killers [a white gang]. When the California House was set on fire, at the corner of Sixth and St. Mary's Alley, I rushed up to try and put it out, and was shot in my right thigh with buckshot, and also received a blow over my left eye—the mark of which is there until this day. I made my escape as soon as possible and went to a doctor's; but the doctor, after looking at me, said, "You are not hurt; go and try them again." I went, and fought harder than ever. The women tore up all the sidewalk, so that the men could get bricks and stones to fight with. At two o'clock in the morning the fighting ceased, but was renewed again at seven

> and I was the first who fired on the Killers that day . . . members of the Goodwill Hose Company, who were on the side of the colored citizens, came to my assistance, and then we had a free fight of it; but I am sorry to say there were seven or eight of that company shot that day. There were also two colored men shot, and several wounded, and the California House was burned to ashes. . . . This riot was created by the Irish democrats.[7]

Such organized and prolonged violence required the state to develop more regimented forms of social control. In 1836, city officials in New Orleans created the first full-time civilian patrol, though unarmed and lacking uniforms. Philadelphia and Boston started similar small-scale experiments around the same time. But it was New York City that created America's first full-time, armed police force in 1845. With an initial staffing of 800 men the NYPD provided round-the-clock security service and was charged with preventing and solving crimes. Initially attired in civilian clothes, the New York cops were soon forced to don what the line officers bitterly called "an expensive and fantastical uniform." Within a few years most other major American cities had also created armed, uniformed "London-style" police.[8] As the interlocking institutions of the law—police, courts, and prisons—developed, so too did the need for more reliable forms of identification and routine surveillance. Again, New York led the way.

The primary task of the early cops was, much as it is today, "maintaining order" by controlling petty offenses like picking pockets, shoplifting, prostitution, forgery, public inebriation, and so on. Among the enemy was a new breed of criminal, confidence men, who hid within the veils of anonymity offered by the new, highly mobile polyglot society created by industrial urbanization and mass immigration.[9] In the modern city of the mid-nineteenth century police faced a society of strangers; miscreants were not simply "known to the community" but had to be discovered and formally tagged as such.

VISIONS OF PUBLIC ORDER

Aiding in this task came the scientific novelty of "painting pictures with sun beams." In 1839 Louis Jacques Mande Daguerre joined with the

French country landlord and amateur scientist Joseph Nicephore Niépce, first inventor of photography, to produce permanent images requiring only twenty-minute exposures. The new glass-plate daguerreotypes gained mass popularity within a few years, and as they did the technology improved and the time needed for exposure dropped.[10] By the late 1840s once numerous "miniaturist" portrait painters were on the verge of professional extinction, driven out of business by inexpensive photographs. By 1853, Americans were buying three million daguerreotypes a year. Typically the images were sentimental totems of middle-class probity in which subjects posed in galleries decked in lavish, theatrical settings complete with velvet drapes, caged birds, and stained glass. In 1841 cheap, quick paper prints became available; competition intensified and portrait prices dropped even further.[11]

Before long this amazing new information technology was taken up by the state. Photography, like the law and science, sought to know and fix as fact "the truth." The realism of photography dovetailed perfectly with criminal justice at both a practical and ideological level. As such, photography extended and enhanced state power, operating at two levels: defining and constructing social types, and identifying individuals. Cesare Lombroso and kindred European criminologists would use photography to "uncover" the "stigmata" of the "born criminal."[12] In the hands of doctors, social workers, or police officials photography could thus "expose" signs of physical maladies, mental degradation, moral decay, or criminality. These photographic "truth claims" could then justify a myriad of interventions ranging from medical help to legal punishment.[13]

ROGUES' GALLERIES

By the early nineteenth century many courts had begun keeping permanent paper records containing the details and descriptions of defendants and prisoners. Some of the earliest such dossiers were established by the French Courts of Assizes in 1808. And even before photography, many police departments in the U.K. had shared bulletins and gazettes containing the physical descriptions of wanted persons. At other times constables in search of fugitives would dispatch descriptive letters to their counterparts in other jurisdictions. Police agencies in France and England also had weekly parades or formations of prisoners at which detectives from neighboring jurisdictions who were looking for suspects would scan the ranks of captives for familiar faces.[14]

By 1841 some police in France had added to these practices the routine photographing of prisoners. A year later, police throughout Britain, starting in Birmingham, were using glass-plate photos called "ambrosetypes" to capture the images of prisoners. In 1853, the New York City Police Department began photographing repeat offenders and publishing their images in a "rogues' gallery." Philadelphia, Albany, and a handful of other cities opened similar galleries soon after; in all cases the public was "invited to call and examine" the images. By 1858 the NYPD had 450 "ambrosetypes" of habitual offenders and a few years later most major departments from Moscow to San Francisco had also opened rogues' galleries.[15]

The optical politics of these spaces worked in several ways. First, there was the obvious function of identifying wanted lawbreakers. But the middle classes who visited the galleries were also performing a ritual of obedience and allegiance to the state. To visit a police gallery was to position oneself as an official "insider" opposed to the state's enemies.

One of the more ardent enthusiasts of early criminal photography was Thomas Byrnes, head of New York's detective bureau and then chief of police until 1895. In 1886 he published *Professional Criminals of America*, a large photobook on known lawbreakers, almost all of them "confidence men" and forgers—scam artists who thrived on the anonymity of rapid urbanization. Under Byrnes the rogues' gallery morphed into an actual intelligence center: fifty copies were made of each mug shot, some for use in local precincts, others for detectives in the field, and still others for mailing to distant departments.[16]

San Francisco seems to have adopted a similar system, with detectives carrying portable "mug books" as early as the first years of the 1870s. One remaining example is the mug book of San Francisco Police Department detective Delos Woodruff, who used his portable rogues' gallery to work the streets of Chinatown in the 1860s and 1870s. This long, narrow leather-bound volume sits nicely in one's hand and could conceivably fit into a large coat pocket. Unclip the leather binding and the pages fall open

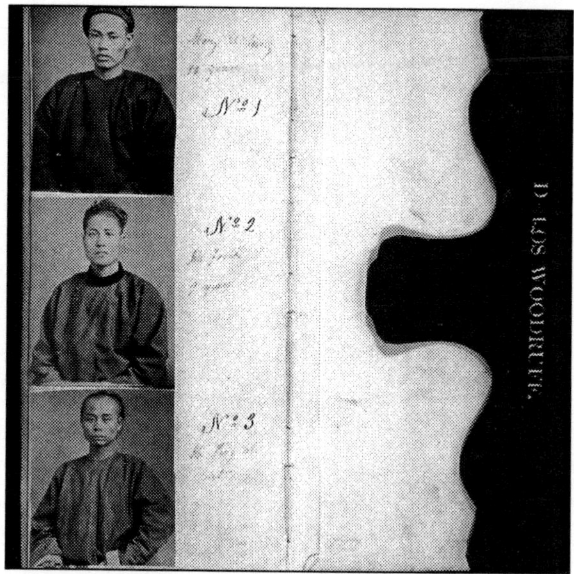

Wong Ah Wing, Ah Foock, and Ping Ah: San Francisco mug shots circa 1870 (credit: California Historical Society)

readily; out from the verso page stare three identically sized portraits of young, hard-looking Chinese men. With little or no writing next to the photos, one might assume that the photo-ledger was less a guide for Woodruff and more likely a tool used to jog other people's memories during curbside interrogations.[17] Whatever the case, Woodruff's book, like a visit to the rogues' gallery, served both technical and moral purposes. His photos identified the presumed hoodlums of Chinatown but also helped construct "insider" and "outsider" identities and in effect recruited rank-and-file citizens into the state's project of surveillance and control.

While a great advance over the subjective, incomplete physical descriptions of earlier gazettes, the new medium had its limits. The rogues' galleries were, like slave passes and wanted posters, haphazard and only vaguely effective. Most important, photography was a powerful tool only if a suspect could be matched to an image, a task that was easier said than done. And the more photos police produced, the harder became the process of sorting, organizing, and using them. With hundreds, even thousands, of images on file, how were the photos to be archived? By name, physical description, numerical code? All of these methods were tried; all were resisted. When departments listed their "rogues" by name, the rogues turned to using aliases. Regardless, once a photo collection reached critical mass, its organization usually fell apart and chaos reigned. Success produced failure.

In San Francisco police tried to track the "criminal fraternity" with a system involving two parallel ledger books. One, "the mug book," contained frontal and profile images listed by number; when trying to identify a suspect officers would flip through this book looking for a match. The number next to each photo correlated to a physical description and a case history held in another ledger, called the "photo key book." These entries were handwritten, replete with misspellings, strange homemade punctuation, and simple abbreviations like PL for petty larceny, SP for state prison, and CJ for county jail. At times the narrative dossiers followed a criminal career from start to finish; a few examples illustrate their episodic and idiosyncratic nature:

> James Simpson ALIAS "Shorty Simpson," Born in Baltimore age 21 years, height 5 feet 3 _ , 155lb—fair complexion—hight full forhead—large gray eyes. short—full nose small mouth—short full face—round chin—dark hair—hair straight—
>
> marks
>
> Two joints off third finger of left hand, two large scares over the temple under hair –
>
> crime
>
> arrested by coffey inness on three charges of burglary sent to county court oct 26 1871
>
> [new entry]
>
> reduced to P.L. Jan 26th 1872. 9 months C.J.
>
> [new entery,]
>
> May 2n 1874 S.P. 6 years, Arst. to Rol. [5979]
>
> May 17, 1878 discharged per Oct. and Pardoned
>
> DEAD
>
> Died from an overdose chloral hydrate on 329 Bush st. 7th 1884[18]

More often the records are brief with barely any history or description.

Lizzie Shrum = born in Irland. Aged 23 years hiegt 5ft–4in
Weight 123 lbs Dark Complexion grey Eyes.
Black hair. full face. nose large + Small Mouth
Sent to jail for 6 days for petty Larceny of twenty one dollars
local officer
becker
[no date][19]

Or this. . .

richard cornell aged 19 years height 5 ft 7inc weight 165 pounds Complexion Rather dark gray eyes hair Black fool face has ben arested several times for Larceny
Offisers A W Stone
And Selinger
June 22/71 Co, court robbery[20]

These files (if they even merit that description) were unhelpfully arranged in chronological order, by date of arrest. Presumably, police officers when seeking to identify suspects would simply flip through the many photo ledgers looking for a likely match and then check the photo key book for a handwritten case history. It's obvious from such records that, in San Francisco at least, the whole intelligence infrastructure of policing was unorganized well into the late nineteenth century.

FROM IMAGE TO BODY

At one level this surviving paperwork is mundane, even prosaic, but read from another angle these records give us significant insights into the micropractices that, in their aggregate form, constitute *actual* state power and bureaucratic social control. Recall Weber's insights: without proper files there could be no modern business firm, no nation state, no functioning criminal law. When the state's files were in disarray, it was for better and for worse a weaker force.[21]

By 1912, the mug shots in NYPD's rogues' gallery were posted on broad, yardwide panels, each of which was mounted on hinges and allowed to turn like the stiff pages of a giant, wall-mounted book. Each page, or panel, extended from a man's waist to his head with ten rows of twelve photos stacked on each page. Facing two open panels the viewer would address a roughly two-foot-high and six-foot-long wall of wallet-sized photo portraits.[22] Needless to say, going through such a mass of photos was a time-consuming endeavor. As jurists in the UK found, "such a vast list of names . . . such a vast mound of photographs . . . became useless as a means of identification."[23]

What police forces needed were systems of information management; reliable methods of *indexing* their photographs. The first forces to develop such means appear to have been in Britain. Originally, jail wardens, detectives from Scotland Yard, and officers from the London Metropolitan Police would gather three times a week at Holloway Prison to visually identify prisoners. To supplement this ritual, some photos and written descriptions were circulated to outlying areas. But starting in 1869 with the passage of the Habitual Criminals Act, police were required to keep an "Alphabetical Registry" and a cross-referenced "Distinctive Marks Registry." The former held names, the latter descriptions of scars, tattoos, birthmarks, balding, pockmarks, and other distinguishing features.

This Distinctive Marks Registry was itself systematically disaggregated into nine general categories pertaining to regions of the body. Thus, there were files for the head and face; throat and neck; chest; belly and groin; back and loins; arms; hands and fingers; thighs and legs; feet and ankles. Police clerks would first check the Alphabetical Registry for an arrestee's name hoping to find a corresponding photo and file. When that failed the clerk would search the prisoner's body for a "distinctive mark" and then check one of the nine body-area files for a match. Simon Coles, an expert on the history of identification, describes the process well: "If a prisoner was found to have a prominent and seemingly permanent burn scar on the inside of his right arm, the clerk would refer to the Distinctive Marks Registry, look under the heading 'right arm,' then consult the subheading 'scars from wounds or burns,' and then the sub-subheading 'inside.'"[24] Other departments had methods that were rather more subjective, imprecise, and labor-intensive, but this organization of the body into a standardized text to be read by the law was a crucial innovation in modern identification.

4

THE ACCUMULATION OF BODIES, PART II: EARLY BIOMETRICS

> The unidentified American—we find him everywhere where trouble is.
>
> — *New York Times*, 1912

Alphonse Bertillon started out as a lowly French police clerk, though he was the scion of an august scientific family and would eventually become so famous that when he died the size and weight of his brain (rather small) made international news.[1] His father, Louis-Alphonse Bertillon, was a pioneer in the fields of demography and anthropology; his brothers, Jacques and George, were also prominent academics. Meanwhile, the young Alphonse was a slacker who drifted about France and Britain until finally Bertillon senior secured his son a clerical job with the Parisian police.

There Alphonse confronted the typical chaos of huge, poorly organized, and therefore practically useless police files. It was a situation made all the worse by the 1871 Paris Commune, during which radical workers on the eve of their defeat took one final act of defiance and burnt all city files predating 1859. This attempt to "smash the bureaucratic-military machine" of the state effectively erased mountains of worker debt as well as the countless criminal histories used to stigmatize the poor, the mad, the Roma, prostitutes, and political subversives. In fact, some of the only "records" left after the uprising were the many documentary photos taken during the Commune's brief reign—these tended to be popular portraits of proud Communards posing on the barricades—taken by photographers like Auguste Braquehais. During the *semaine sanglante* in which French authorities took their revenge and massacred thousands, the execution squads used these same photos to identify former Communards.[2] Nonetheless, at the end of the Commune Parisians over the age of twenty-one were largely free to invent any identity they pleased.[3]

INDEX AS IDENTITY

Disgusted by the organizational chaos of post-Commune Paris, Bertillon set to work rectifying the mess. By the late 1870s he had devised a solution: the trick was to use the anthropometric tools and principles of colonial anthropology in the police prefectures at Montmartre and Belleville.

As Europe conquered much of the planet, the first generation of anthropologists and phrenologists—among them Bertillon senior and his elder sons—devoted themselves to "discovering" the macro-level human types of modern race theory. The methods always involved measuring "savage" bodies in search of "racial phenotypes." Alphonse Bertillon saw in his father's tools a methodology that could be redeployed down to the scale of individual bodies. Using the same awkward metal calipers and taxonomic methodology he sought to produce *exact* statistical portraits—not of groups—but of individuals.[4]

The system, eventually called "Bertillonage," began as a means of cataloguing and retrieving mug shots and police files, but soon become a form of identification in itself. Before long, Bertillon's system of body measurement identification was more trusted than the photography it was supposed to index. In the Bertillon system each prisoner's dossier held a card containing the usual mug shot and description of distinguishing marks, as well as eleven different categories of exact bodily measurement. Each numerical value was the product of a tightly choreographed scientific procedure in which only a trained "Bertillon operator" would manipulate and measure the prisoner's body from head to toe. As the great identifier himself put it, "The anthropological length of the foot is different from the *measure* taken by the shoemaker." The Bertillon operator's aim was to elicit from the body a set of constant, nonsubjective measurements that could be reproduced exactly by any other operator applying calipers in exactly the same way. Such measurements were then translated into an elaborately coded vocabulary that was itself abbreviated. To its credit, this fussy chain of rituals produced dramatically consistent numerical portraits.

As Simon Coles points out, this "digitalization" of the targeted body allowed the law to track a subject across time and space in ways photography alone could not. With Bertillonage, a police clerk in one jurisdiction could telegraph numerical information to a counterpart in any other jurisdiction and receive an electronic answer within minutes.[5] The repeat offender—a category that dovetailed nicely with prevalent notions of the "born criminal"—could no longer hide behind an alias, disguise, or even the wear of aging. This coordination of everyday police practices marked a seismic shift in the politics of identity and routine surveillance.[6]

IDENTIFYING ANARCHISTS

By the beginning of the 1890s police and colonial administrators throughout the world were using Bertillonage, or at least versions of it. One catalyst for this proliferation was the new level of international cooperation among law enforcement agencies, which was itself partly a response to increased immigration and the rise of international anarchism. Unlike the Black Bloc of today's global justice movement, these anarchists really did make war on capital and the state.

During the late nineteenth century the US faced a wave of militant labor organizing, strikes, and anarchist bombings. Composed mainly of Italian, Russian, and Polish immigrants, a radical "new left" was gaining ground throughout the country, spurred in part by the hanging of the four labor activists known as the "Haymarket martyrs" on November 11, 1887, in Chicago. During the next two decades anarchists, who were often skilled, highly mobile, hard-to-track immigrant workers, assassinated six heads of state (including President William McKinley, shot down on September 6, 1901, by the young blacksmith Leon Czolgosz). Even Alexander Berkman—Emma Goldman's comrade-lover—made a move on Andrew Carnegie's associate Henry Clay Frick. In 1892, Berkman blasted the plutocrat three times with a pistol and then stabbed him seven times; miraculously, and to the shame of anarchists ever since, Frick lived. At the same time the Industrial Workers of the World (IWW)—using the transport arteries of the railroads as their political and information networks to organize workers—led strikes and otherwise caused trouble for the rich and their corporations.

Thus, it was not simple happenstance that the *New York Times* placed an article on the "world wide" effort to identify criminals using Bertillonage just above a profile of "international" anarchist Emma Goldman.[7] In fact, a lateral reading of that era's newspapers reveals numerous such connections, indicating a general field of interlinked issues. The project of identifying common outlaws was bound up with the war against rising political radicalism.

But Bertillonage had its weaknesses. Capturing *exact* measurements required extremely precise and consistent procedures. To achieve this precision Bertillon created a Taylorized choreography of movements that his "operators" were required to follow in every detail. For example, measuring a foot required twenty exact movements, which combined were designed to force subjects to press their full weight on the measured foot, thus causing maximum extension of the toes and thus an exact measurement. The problem was that not all Bertillon operators used the same procedures or codes. Instead, many local police forces—too proud or lazy to do what the French experts demanded—simplified and changed Bertillonage as they saw fit. In 1896, for example, the admissions registry at New York's Sing Sing Prison measured shoe size rather than anthropometric foot length.[8] Such vernacular versions of the systems worked only in relation to themselves; as soon as information was traded across jurisdictions, chaos returned and the rigid system of biometric values was transformed into just so much numerical noise. From the start, Bertillon's overly complex system was vulnerable to better ideas.

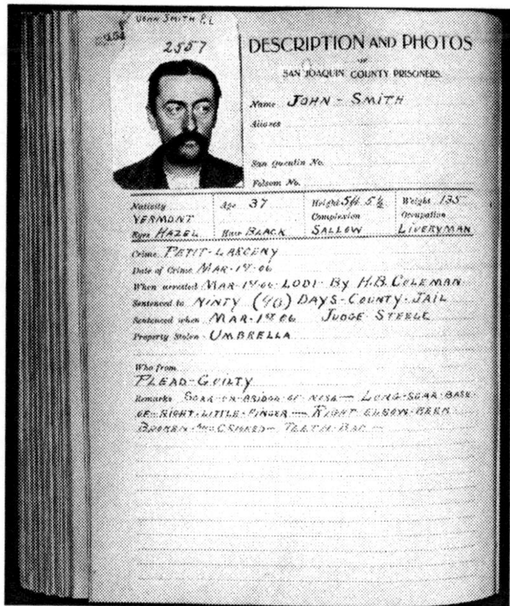

2557

DESCRIPTION AND PHOTOS OF SAN JOAQUIN COUNTY PRISONERS

Name JOHN - SMITH

Aliases

San Quentin No.

Folsom No.

Nativity VERMONT | Age 37 | Height 5 ft. 5½ | Weight 135
Eyes HAZEL | Hair BLACK | Complexion SALLOW | Occupation LIVERYMAN

Crime PETIT-LARCENY

Date of Crime MAR-1st-06

When arrested MAR-1st-06 LODI By H.B. COLEMAN

Sentenced to NINTY (90) DAYS-COUNTY-JAIL

Sentenced when MAR-1st 06 JUDGE STEELE

Property Stolen UMBRELLA

Who from

PLEAD-GUILTY

Remarks

John Smith, San Joaquin County prisoner, 1906
(credit: California Historical Society)

DACTYLOSCOPY AS SCIENTIFIC HOBBY

In 1857 the Sepoy mercenaries of the British East India Company rebelled and temporarily overthrew British rule in northern India. Massive and bloody repression eventually righted the ship, but the "Indian Mutiny"—as it is known among the English—transformed British rule in the subcontinent. For one thing, it led to the end of the East India Company. In the chaotic years following the rebellion violence, theft, and fraud surged.

To combat this disarray, the chief administrative officer of the Hoogley district of Bengal, William Herschel, began experimenting with the use of inked handprints on documents as a means of verifying the identity of contractors, pensioners, and other local people with whom he had official dealings. In all probability Herschel gleaned this technique from similar ancient Hindi practices that were themselves most likely borrowed from China.[9] Whatever the case, Herschel's prints served to exert

British control in the field of identity. With handprint records the British could shape and control knowledge and thus political situations. Herschel created a technology of "truth" from which flowed legal power, legitimation, and accountability. More specifically, handprints on documents enabled Herschel to catch imposters attempting to collect pensions fraudulantly or contract payments owed to others. But the innovation had another, less instrumental, heuristic impact. Catching forgers forced Asians to "internalize the gaze" of the British overlords just a little bit more.

Simultaneously, several other members of the gentlemanly class were also "discovering" the papillary ridges of the finger tips and "inventing" fingerprinting. Most prominent among them was the eccentric Francis Galton—father of eugenics and cousin of Charles Darwin. (In his youth Galton had conducted experiments on himself with medical and psychoactive drugs, going through the pharmacopoeia in alphabetical order until finally quitting at the end of the letter C. He recalled in his memoirs that "it was an interesting experience, but had obvious drawbacks.")[10] Galton's study of fingerprints, like the senior Bertillon's use of body measurements, operated at the macro-level in search of "race" and heredity. Though a racist and keen to rank darker people as inferior and distinct from whites, Galton was at least honest enough with his evidence to admit that there was no link between the papillary ridges of the human digits and the political category of race.

However Galton's experiments did yield a system of classification that divided all human prints into three basic subpatterns: loops, whorls, and arches. These categories were refined further by Edward Henry, another colonial administrator, who by counting papillary ridges was able to break loops, whorls, and arches into even smaller subsets.[11]

The first person to float the idea of using prints for criminal identification was Henry Faulds, a British physician working in Japan; his famous suggestion appeared as a letter to *Nature* in 1880.[12] Faulds, a classic Victorian modernizer, expended much effort in the following decade attempting to persuade police to include fingerprinting in their ever-growing dossiers. Few officials were interested, and "dactyloscopy"—as print reading was known—failed to become a standard law enforcement tool for another generation.

PRINTS AS A POLITICAL TOOL

Among dactyloscopy's chief advantages—or so believed white colonial administrators, police, and bureaucrats—was its ability to compensate for the homogenizing effects of racist perceptions. Edward Henry's innovations, for example, were explicitly driven by this idea. Like many white men, Henry doubted the utility of photography or Bertillonage when applied to black and brown bodies. How was a white warden or cop to recognize one dark face from the next? Dactyloscopy seemed to offer a way out. As one identification expert noted in 1902, fingerprinting would help "in the official identification of Chinese, Negroes, and other races the features of which at least to the Caucasian eye, offer hardly sufficient individuality to be at all times trustworthy."[13]

Thus, following the lead of Herschel in India, white administrators and police who saw (or imagined) Asians, Africans, and Native Americans as bafflingly homogeneous began to fall back on the infinite uniqueness of fingerprints. Thus, fingerprinting literally migrated from colonial periphery to the economic core. In the United States the first populations to be fingerprinted en masse were convicts, petty criminals, soldiers, and Native peoples.

The historical record offers conflicting accounts as to which constabulary force first deployed dactyloscopy, but it was most likely the Argentine Central Police in 1891. The "system builder" leading this revolution was a Croatian immigrant named Juan Vucetich, who eventually became chief of the Office of Identification. Since all the European print classification systems (and there were many) appeared inadequate in the eyes of Vucetich, he reworked Henry's modification of Galton's arches, loops, and whorls. In 1892, Juan Vucetich made his first positive identification, catching a repeat offender who had been using an alias. (As yet, lifting "latent prints" at crime scenes was not possible.)

Colonial police in India began using the Henry system in 1897, and by 1902 Scotland Yard had incorporated a form of fingerprinting into its Bertillonage. The first real working fingerprint file in the US was used by police brass upon other would-be cops. Among the myriad forms of corruption plaguing New York's Finest at the turn of the century was mass cheating on civil service exams. In fact, some police applicants were so illiterate and unprepared that they resorted to hiring imposters to sit the exams in their stead. One stand-in, who had taken the test for at least twelve different officers, blew the whole scam when he sued several ungrateful cops who had failed to pay him!

For their own reasons, the city fathers wanted a more reliable and professional police force, so the Police Commission ordered Chief Medical Examiner Hennery Deforest to devise a system of identification that would cut down on testing fraud. He visited Scotland Yard and returned a booster of fingerprinting. Several other police agencies began investigating similar uses of fingerprints at the same time.[14]

But it was the flamboyant demonstration of dactyloscopy by a dashing young Scotland Yard detective named John Kenneth Ferris at the 1904 St. Louis World's Fair that led to the fingerprint revolution in US police departments. Within a few years of the fair, attended by many important law enforcement players, most major departments were using dactyloscopy, among them: Boston, Baltimore, Washington, D.C., St. Louis, Cincinnati, Cleveland, Louisville, Indianapolis, and Memphis. The navy, too, began printing sailors and in 1907 started using its files to bust deserters. Meanwhile, the popular press started touting the ability of fingerprints to identify war dead and the mutilated victims of accidents. Two years after the fair the NYPD brass sent another representative—Sergeant Joseph A. Faurot, who would later lead the department's Identification Bureau—on a junket to Scotland Yard. He too returned "completely converted to the finger print system," and the department added the technology to its Bertillon files. So too, did Leavenworth Penitentiary, and these files soon formed the basis of the federal government's first National Identification Bureau, which eventually become the FBI's Bureau of Identification.[15]

Around the same time, less than ten years after the last army massacre of Native Americans, the Commissioner of Indian Affairs of the Department of the Interior started inking hands on the reservations in conjunction with payment records and land deeds, such as the ones in which the Lakota were forced to privatize and surrender much of the Rosebud Reservation in 1907. In fact, nationwide dactyloscopy on reservations coincided with a major white land grab. Thanks to late application of the 1887 General Allotment, or Dawes Act the turn of the century brought with it a new wave of enclosures on Indian land. Native people were forced to break up, commodify, and sell off their tribal commons.

The government agents in charge of building dossiers on native people and of overseeing reservation economics were urged "to use the greatest care in carrying out this plan, as it is desired to have, within the shortest time possible, an infallible method of identification in case of dispute or attempted fraud."[16]

PROLIFERATION

By 1910 prosecutors and cops had their first criminal convictions based on fingerprints. Here, too, race and racism greased the skids of a new technology of identification. The defendant in this landmark case was a Black man accused of robbing and killing a white woman. The only evidence against housepainter Thomas Jennings was a set of prints left in the still tacky paint of a porch railing. Police, ready to blame Jennings, removed the railing, photographed the prints, and showed them to have thirty-three points of similarity with those taken from Jennings. Even the editors the *New York Times*, ardent advocates of dactyloscopy and not particularly forward thinking on race relations, were disturbed by the ruling. They noted that even if Jennings "had left the marks on the railing, that is no absolute proof that he committed the murder." The case went all the way to the Supreme Court, where Jennings's sentence of death was upheld and with it the power of this latest technology of routine surveillance.[17]

Here, increased registration and identification was clearly part of a broad project of racial, gender, and class discipline. Dactyloscopy and criminal photography helped create a new type of, what Foucault called, "governmentality," that is, the self-control necessary to be governed.[18]

THE DRIVE FOR MANDATORY IDENTIFICATION

As the Progressive Era hit its stride and the utility of fingerprinting became widely accepted, there arose a clamor among the better classes for mandatory identification and registration of the entire population. This message was promulgated most aggressively by "good government" reformers showboating, media-savvy cops like Captain Faurot and Argentina's Vucetich. In fact, many leaders in law enforcement, Vucetich in particular, wanted a worldwide system of registration; by 1900 everyone in Buenos Aires already had their prints and photographs filed with the police, the military, and the Interior Department.[19] By the mid–1910s the call for wider use of fingerprinting grew particularly vociferous across the US. World War I added momentum to the crusade as opinion makers debated fingerprinting all "aliens" and most applicants for the military were being photographed and fingerprinted (so as to prevent deserters from reenlisting). Throughout this clamor pundits proffered a steady stream of apolitical justifications. In response to a letter decrying military use of fingerprinting and photographs the *New York Times* wrote: "The world, like the army, is full of cruel wrongs and bitter insults for those who look for them, but why manufacture more out of nothing—or of easily tolerable things like having one's picture and finger prints on record?"[20] But for many citizens, giving one's fingerprints to the police was seen as an insulting mark of incrimination. Resistance to dactyloscopy began to mount.

NO TO PRINTS!

It was early June 1916 and NYPD officer Frank Rice had been detailed to Washington Heights, where he was to stake out and bust cases of "disorderly conduct." Among his captives that day were three teenage boys playing baseball. Officer Rice made his arrests and the lads were convicted, fined, and ordered to submit to fingerprinting in accordance with a 1913 disorderly conduct statute. That would have been that, but the mothers of the disorderly boys in question protested and went to the press. Public outrage followed. Crucial to the case was the symbolism of *baseball*. The all-American game could now get you jail time and a permanent record? As usual, officialdom attempted to calm public passions with appeals to the *scientific* and *expert* nature of the discourse within which recorded fingerprints circulated. "The fingerprint," assured Police Commissioner Burdette G. Lewis, "is the most scientific record that can be kept. It cannot be placed in the Rogues' Gallery, where it may be seen and recognized. Unlike hand writing it can not be read by the average individual; it can only be read by an expert."[21] A court official explained the need for fingerprinting petty violators more candidly: "In the cases of persons who have been convicted three or more times for disorderly conduct or vagrancy within one year, the Magistrate shall have the power to commit the offender for an indeterminate period not to exceed to two years. This . . . provides a much needed check upon habitual offenders."[22] In other words, widespread fingerprinting was an indispensable tool for effectively punishing the visibly poor.

Later that year, the courts drew up a more precise definition of which offenses and what types of people would require fingerprinting: "jostling, trying to pickpockets, rowdyism in public conveyances, mashing of women in public streets, degenerates, beggars, confidence men, swindlers, and offenses involving riotous conduct . . . disorderly women, intoxicated persons and vagrants." Thanks to public pressure, the American Pastime and "ordinary street brawls" were exempt.[23]

BOMBS, FINGERPRINTS, AND RED RAIDS

As World War I ended, the call for universal fingerprint registration increased. The late 1910s and early 1920s were a dangerous and volatile era in which the pent-up political and economic demands of workers burst forth. During the war workers had effectively signed a truce with employers. In exchange, recalcitrant employers had finally recognized the American Federation of Labor's right to organize skilled workers in exchange for a no-strike pledge, because, as Woodrow Wilson put it, "America is on strike against Europe." But when the war ended in victory and a booming economy (soon to be a slump), workers expected and demanded more. What ensued was the last great armed conflict between American labor and capital.

The far left was bitterly opposed to the Great War, which it saw as a senseless fight between rich men, paid for with the blood and money of working people. Between 1914 and 1917, anarchist cells set off bombs in New York, Boston, and other cities. Most caused only minor injuries, except for a 1917 explosion in Milwaukee that dispatched ten policemen to an early grave.

However, much of the left was not so active. Early in the war years, patriotism and conscription, a halt to immigration, and the wartime economic boom had effectively demobilized labor: the working class was busy with war and production. What jingoism and economic expansion did not achieve, government surveillance and repression took care of. All factories with government contracts were subject to "plant protection"—a system of federally organized volunteer spying on a mass scale. There was also the Espionage Act, passed in 1917, and the Sedition Act of 1918, which made it illegal to advocate opposition to the federal government or to the war effort.[24] But with the economy under state regulation and industrial production going full steam, union strength eventually began to grow: the American Federation of Labor (often an openly bigoted organization of skilled white tradesmen) increased its ranks by some two million while the racially integrated and more radical IWW also increased its strike activity and membership as victory in Europe became inevitable. Then came a further spur: the Bolshevik conquest in Russia. The wartime dam of worker restraint finally gave way with a massive labor offensive after the armistice of November 11, 1918.

The first city to go was Seattle in late January 1919, when 35,000 mostly skilled shipyard workers dropped their tools to demand a wage increase. The federal government, still the ultimate authority in the semi-nationalized wartime shipyards, told the owners to hold fast against the militants. In short order the walkout blew up into a highly disciplined citywide general strike. Nothing moved without approval of the strike committee. Inspired by the Russian soviets, strikers seized and began autonomously operating numerous industries and set up laundries, dairies, public kitchens; public safety—or armed security—was managed by the central strike committee. Other cities saw less dramatic but still very militant labor offensives.

In response came a massive wave of government repression and surveillance. Led by the War Department and Attorney General A. Mitchell Palmer, the crackdown involved everyone from postal inspectors to regular federal troops; the counterattack made the domestic military campaigns of the 1870s and the 1890s look quaint. Most radical publications were destroyed, their mailing permits revoked and their offices raided. Of the rural socialist papers that existed in 1916 no more than 10 percent were left by 1920. Cultural institutions and workers' organizations were spied on, sabotaged, raided, and closed. Federal troops crushed organizing efforts by miners in Montana and Arizona, while state militias did the same in California and Minnesota. Special agents patrolled the rail lines, ejecting and sometimes killing IWW organizers. Vigilantes operating with the connivance of local authorities intimidated, tortured, and lynched organizers such as Frank Little, who was first castrated then hanged. The head of the Socialist Party, Eugene Debs, was imprisoned. Then in 1920 Palmer and his young protégé J. Edgar Hoover launched a series of massive nationwide raids, detaining 10,000 radicals and deporting thousands of others on so-called "red barges" and "red arks." For many comrades watching the American left being smashed to pieces, the late 1910s and early 1920s must have seemed like a political Armageddon.[25]

THE CULTURAL CAMPAIGN FOR REGISTRATION

During this season of terror there emerged again among the better classes a renewed push for universal fingerprinting and creation of standard everyday identification. The popular press was replete with stories about amnesiacs who, so unfortunately, did not have registered ID. Without fingerprints and photo IDs such people were forever lost to their families. (Never mind that this was an extremely rare problem—it warranted a national ID system!) So too did the theme of the kidnapped child, untraceable for lack of prints, suddenly become a national obsession (or at least it was for journalists and editors). And to give it all a sugary coating there appeared regular pieces on how the security-conscious rich expressed their privilege by filing their prints with the local police—the not-so-subtle logic here being if it's good enough for the great and the good, why not the hoi polloi as well?[26]

Some of this pro-registration PR was the work of the First National Scientific Registration Society, which had been founded in 1917 by a group of New York socialites with Mrs. John King Van Rensselaer at the lead. The group's purpose was simple enough—push for mass registration of fingerprints and photo identification. The conservative *Literary Digest* captured well the problem at hand in a 1919 article that lamented the "unfortunate" close association between criminality and "the taking of finger prints," which had caused the latter to be seen as a "disgrace." Attempting to assuage its readers the *Digest* explained that "identification is of supreme importance in hundreds of fields far removed from crime and criminals, and . . . it is a desirable thing to have on file somewhere the finger-prints of every man, woman and child in the United States."[27] A few months later the *New York Times* chimed in with an editorial that also fretted over the association between crime and fingerprinting: "Respectable and honest people are quite as reluctant to have the markings on the ends of their fingers taken and preserved as are professional burglars and pickpockets."[28]

A favorite Trojan horse for encouraging fingerprinting was the call for printing all babies—the natural precursor to printing all people. In New York, Deputy Police Commissioner Joseph A. Faurot was particularly aggressive in pushing for the use of prints on birth certificates.[29]

EXCHANGING FILES

The class struggle of bloody 1919 helped push cooperation between police departments in the way only crisis can. That summer New York Police Commissioner Richard Enright proposed that New York and Chicago "bring about closer co-operation by interchanging finger prints and criminal records." This official attempt at networking had been preceded in 1916 by the efforts of a private professional organization, the International Association of Chiefs of Police.[30]

The point here is not that there was a unified plan by elites to register the population so as to crush the left, but rather that there was an elite *reflex* toward fingerprint registration and identification that was itself just one manifestation of a general attempt to maintain control in a volatile political situation. Even in the best of times political elites often see the people as ignorant, dangerous, lazy, and in need of external control. Accordingly, many in the working classes had both general and specific reasons to fear the proliferation of fingerprinting.

Even before the season of the red scares employers were using the new biometrics to enforce black lists against radicals by preventing organizers from using multiple identities. As one glowing report in the *New York Times* explained, "The United States, Cambria and Minnesota Steel companies were leaders of the industrial corporations in introducing fingerprinting among employees." Carnegie Steel also used fingerprinting at its adjacent Homestead and Duquesne mills, where "workers discharged in one plant drifted across the river to the other. They readily found employment until the company finally began fingerprinting applicants. It then was able to detect those who had been discharged or rejected at another plant."[31] One company, demanding the fingerprints of all employees, found that only one man refused and as a result quit. "Subsequently," as the *Times* delicately explained, "the company, which had kept track of him, learned that he had fallen into the toils of the law in connection with a bolshevist meeting raided by police."[32] It was in this context that organized workers first opposed the proliferation of dactyloscopy.

THE ANTIPRINT STRIKE

On May 23, 1920, the vast majority of Cleveland cabbies walked off the job. Included in their demands were the usual economic elements, such as better pay, but at the heart of the matter was a new and offensive fingerprinting ordinance. Less than a month earlier Mayor W. S. Fitzgerald had signed an ordinance requiring all cab drivers to be fingerprinted by the police. The few drivers who did cross the antifingerprint picket lines risked beatings at the hands of strikers, who in turn had to fight it out with cops. The *Plain Dealer* reported that "No cars were available in any part of the city last night."[33] Despite police pressure and public reassurance that fingerprinting was not an impugning mark of criminality, the drivers hung tight. "We will continue our protest strike until we are given a square deal and until the finger print clause in the new taxicab ordinance is waved," explained the drivers' business agent, Max Levin. "Not a man will go back to work before that time."[34] Eventually a compromise was reached, but the strike was the first and perhaps last that had as its central issue the question of everyday surveillance.

THUMBS DOWN!

Over the next two decades the drive for universal fingerprint registration continued and so did resistance against it. Within law enforcement, the more exact dactyloscopy finally displaced the Bertillon system. And fingerprinting did expand in other realms of life, but slowly. Most legislation to create universal registration at the state level was shot down, as were all attempts in Congress. J. Edgar Hoover, an architect of the antileft blitzkrieg of 1919, did his best to coordinate the registration drive of the 1920s and 1930s. But, the libertarian vein in American culture and the organized opposition of targeted groups—such as African American domestic workers and hotel employees—kept compulsory printing in check. By the late 1920s registration campaigners had shifted their efforts from compulsory to "voluntary" fingerprinting.[35]

From the private sector, with money and support, came the US Chamber of Commerce; the National Association of Manufacturers; the American Bankers Association; the Daughters of the American Revolution; the American Legion; the Hearst newspaper empire; and the openly racist American Coalition, whose ridiculous subtitle was "An Organization to Coordinate the Efforts of Patriotic, Civic and Fraternal Societies to keep America American." Prominent writers like Rupert Hughes, Vera Connolly, and Will Irwin were recruited to pen panegyrics to the inky records that would keep America safe from itself. The Boy Scouts signed up en masse—one million in all. Meanwhile, society types in coordination with helpful newspapers made great displays of being fingerprinted by the police. Always the propaganda appeal—usually little more than recycled FBI boilerplate—was the same: fingerprinting is good for you! Always the same implausible arguments: fingerprinting automatically reduces crime; fingerprinting helps identify amnesia victims; fingerprinting somehow prevents child kidnapping; fingerprinting prevents clerical errors by government and business.[36] Never, of course, were heard the more cogent political reasons: fingerprinting will help us control reds, Negroes, vagrants, and footloose young women.

One particularly extreme example of the campaign was the fingerprint drive in Berkeley, California, which began in 1936 thanks to the coordinated efforts of the police chief and local businesses. The goal was to create police print files for the town's entire population. Toward that end, fingerprinting stations were set up in public buildings, shops, and on street corners and were staffed by laborers from the Works Progress Administration and the National Youth Administration. Exhorting cooperation from the public came a wave of advertisements, window placards, supportive newspaper articles, harangues from soap-box speakers, *and* 5 percent discounts for citizens who could show merchants their police-issued "merit cards" stating in bold print "I have been fingerprinted." Even Robert Gordon Sproul, the eminent president of the University of California, submitted to fingerprinting as local newsreels relayed the happy occasion to a wider audience.[37]

Why this absurd circus?

The police had a very clear explanation: fingerprinting would "bring about the identity of, and enable us to follow the movement and activities of, Communists, Anarchists and Radicals."[38] One of the few artifacts remaining from the Berkeley experiment is a pamphlet called *Why Fingerprinting?* published by the "Citizens' Committee on Universal Registration in California." Filled with supportive ads from organizations like the local Kiwanis Club and the Pacific Guano Company, *Why Fingerprinting?* presents a long, strange defense of universal registration. But the punch line boils down to a simple and revealing Us vs. Them litmus test: "Fingerprinting means merely positive identity. It means that whoever so registers himself is proud of being identified with modern society and is willing to play the game according to the rules."[39] The reactionary tone here should be no surprise, since one of the key groups in the Berkeley drive was the California Junior Chamber of Commerce, whose "Prospectus for a Better Life in America" contained this frank provision: "A law should be passed under the terms of which an individual convicted of revolutionary activity should be incarcerated, and continually held in a concentration camp."[40]

In 1938 the ACLU answered Berkeley and the rest of the registration hawks with a scathing assault on the post–World War I fingerprinting drive in the form of a pamphlet called *Thumbs Down!* This brisk essay skewered everyone from Hoover on down. Throughout its pages one point emerges again and again: fingerprinting was about class and racial control, not public safety.

The ACLU asserted that fingerprinting "provides the basis for a labor blacklist . . . offers employers an easy means of control over and intimidation of their employees . . . would curb severely the movement of citizens . . . would be intended as a whip for the persecution of aliens . . . [and] subjects the whole populace to police surveillance."[41] The *New Republic* also exposed the real meaning of the engineered craze for registration: "There seems no doubt that the instigators of the Berkeley fingerprinting jamboree are in fact people with strong fascist leanings, who hope to use the device against labor and 'radicals'—a term that, to the Pacific Coast's high blood pressure, includes even the mildest liberals."[42]

No national registration law was ever achieved but by the end of the 1930s piecemeal registration drives and local laws requiring prints for more and more types of documents from birth certificates to commercial driver's licenses, had made fingerprinting and photo identification a regular part of American life. And once established as such it became harder to imagine life without registration and therefore harder to oppose or undermine the next big cycle in the development of a soft cage of routine societywide surveillance.

5

CRUEL GAM *SAAN*: SURVEILLANCE AND CHINESE EXCLUSION

For a paper son, paper is blood.

— Fae Mynne Ng
Bone 1993

America has power, but not justice.

— Chinese detainee
Graffito from Angel Island Immigration Station

For more than sixty years Chinese immigration to the US was almost completely illegal. Only a few exempted classes of migrants, such as merchants and students, were allowed in. To stop the flow of newcomers and keep track of the Chinese already residing in the United States, the federal government in 1882 created what was then the country's most complete system of registration, identification, and routine surveillance; It lasted until 1943. Yet, despite this sweeping ban, thousands of Chinese laborers continued traveling back and forth between China and the American *Gam Saan*, or "gold mountain." During the 1890s, the vast majority of all Chinese migrants who attempted to enter the US were admitted, and between 1910 and 1940 some 175,000 Chinese migrants moved to America.[1]

How did they do it?

For the answer, step back into old San Francisco, before the dot-coms, before the Beats, before the Bay Bridge. . . . Meet Lee U Ong, a merchant with a store at 1027 Stockton Street, in Chinatown. Mr. Ong sold only Asian imports because the law prevented him from directly competing with shopkeepers of European descent. Like many other stores in "the quarter," Ong's was a hub of social activity: one might go there to buy sundries, play Wei Qi, smoke cigars, or drink tea and escape the ubiquitous San Francisco chill. In the eyes of most white San Franciscans, Lee U Ong was just a merchant. But like all Chinese merchants Lee U Ong was a member of several overlapping associations and benevolent societies, and these created a dense web of contacts that aided Ong in his primary business, the "paper sons" industry: the buying, selling, and concocting of false identities for illegal Chinese immigration.

Though it was only 1916, Ong had jacked into the underbelly of a low-tech information economy as cyberpunk as any William Gibson novel. For a price he could get you from China to *Dabu* (that is, "first city" or San Francisco). He could also bring in one's wife, son, daughter, or possibly a "sing-song girl" to work at a brothel. Messy paperwork? Possible detention in an "immigration shed" on Angel Island in the middle of the bay? No problem: Ong was friendly with some of the *luk yi*, or "green clothesmen" who interrogated all incoming Chinese and made the key decisions. To ensure smooth operations, he kept things "greased" with regular $10 payments to interpreters and bureaucrats as far away as Sacramento. No relatives to join in the US? He would invent whole families and send would-be migrants to a "coaching school" in Hong Kong where his people would outline the details of one's new "paper" identity. If you had immigration problems of any sort, Lee U Ong was your man.[2]

THE CHINESE MUST GO!

When the first Chinese miners came to California they were *not* greeted with mass hostility; in 1850 the Chinese participated in civic ceremonies as equals with whites. Nor was California Justice Nathaniel Bennett unusual in his amicable sentiments toward the Chinese: "Born and reared under different Governments and speaking different tongues, we nevertheless meet here to-day as brothers. . . . You stand among us in all respects as equals. . . . Henceforth we have one country, one hope, one destiny."[3] Until the late 1860s Chinese residents marched in San Francisco's Fourth of July parade.

The Chinese were, in fact, essential to the economy of the West, which was resource rich but short of labor. Chinese worked the mines, drained the swamps of what is now the extremely fertile Central Valley, planted the orchards, and taught Europeans how to tend them (the famous Bing cherry was a Chinese invention). Chinese immigrants provided fully 90 *percent* of the labor for the Central Pacific Railroad.[4] But by the mid–1870s the economy had crashed into a brutal depression and a simmering Sino-phobia now boiled over into organized hate.

The standard story of this racist upsurge blames organized labor, particularly the western elements of the Workingmen's Party led by the Irish demagogue Denis Kearny. A bombastic, bullying self-promoter, Kearny ended all his speeches with "and whatever else—the Chinese must go!" While it is true that this fanaticism preached in the sandlots of San Francisco had an important impact on the white working classes of the West, new scholarship complicates the prevailing assumption that it was workers who demanded the Chinese Exclusion Act.

According to the standard history, both major parties in the East adopted "sandlot-ism" and made the materially irrelevant issue of Chinese exclusion into a national cause and a federal law solely to placate the West, in specific, and the labor vote generally. However, as historian Andrew Gyory details in his excellent book *Closing the Gate* a more accurate story shows labor's role as contradictory. In fact, business and the political classes were *autonomously* racist and acted on their own to hype the alleged threats—economic, cultural, and moral—of Chinese immigration.

Their real concern, argues Gyory, was worker unrest during the economic crisis of the 1870s, which began with the collapse of the railroad boom and was exacerbated by a long drought. In this context, the Chinese became a useful political lightning rod. Organized labor played its shameful part to be sure, but, to take one example, Kearny's demagoguing tour through the East was cut short due to lack of popular support. And much of the labor press actively *opposed* anti-Chinese racism, calling it divisive and irrelevant.[5]

The real catalyst for the Exclusion, or Geary Act, of 1882 was the near civil war of the Great Upheaval of 1877–78.[6] It was the spectre of St. Louis's industries being run by armed workers for almost two weeks and the nightmare of German, Cuban, and Chinese cigar makers standing united in their bitter battle for restored wages that really worried the captains of industry and press magnates.

THE LEGAL MACHINERY OF EXCLUSION AND RESISTANCE

The first legislative move toward exclusion was aimed at Chinese women, who throughout the era of Chinese exclusion were policed with extra vigilance. It began in the early 1870s with several Californian legislators, among them Horace F. Page, who pandered to employers on the West Coast who wanted Chinese labor but also wanted the Chinese to be scared, disorganized, and thus cheap to employ. Page and his crew spent several years foisting their regional issues on an uninterested national congress in Washington, D.C. Since in the early 1870s there were very few Chinese anywhere east of the Rockies, the whole issue was rather abstract for voters in most of the country. However, within a few years Page and his allies had made considerable headway by claiming that most Asian women in the US were dangerous harlots, a threat to American manhood and purveyors of disease. In 1875 Congress passed the eponymous Page Act, which banned the immigration of women from "China, Japan or any Oriental country" who were arriving with the intent to work as prostitutes.[7] (Never mind that prostitution was legal in San Francisco and other parts of California until the early 1920s.)

Seven years latter came the Geary Act, which prohibited the entrance of all Chinese laborers, skilled and unskilled. The law would be updated and modified many times in the following decades, always emerging with tougher language. The few groups exempted under the act, such as merchants, students, and travelers, were now required to get special identification called "Section Six" or "Canton certificates," which were obtained from either the US embassy or Chinese authorities before embarking on the voyage to America, the "Flower Flag Country."

All Chinese people residing in the States ninety days prior to the Geary Act were allowed to stay and had the right to leave and reenter the country. But they too would have to obtain certificates of identification from the collector of customs at their port of departure. According to the woefully inadequate 1880 Census, there were at least 105,000 of these "prior residents."[8]

These identification documents, eventually known as "431 papers," would state "the individual, family, and tribal name in full, the age, occupation, when and where followed, last place residence, physical marks or peculiarities, and all facts necessary for the identification of each such Chinese laborer. . . ."[9] The collector in turn was to keep a "registry book" in which a duplicate of such information was copied. When a laborer returned from China he or she would have to present their certificate of identification and have its details compared with those in the collector's registry.

In one regard these practices were rather traditional. In 1837 the Supreme Court upheld a state's right to demand that all "Ship's Masters" keep and provide to port authorities identification lists containing the "name, place of birth and last legal settlement, age, and occupation of every person brought as a passenger."[10] But the requirement of a descriptive certificate to be carried *as identification* by the passenger once landed was a powerful new extension of state bureaucratic power into everyday life.[11]

Predictably, this strategy met immediate resistance. By 1883 many Chinese had stopped bringing their "Canton certificates" and were attempting to land as "prior residents" using affidavits and the testimony of local witnesses to argue their cases before the dockside clerks of Customs Houses and, when needed, in federal court. After all, complex and tyrannical bureaucracies were a normal part of life back in China. Instead of

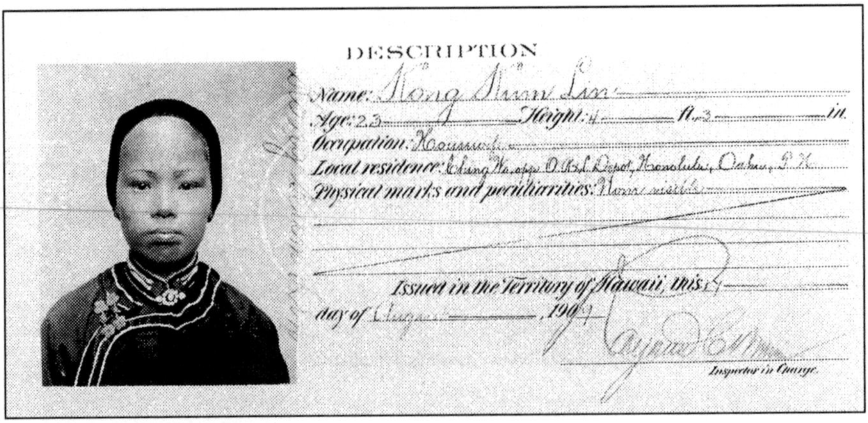

Certificate of Identity 4511: Kong Kum Lin, 1908-1943

haughty Manchu Mandarins demanding taxes, documents, and affidavits the immigrant now faced the relatively unsophisticated and corrupt officials of America's nascent immigration bureaucracy. And the new fight was not dissimilar to the old: when denied entrance migrants logged administrative appeals, submitted new evidence, and filed writs in courts. As Lucy Salyer, a leading authority on Chinese American legal struggles, shows, the migrants had quick and numerous legal victories and began pushing back the language of the Geary Act. For example, by 1884, Chinese court victories had exempted all prior residents from exclusion and shifted much of the burden of proof onto the collector of customs, who now had to show that the migrant was carrying fraudulent documents. One estimate held that the federal courts were directly or indirectly responsible for the entry of one-third of all Chinese immigrants who successfully landed during the first fourteen months the Exclusion Act was in effect.[12]

FIXING DOCUMENTS

Any successful landing, adjudicated or not, required proper paperwork: a "Section Six" certificate, whether genuine, doctored, or confected. One could enter as the daughter or son of someone in an "exempted class," such as a merchant or native-born Chinese American. In either case, getting paper was the key. One way to do so was by creating fictitious

FORM OF CHINESE CERTIFICATE.

In compliance with the provisions of Section 6 of an Act of the Congress of the United States of America, approved July 5, 1884, entitled An Act to amend an act entitled An Act to execute certain treaty stipulations relating to Chinese, approved May 6, 1882.

THIS CERTIFICATE is issued by the undersigned, who has been designated for that purpose by the Government of China, to show that the person named hereinafter is a member of one of the exempt classes described in said Act and as such has the permission of said Government to go to and reside within the territory of the United States, after an investigation and verification of the statements contained herein by the lawfully constituted agent of the United States in this country.

The following description is submitted for the identification of the person to whom the certificate relates:—

Name in full, in proper signature of bearer: Hu Kia Noong

Title or official rank, if any:

Physical peculiarities: no special peculiarities

Date of birth: March 13 1884

Height: Five feet 3 inches.

Former occupation: a student

When pursued: 1905 — 1907

Where pursued: Soochow University

How long pursued: two years

Present occupation: Pharmacist & teacher

When pursued: 1909 – 1910

Where pursued: Soochow Hospital

How long pursued: three years

Last place of actual residence: Soochow

NOTE.—If a merchant the following blanks should be filled out:—

Title of present mercantile business:

Location of said mercantile business:

How long said business has been pursued:

Amount invested (gold) in said business:

Present estimated value of said business:

Specific character of merchandise handled in said business

NOTE.—If bearer is a traveller the following blanks should be filled out:—

Financial standing of bearer in his own country:

Probable duration of his stay in the United States:

Issued at Shanghai, China, on this 3rd day of

(VISÉ.)

I, the undersigned duly authorized consular officer of the United States Government for the territory within which the person named in the above certificate resides, have made a thorough investigation of the statements contained in the foregoing certificate and have found them to be in all respects true, and accordingly attach my signature and official seal in order that the bearer may be admitted to the United States upon identification as the person represented by the attached photograph, over which I have partly placed my official seal.

Port of Arrival San Francisco

Hu Kia Noong. The English-language side of a Chinese-issued Certificate of Identity, circa 1905

businesses that included on their charters many more partner names than actual partners. As one investigation revealed, "Partnership lists filed at Angel Island were padded; that is to say the store may have 5 or 6 members in all, but the lists filed at Angel Island would contain 20."[13] The slots of these "merchants" could then be sold to laborers and others wishing to enter *Gam Saan*. A confiscated Chinese-language partnership book from 1914 states: "The purpose of this firm is to bring profit to ourselves with the benefit to others. It benefits others because it provides headquarters for our relatives. . . . Any person who should use the firm's name to enable boys to come to the United States as his sons must pay the firm Fifty Dollars ($50) for each boy." And finally: "Should anyone outside of the present partnership desire to use the name of our firm for making a merchant paper he must pay the sum of Fifty Dollars and then he will be rated as a partner."[14]

Those who could not enter as "merchants" would attempt to enter as the "paper" daughters, sons, or wives of documented residents, or of Chinese American citizens who had been born in the US before Exclusion. They might also attempt to enter as a returnee, using the identification papers of someone who had gone back to China. Different classes of documents commanded a range of prices: "son-of-native" identification papers were always the best. As one migrant advised: "If you can get paper for him . . . to come as a son of native, rather than as a son of merchant, the examination of the case will be much shorter."[15] Or from another missive: "If you have any 'son-of-native' paper that fits. . . ."[16]

INTERROGATIONS AND COACHING

Regardless of documents, every Chinese traveler entering the United States was subject to a series of long and detailed official interrogations. In San Francisco these took place at the Immigration Station on Angel Island. At first the exams were rather lackluster, but by the 1890s the process had become a grueling and intricately bureaucratic affair; immigration officials now photographed the travelers and typed up the transcript of each interrogation. These files, kept for decades, were used to cross-check the testimony of alleged sons, daughters, and returnees. At times the interrogations were absurdly detailed; regular questions included: Where did your mother keep her rice bin? Where was the well in your village? Where was the temple?

If an immigrant returned to Guangdong (the province from which almost all Chinese immigrants to the US came until recently) and then traveled back to California, they—or the person pretending to be them—would be re-interrogated and every answer checked against the transcript of their original interview.

To help "paper sons" pass these exams "steerers"—professional smugglers like Lee U Ong—created "coaching letters" that would map a traveler's new identity. "If the inspector asks you how far your village is from the Bamboo tree," instructed a typical coaching letter confiscated in 1917, "you answer 'I have no bamboo trees in my village, there [are] only bamboo and trees behind the hill of Jeung Bin village.'" The same note ends with a word on security: "Be sure to study and memorize the above questions and answers right away. After you get through with them, don't forget to destroy this letter. I herewith enclosed . . . a photo of [your 'paper' father]. Study his features and do not fail to recognize him."[17]

Coaching letters could be as brief as a few lines, or they might constitute an elaborate counter-dossier, complete with old interrogation transcripts, photos of one's "paper" family, and even maps of one's purported "home" village. Sometimes Chinese American kitchen staff passed coaching materials to the detainees held in government barracks on Angel Island. But more often coaching material was sent to China for the travelers to study on their steamer trips to America. A few very well organized steerers, like Lee U Ong, even had schools in Hong Kong where they prepped travelers for the inevitable interrogation.

Back in the US, paid witnesses were another crucial part of the process. If someone was entering as a returnee they would need their alleged friends, business partners, and neighbors to visit the immigration station and vouch for them. These paid witnesses, who very often knew neither the real person nor the details of that person's false identity, also required coaching. For this there were schools in the US. Henry C. Kennah—a stout, prematurely graying immigration attorney who was a partner of Lee U Ong—operated just such a coaching school in San Francisco's Chinatown. As one government informant explained, Kennah "taught Chinese [migrants] facts about things that happened in Chinatown in previous years, iron fence around Portsmouth Square, the killing of [underworld boss] little Pete, and lots of other things. . . ."[18]

INFILTRATING ANGEL ISLAND

The linchpin to this whole system was, of course, information—or more specifically, access to the vaults and dossiers kept by officials on Angel Island. Both sides in this game used knowledge as a weapon. If the *luk yi* ran their investigations and built up their files and used every detail they could to keep the Chinese out, the Chinese in turn did their best to get into, steal from, and rewrite the files of the US government. In that respect the Chinese steerers of yesteryear were much like today's computer hackers.

To crack the government vaults steerers like Ong and Kennah kept a bevy of corrupt immigration inspectors, clerks, and interpreters on healthy stipends. "It was current rumor around Chinatown that all of the inspectors engaged in Chinese work were grafting," explained one government memo.[19]

And during the early 1910s one of the most active "grafters" was a young stenographer named Robert T. Fergusson. Known as "Fook" in the stores of Chinatown, Fergusson was eventually arrested and under pressure started informing on his business partners with a flood of detailed and incriminating confessions.[20] From Fergusson's panicked logorrhea we have numerous typed confessions that paint a fairly detailed picture of how immigration documents were stolen, copied, doctored, and then placed back into government vaults.

First, Fergusson would "abstract" or steal whatever file Ong and Kennah requested. Next Ong and Kennah would replace the existing identification photo with an image of the alleged "returnee" or merchant's "daughter" or "son." Then, more often than not, the dossier's testimony would have to be rewritten, usually so as to increase the number of children claimed by a legal immigrant. Each of these new children became yet another identity that Ong and Kennah could sell for hundreds of dollars.

But altering testimony was tricky. It could involve simply removing a few pages or it could require adding new pages and changing old answers. And if the interrogation transcripts being doctored were ten or twenty years old, rewriting testimony required getting or creating credibly "aged" paper. Luckily, Ong and Kennah had an expert close at hand—a Mr. E.L. Mills of San Francisco. "Mills made a practice of taking testimony paper and aging it by some process," explained Fergusson. The steerers "paid $25 a sheet for doing this and furnished Mills many sheets for this purpose." Later on, Fergusson explained how "Lee U Ong at one time took some testimony paper that I gave him and soaked it in tea to make it look yellow."[21]

Another challenge was changing photographs. Since most photos affixed to immigration records were stamped or even embossed, replacement photos had to match the markings on the original documents. Thus, Fergusson told investigators that: "Lee U Ong had the landing stamp made, 'Landed, San Francisco, etc.,' and I understand he used it frequently himself, changing a lot of pictures. I left it in Mills' possession to use in changing pictures but afterwards Lee U Ong demanded it and I took it back to him. Inthemeantime [sic] Mills had taken a soft rubber eraser and made one for himself just like it."[22] And for those cases where the photos had to be artificially aged, there were specialists in Chinatown to handle the job.[23]

Finally, these reengineered files were smuggled back on to Angel Island and placed again in their proper vaults. Thus, when a paper son, or "native born" returnee disembarked for the first time on Angel Island, the hostile *luk yi* would find in their files the migrant's photo affixed to official documents that were four, five, or even ten years old *proving* the traveler had the right to land.

But inspectors were always on the lookout for just such contraband. A typical memo states: "The coaching material with this letter is found to be identical with the testimony given by Louie Fon Gim upon his arrival in the United States in 1913."[24] To prevent such exposure, steerers emphasized the need for secrecy: "Study thoroughly the testimony and the diagram of the village with the nearby houses and their occupants. When you have learned them and when the steamer arrives at port, burn the testimony paper and the diagram of the village. Be sure not to keep them, so as to avoid their being found by the inspector."[25]

Sometimes things went wrong, stories got confused, and emergency communications had to pass between the immigration station and witnesses in Chinatown. Take for instance this note from a detainee to an outside witness: "The inspector asked me where Yip Yin was buried and I answered him that he was buried in 'Gim-san' [Gam Saan].. . . If he is not buried in the United States and if there will be a rehearing, say Yip Yin is buried in China in a hill called 'gim-san.'"[26] And just in case, last-minute reminders were sent: "At the conclusion of the hearing you two, [paper] father and son, will be asked to stand together in the examination room to be compared as to physical resemblance. When Fon Ging is asked to come out or appears, you must be sure to call out 'Ah Pa' (or papa)."[27]

On several occasions these corrupt practices were investigated by the Secret Service, but to little effect. However, by 1916 shenanigans on Angel Island had gotten so out of control—renegade inspectors were beginning to routinely extort payments from even legitimate Chinese travelers—that the government was forced to launch a serious undercover investigation. Leading the charge was John B. Densmore, solicitor of the Department of Labor and former editor of the United Mine Worker's house paper. His inquiry started in March 1917 and lasted seven months, and during that time he uncovered a "ring"—actually it was more like a loose network—of Chinese steerers, white immigration lawyers, and numerous inspectors, interpreters, record clerks, and night watchmen on Angel Island.[28] Ultimately some twenty-five employees were dismissed and two dozen people were indicted, including several "paper relatives."[29]

ORGANIZED RESISTANCE AND THE FACILITATION OF FRAUD

Chinese immigrants also fought Geary Act surveillance in organized and overtly political ways, like mass refusal to register in 1892 and a boycott of American-made goods in 1904–5.

The original Geary Act required all Chinese people in the US to register with their local collector of internal revenue, who was to issue registration/identification certificates. But practices in western ports like San Francisco, Los Angeles, and Portland took some time to catch up with the letter of the law. The US Customs Service, the bureaucracy tasked with policing the Chinese until 1903 (when the Labor Department's Bureau of Immigration took over), was woefully understaffed, disorganized, and corrupt. As a result, very few Chinese registered. Local xenophobes complained, but the majority of Chinese people who had entered the US prior to Geary remained "at large" with no official identification, unregistered and unknown to the government.

The officialdom's benign neglect was short lived. When the Exclusion Act was amended in 1892 Sinophobic politicians again demanded the full registration of all Chinese laborers in the United States. "We have been mocked, and that is why we are angry," sputtered the Montana Senator Wilbur F. Sanders. This time the Geary Act required all unregistered Chinese immigrants to apply within one year to the collector of internal revenue for a certificate of residence; any who failed to do so would be hunted down and deported.

As the new law went into effect San Francisco–based Collector of Revenue, John Quinn, informed the people of Chinatown, "I am now ready and willing to register all who may apply."[30] Adding to the threat of this legal offensive was the racist vigilantism of the previous decade. After the first Geary Act white thugs had robbed, beaten, and killed Chinese people throughout the West; once thriving Chinatowns, a standard feature of the Western frontier, were depopulated. Even around San Francisco, the heart of Chinese America, Cantonese fishing villages on the north and east coasts of the bay and farming communities in the Sacramento River Delta were "ethnically cleansed" out of existence through a mix of legalistic legerdemain and simple terror.

Despite all this, the Chinese community, riven with bitter and fratricidal fault lines, closed ranks and refused en masse to register. The usually conservative Six Companies—which were neither companies nor six in number, but rather clan-based benevolent societies known as *huiguan*, which acted as an informal government in Chinese communities—posted fliers throughout the West strongly advising people *not* to comply with this "cruel" and "unjust" law. In San Francisco's Chinatown, people stayed away and by year's end only 439 of an estimated 26,000 unregistered Chinese had presented themselves to authorities. The eponymous San Francisco Democrat Thomas Geary went ballistic, demanding that the US Attorney indict the leadership of the Six Companies. Meanwhile, the Treasury Department—in charge of overseeing Chinese exclusion—tried to coax unregistered immigrants to comply with the act by offering to drop the newly introduced and highly offensive use of *photography* in identification papers for Chinese residents who had arrived before Exclusion.[31] It was no use. Even this significant concession—a loophole that would facilitate continued identity fraud—was inadequate. The Chinese ignored federal demands to register. White San Francisco began to worry.

As the deadline for final registration neared, tension mounted. Rumors and threats circulated that all unregistered Chinese people would be rounded up in armed sweeps. The *tongs*, which were sub-rosa, political, often semi-criminal lodges or associations, prepared to flex their muscle.

Rank-and-file members bought guns and prepared for war. As one fretting newspaper article put it, the "Chinaman . . . usually purchases the most deadly and effective weapon he can find."[32] But on the deadline, Collector Quinn preempted an uprising with a force of 180 armed federal marshals to flood San Francisco's Chinatown, the epicenter of resistance.

There were no immediate roundups, and the question headed to federal court. The Six Companies had hired three of the best appellate attorneys in Washington, DC, to fight the Geary Act with a series of test cases. Their team included J. Hubby Ashton, counsel for the mighty Southern Pacific Railroad. Nevertheless, the main test case *Fong Yue Ting v. the United States* was thrown out, to the shock of the mainstream Chinese leadership. Thousands again faced deportation.[33] But the Treasury Department estimated that deporting all "illegal" Chinese would cost an impossible sum: $7,310,000 to be precise. On top of that, the fruit barons of the Central Valley—dependent as they were on Chinese labor and technical know-how—would have been ruined if their work force disappeared. Deportation did increase, but so too did trafficking in paper sons.

One interesting side-effect of the showdown was to upset the balance of power within the Six Companies and between the *huiguan* and the *tongs*. The details were worked out in the alleys and opium dens of Chinatown during a decade of bloody gangland warfare that eventually saw the Sam Yup *huiguan*—which had dominated the Six Companies since the Gold Rush—displaced by the now more numerous Sze Yup *huiguan*. At the same time, the *tongs* rose to challenge all *huiguans* of the Six Companies.[34]

The next wave of organized resistance arose in 1905 when Chinese Americans and tens of thousands of consumers in mainland China boycotted US goods. In 1904 the Geary Act was again up for renewal and addition of more rigorous conditions, but the immediate trigger for the boycott was a series of ugly assaults on Chinese individuals and collective Chinese dignity.

First there was a mass raid on Boston's Chinatown in which any Asian person not carrying government-issued identification was hauled off to jail. Without a single warrant, the sweep captured 250 people. Here the politics of everyday surveillance served as a justification for state repression. A year later SFPD officers severely beat a Chinese diplomat named Tan Jinyong. Before hauling the bloodied dignitary away they tied him to a lamppost by his queue (a long, traditional braid). Despite Jinyong's diplomatic immunity and innocence of any crime, the district attorney put him on trial for assault of a police officer. Before it was all over, the disgraced and politically powerless Tan Jinyong had committed suicide. In 1904, the Chinese delegation to the St. Louis World's Fair, headed by Prince Pu Lun, was subjected to prolonged anti-Chinese insults, threats, and humiliation. Then in April 1905 an angry blue wall of cops attacked New York City's Chinatown in a big antigambling raid in which 200 members of Chinese literary societies were arrested.[35]

Once the humiliated Chinese delegation returned from the St. Louis Fair they began agitating in Beijing for the Chinese government to pressure the United States to scale back its racist immigration laws. In the US the Chinese Vice-Commissioner, Wong Kai Kah, penned a sharp and widely read warning to US business in the *North American Review:* continued abuse of the Chinese in America, he warned, would backfire in commercial retaliation.[36]

What really motivated Chinese people to start boycotting American goods was increased use of the newly popular Bertillon system. Lang Qiche, a much-read Chinese author of that era, noted how his country people were measured "as if they were criminals." Like many others he found this "an insult to our nation's dignity."[37]

By summer 1905 the streets of towns and cities on the south coast of China were plastered with broadsides demanding that consumers avoid imported goods from the Flower Flag Country and substitute homegrown products instead. The overall economic impact of the boycott was minimal but the psychological impact was enormous. The Chinese government, pressured by the Chinese Consulate General and the Six Companies, leaned on the US government to reconsider its campaign of official discrimination. As soon as the boycott was shown to be working, President Theodore Roosevelt, who had been a gleeful supporter of Chinese exclusion, started backpedaling, holding a cabinet meeting to discuss the boycott and ways to make exclusion enforcement less offensive. Before year's end the boycott was petering out, but the federal government had made numerous concessions to Chinese Americans, easing and dropping some of the most offensive and effective elements of its surveillance regime.

Beginning in 1894 the Chinese exclusion portions of the US Code provided "for the Bertillon system of identification at the various ports of entry, to prevent unlawful entry of Chinese into the United States."[38] Lack of funds made this provision largely moot before 1905. After the boycott, proper Bertillonage and fingerprinting were formally dropped until the Chinese Exclusion Act expired in 1943. In other words, the collective transpacific boycott successfully checked the growth of effective federal surveillance and that allowed the paper sons industry and Chinese migration to continue, though never at its pre-exclusion levels.

Ultimately, Chinese exclusion was the first campaign of mass identification and registration of a civilian population by the US federal government. Conversely, the paper sons industry was the largest informal anti-surveillance movement in US history. If there is a lesson here, it is that individual survival strategies were in this case dependent on the broader social spaces created by collective political action. If fingerprinting and Bertillonage had been more widely used, evasion of the immigration laws would have been exponentially more difficult. The blind spots in the bureaucracy of identification and racial control were preserved, in large part, by organized political struggle.

Another factor made the paper sons industry possible: the primitive nature of information technology. By the time the Exclusion Act finally expired in 1943, early mechanical computers were in fact making their operational debut. And as we shall see in the next chapter the Census Bureau had used mechanical proto-computers from the turn of the century onward (so too did the Nazis). But the early Customs Service and the Bureau of Labor did not have such gear. However, over the next sixty-odd years the steady introduction of computers would radically transform the terrain of everyday surveillance in ways both subtle and profound. It is to that political rupture, the digital revolution, which we now turn.

6

OF ONES AND ZEROS: DIGITAL SURVEILLANCE EMERGES

Although you may never have seen a computer and almost certainly won't be able to afford a big one—they can cost ten million or so—your life is almost certainly going to be affected by these mechanical wizards. In other words, they think about you even if you don't think about them.

—*The Story of Computers*
A book for young adults, 1964

I am data.

—Advertisement for SBC Telecom, 2000

The literary and cinematic imagination is rich with surveillance imagery. In George Lucas's film *THX 1138*, an underground slave class reports to video confessionals and imbibes mandatory medication. The film *Gattaca* portrays a massive corporation guiding a system of genetic tyranny, while *Enemy of the State* sets loose the National Security Agency's omniscient satellites, tracking phone calls and photographing suspects from afar. Reigning supreme over the entire genre is the paranoia of *1984*, where oblong telescreens sit beside posters announcing "Big Brother Is Watching You."

In reality, the emerging architecture of the soft cage of total surveillance is perhaps most frightening because it is so mundane, decentralized, and even convenient. Thanks to computer informatics and microtechnology, the gates, meters, and identification badges of routine surveillance now dovetail perfectly with the contours of everyday life.

Unlike the paper sons of the last century, we do not carry "section six certificates," fake or otherwise; instead we carry credit cards and bankcards that informally log our movements and lifestyles more effectively than any formal efforts did in the past. When viewed in isolation, each component of the new digital surveillance seems quite reasonable. But each new camera, database, or ID operates in relation to a larger societywide momentum toward increased observation.[1]

THE QUALITATIVE SHIFT

To best unpack the new superintendence, follow the path laid by scholars such as David Lyon, John Rule, Gary Marx, and Reg Whitaker.[2] These writers and others have noted how the computer revolution has caused a qualitative shift in the politics of surveillance. Their argument is that the *quantitative* increase in the speed and amount of data that computers can process has led to a *qualitative* transformation in the political uses of such data. As digital technology spreads, surveillance becomes more ubiquitous, automatic, anonymous, decentralized, and self-reinforcing. Computers create a parallel realm of ones and zeros, of interconnected records and databases, in which we all exist and in which we are all watched.

This informal system of tracking is built on three key components: First it needs "tags," or universal personal identifiers, that can uniquely identify specific individuals within large populations. Second, it requires databases and powerful processors that can store and search previously unwieldy amounts of information. Finally, it requires telecommunications networks to link disparate, unrelated files into technologically and politically coherent systems. All of these components have multiple uses, some of which are quite benign. Consider the Social Security number, which helps keep many people from penury in old age, or school records, which provide necessary proof of qualification. And all the bounties of consumerism flow more freely when we purchase with plastic. Yet Social Security numbers, school records, and credit profiles, when computerized and stitched together by computerized network, can triangulate on and expose individuals and demographic groups in politically dangerous ways.

Thus computers transform once meaningless data into the ore from which are refined the precious informational alloys of the soft cage. Instead of observation towers, checkpoints, and the low-flying black helicopters of dystopian fantasy the emerging surveillance society is characterized by innocuous passwords, swipe cards, automatic toll lanes, and workplace IDs. Everywhere we leave digital footprints.

We are not "being watched" so much as we are voluntarily "checking in" with authorities. If looked at from this view, the landscape is now littered with registration kiosks—ATMs, automatic ticketing machines, electronic tolls—where we deposit personal information in exchange for services. These nodes upon what Mike Davis called the "scanscape" can also be seen as altars where we genuflect to authority, performing the quiet rituals of obedience by registering our locations in time and space.[3]

THE THINKING MACHINE IS BORN

The prehistory of the digital revolution extends back to the very beginnings of the Age of Reason. The first rudimentary "calculating" machine—other than the ancient abacus—was the "Pascaline," invented by the young Frenchman Blaise Pascal in 1645. Compared to postmodern super-servers the Pascaline was the evolutionary equivalent of amoebic life, a copper box containing a series of interlocking gears, much like a modern odometer. When a gear with ten teeth made one rotation, a second gear would shift one tooth until that gear rotated ten times; it would then shift another gear, thus "carrying the decimal" mechanically.[4] Though technically complex, the contraption was not much of an improvement over the abacus and really nothing more than a novelty.

Building on the Pascaline came Gottfried Wilhelm Leibniz, who redesigned it to include a stepped cylinder, giving the machine the ability to divide and extract square roots without error. By 1694 Leibniz had constructed a functional model of his calculator and with it created a new division of intellectual labor. As the inventor explained, "It is unworthy of excellent men to lose hours like slaves in the labor of calculation which could safely be relegated to anyone else if machines were used."[5]

The next informatics breakthrough came 150 years later when Charles Babbage, invented the so-called "Difference Engine," a contraption able to automatically calculate logarithms. Later Babbage also designed the "Analytical Engine." Though never built, this second "engine" is now recognized as the basic template of modern computing. Like the ThinkPads and mainframes of today, Babbage's analytic engine had an anatomy of five components: the store (or memory), the mill (or processor), the control (a sequence of operations on punch cards similar to programs), and the two input/output devices. More important than Babbage's actual technological breakthroughs were the implicit politics of his worldview. His treatise, *On the Economy of Machinery and Manufactures*, made an elaborate case for deskilling and fragmenting the labor process so as to weaken the political power of labor. In other words, Babbage presaged F. W. Taylor's *Principles of Scientific Management* (on which more later) and saw technology as a weapon in the struggle between employers and workers: "The master manufacturer, by dividing the work to be executed into different processes, each requiring different degrees of skill or of force, can purchase exactly that precise quantity of both which is necessary for each process."[6] It was a fight he knew intimately: the production of his various contraptions was itself vexed by conflicts between him and the skilled craft laborers he employed. In dreaming of a technological escape from (or conquest of) labor, Babbage went so far as to imagine a complete recomposition of social relations, with a "new class of managerial analysts" ruling and guiding society as they saw fit.[7]

Though Babbage is an interesting harbinger of modern computing, the real political arrival of computers occurred thanks to Herman Hollerith. Like Babbage, Hollerith's work and technological legacy was bound up with measuring and managing populations. As a nineteen-year-old clerk with the US Census Bureau in the early 1880, Hollerith labored to devise an automated means to tabulate the nation's decennial count. At that time the government's enumeration of the population was done almost entirely by hand. Census questions had to be kept to a minimum, and the analysis, such as it was, took almost a decade to complete. The result was little more than a simple headcount. Hollerith, imbued with the technological dynamism of his era, strained against these limitations.

In search of a solution the young clerk focused on the pattern programming cards used in mechanized looms. Interestingly, these were the very same machines that kicked off the Industrial Revolution and almost simultaneously modern workplace sabotage. After all, the armed and clandestine Luddites who rebelled against England's emerging industrial system in 1811 and 1812 smashed power looms with black hammers called Enochs.[8] Little did they know what great transformations the memory cards of the looms would later unleash.

Hollerith disassembled these same machines, but toward a different end: he searched for a way to mechanize thinking and transform the politics of information. More specifically, automatic looms—operating much like player pianos and music boxes—used punched cards to recreate visual patterns by directing the spindles of colored thread. Patterned cloth was woven according to "programmed" instructions that were laid out on the punch cards, which, when inserted into looms that could mechanically "feel" or "read" the instructions. The question was how to apply this technology to processing the variables of the national census?

Fittingly, the answer came to Hollerith while observing the routine surveillance and policing practices of a railroad conductor punching tickets. In those days fraud on railways was rampant: the poor stole and recycled tickets in order to travel; so too did union organizers, who saw the rail system as crucial political terrain. To prevent passengers from sharing or recycling tickets, most rail companies transformed their stubs into so-called "punched photographs." Each stub had printed on it a set of possible physical descriptions: hair, dark or light; nose, big or small; eyes, blue, brown, or green. From these basic choices the conductor could punch out the passenger's appropriate description. Watching this process, Hollerith realized that the Census Bureau could do the same.[9]

The idea was to create a card set with standardized holes, each representing a different demographic trait—national origin, gender, age, occupation—and then feed these cards into a reader or tabulator that could automatically detect and count which holes were punched. Such a system could aggregate and disaggregate the cards according to different combinations of variables. With it, government agencies could search census data for all employed women, or unemployed men, or draft age men, or whatever else might be worth knowing. If properly applied, the new technology would revolutionize the census and render the American population more transparent, more useful, and ultimately more governable.

By 1884 Hollerith had his patent and a large, solidly built prototype containing scores of intricate, spring-loaded electric brushes that could "feel" which holes were punched and thus sort the cards accordingly. By 1890 Hollerith's new Tabulating Machine Company was under contract with the Census Bureau to analyze that year's count. Whereas the 1880 Census had asked only five questions and took most of the next decade to tabulate, Hollerith's number-crunching engines processed forms with over two hundred questions, got the job done in a fraction of the normal time, and did it for only two-thirds the standard price.[10]

Thus began a true revolution in political record keeping and informatics generally. A new "take off" in the "accumulation of men" was under way. State agencies, from American county governments to the great powers of Europe, took up Hollerith's technology with an ardent modernizing zeal. Just as the proliferation of the automobile, electricity, and the telephone served to broaden and deepen modern bureaucratic power—in what Giddens calls "internal pacification"—so too did early computers transform statecraft, military organization, and the commercial allocation of people and supplies.[11]

THE INFORMATICS OF GENOCIDE

But "progress" always has a grim side, and so it was with counting populations. By the early 1930s the right to lease Hollerith machines belonged to International Business Machines Inc. (the technology was always leased, never sold). This upstart firm was itself the bastard child of the National Cash Register Company—aka, "The Cash"—which had shunted aside its prodigal vice-president Thomas Watson. Ruthless and driven,

Watson hooked up with Hollerith, then pushed aside his elder partner and went on to make IBM into the mammoth central hub of the Information Revolution that it is today.

Big Blue's best customers, then as now, were large institutions managing major projects. Among them: the National Socialist government of Germany. The horror that issued from this union of the technical best and the moral worst of high modernism is chronicled in Edwin Black's superb book *IBM and the Holocaust*. The sad fact is that IBM's computers and the everyday surveillance they allowed were as integral to Hitler's Final Solution as was Zyclon-B. In fact, Hollerith-style computers were in use well before the Nazis, worried about the psychological stress on their executioners, switched from machineguns to gas.

Immediately after the Nazis took power in January 1933 they set about redesigning the national census, transforming it from a muted, generalized profile of the people and the economy into a demographically exact instrument for focusing on and targeting sub-populations. Before the master race could fully blossom and rule the world, genetic deficiencies in the national stock would have to be located and excised. So the Nazis contracted with IBM through the firm's German subsidiary, Dehomag, (short for Deutsche Hollerith Maschinen Gesellschaft). By May 1933 the deal was sealed: Dehomag, under the close supervision of Watson and IBM in the US, would handle the entire German census project. As Edwin Black put it, the company "would design a census package counting and classifying every citizen. Moreover, it would recruit, train and even feed the hundreds of temporary workers needed to process the census and perform the work on Dehomag's own premises."[12]

The first piece of this task was to retool the Hollerith machines so they could process punch cards with twice as many holes as normal. The new cards, with space for eighty variables, created *super detailed* population profiles that allowed the Nazis to identify not just Jews, but even select subsets of Jews. This precision allowed the Nazis to ramp-up their death machine one gear at a time. The first to go were wealthy Jews of Eastern European extraction, who as rich "outsiders" were easily targeted. Then came the round up of half-Jews, then quarter-Jews or *Mischling*, and then even people of one-sixteenth Jewish ancestry. In other words, Jews were taken in a scientifically targeted and politically efficient fashion.[13]

IBM's informational architecture—identifying individuals and mapping populations—also helped run the slave labor camps and factories that fueled the German war industries of Krupps, I.G. Farben, and Bayer. All factories and work camps had Hollerith machines for selecting the type and amount of labor needed, directing supplies, managing accounts, and compiling reports. Indeed, the trains ran on time and they were headed east, full of Jews, communists, Roma, and homosexuals. Even the infamous ID numbers tattooed on concentration camp inmates' forearms correlated to each prisoner's Hollerith card and the census data it contained: the tattoos were death camp barcodes. And when updated Hollerith-based data showed that a Jew was too weak to labor on, an IBM-owned computer would route the victim to a crematorium or liquidation center. As one Dehomag poster explained, "Hollerith illuminates your company, provides surveillance and helps organize."[14]

The point here is simply to problematize the political implications of everyday surveillance and information technology. Excavating IBM's role in the Holocaust should destabilize one's comfort with the proliferation of routine digital surveillance. The central fact is this: most Jews were not rounded up by means of special police investigations, but rather with the most enlightened tools of statecraft—the census, proper identification, and the managerial know-how of Big Blue.

IDENTIFICATION BY NUMBERS: SOCIAL SECURITY

Using the three components detailed above—universal personal identifiers, databases, and networks—the current landscape of digital surveillance opens before us. Dataveillance both individualizes and totalizes, constructing individual political subjects and demographic groups. Instead of watching the body, dataveillance monitors one's digital shadow. In unpacking computer surveillance we move from identification to data collection and analysis.

In the wake of the terrorist assaults of 9/11 there was much talk of creating an American national ID card. Oracle CEO Larry Ellison said that he would donate the necessary software and even had an audience with the government's mullah of social control, John Ashcroft. Even the formerly stalwart civil libertarian, Harvard law professor Alan Dershowitz, endorsed the notion of a national ID in a bombshell *New York Times* op-ed piece.[15] But, Americans probably won't get high-tech national ID cards in the near future. The more relevant question is: How are we already numerically identified and tracked?

In reality, we have a haphazard but fairly complete and coherent system of national identification. Instead of one ID number we have a set of easily connected numbers that serve as de facto digital tags; foremost among these are the Social Security number, credit card numbers, and driver's license number. When cross-referenced, the information in these various dossiers can be combined into unitary metafiles. Innocent numbers with nominally limited uses are thus transformed into powerful political tools for monitoring groups and individuals. Sociologists call this process "function creep," and nothing illustrates it better than the evolution of the American Social Security number.

Passed in August 1935, the Social Security Act did not at first require an identification number. When the necessary identification requirements of the law became apparent, both the left and right attacked. GOP heavyweight John D. M. Hamilton attacked Roosevelt's Social Security system as crypto-fascist, claiming that all Americans would be forced to wear metal ID tags.[16] William Randolph Hearst's *New York Journal-American* declared the new pension system a form of "snooping and tagging" that would require workers to wear dog tags "for the privilege of suffering a pay cut." In fact, the Addressograph Corporation created a prototype metal tag and tried selling it to the Social Security Board.[17]

The United Mine Workers and the United Steelworkers unions worried that Social Security numbers would be hijacked by bosses to track and blacklist organizers. "The unions, in fact, persuaded friendly officials in Franklin D. Roosevelt's New Deal Administration to include in the Social Security Act of 1935 a provision allowing an individual to replace an existing Social Security number with a second one when 'showing good reasons for a change.'"[18] And the *Boston American* warned that "your personal life will be laid bare, your religion and the church you attend will be listed. Your physical defects will go down in black and white . . . your union affiliation will be stated. . . . even your divorce, if you have one, will be included."[19]

In response to such fears, the Roosevelt administration was very careful with its language. As Arthur Altmeyer, one of the system's architects and political stewards, recalled: "The use of the word 'registration' was avoided because it might connote regimentation. An analogy was drawn between the issuance of a social security account card and the issuance of a department store credit card, which was the only form of credit card in common use at the time."[20]

Despite soothing reassurances that the new numbers would be employed only to administer benefits, function creep quickly set in. By 1939, J. Edgar Hoover had badgered President Roosevelt into issuing an executive order authorizing FBI access to Social Security files in any federal criminal investigation.[21] Throughout the 1940s and 1950s there was, according to the official history, "a gentle evolution" in the disclosure policies of the Social Security Administration (SSA). By 1945 the SSA's eight-column punch card files took up six acres of storage; eleven years later the administration had switched from punch cards to an IBM 705 vacuum-tube electronic computer.[22]

THE PRIVATE SOLUTION

Though law enforcement had increased its access to Social Security files, there was no functional equivalent of a national identification number in other fields of life. Considered from today's political vantage point this is an astonishing fact; both government and industry usually kept records based on name and address.[23]

The lack of any such enumeration became increasingly problematic with the proliferation of Hollerith-style automatic data processing and then magnetic tape-based mainframe computers. Name and address-based files worked only as long as the files were retrieved by hand and analyzed by actual people, because for every measure of human error there was an added measure of built-in human analytic processing. A clerk might notice and correct inconsistencies and redundancies, facts to which many computers were blind. Name and address dossiers plus large bureaucracies plus computerization created loopholes that allowed people to escape debt, the blacklist, and their own criminal records.

A *Harvard Business Review* article from 1961 illustrated the problem thus: "Mrs. John H. Johns wishes to open a charge account. Is she the same Mrs. Johnson H. Johnson who at an other address, has a two-year-old outstanding account?" The solution, according to the *Review,* was a national numerically based system of identification that would impose financial discipline with an even and efficient uniformity by eliminating the public's ability to reinvent identities and escape debt.[24]

This was not a new idea, but by the early 1960s calls for a national ID number were at an all-time high, particularly among banks and credit bureaus. But after decades of legislative attempts, all of which failed, there was little hope that Congress would save the day; national ID numbers were just too unpopular. If the government, stymied by America's folksy mistrust of being counted, would not impose a national ID, then, as the *Harvard Business Review* suggested, bankers and credit bureaus should use their economic power to impose such a system through economic fiat. In concert America's large businesses could transform the Social Security number into a de facto national identification by simply *demanding* the Social Security number in exchange for services.

As for privacy concerns? "This is the regimentation bugaboo again," sniffed the *Review.* "If an applicant refuses to give his number, the answer is obvious; he doesn't get credit, his check is not honored, or his insurance application is rejected."[25] The power of business to impose legislation was beyond question. The same year also saw an amendment to the tax code that allowed the Internal Revenue Service to use the Social Security number as an individual taxpayer identification number.[26]

Now financial data of all sorts would be permanently linked to a national identification code, the SSN. One of the most important firewalls in the structure of modern privacy had been quietly demolished. And lest one miss the larger implications here, suturing together disparate financial dossiers is not solely a question of money. Such files can contain information on a subject's residence, employment, and medical history. Thus were illuminated huge fields of demographic data. Accelerating this collapse in privacy was the rapid computerization of American life. One indicator of this: between 1956 and 1965 IBM's gross revenues almost tripled.[27]

State-of-the-art government-owned IBM 729 computer, 1969

LEGISLATIVE BAND-AID

By the early 1970s a popular backlash of sorts was forcing government to regulate the use of the personal information it collected. The Department of Health, Education and Welfare issued a landmark study and made a series of innovative privacy-protection proposals. These eventually morphed into the anemic Privacy Act of 1974, a law that limited the uses of government-collected data and of Social Security numbers by state and federal agencies. Unfortunately, the act left totally unregulated the routine surveillance practices of "banks, credit-card companies, employers, and health-care providers." Two years later Congress loosened even these restrictions and allowed the expanded use of Social Security numbers as IDs by state motor vehicle departments and social service agencies. Even before this, the SSA had been sharing location information on suspected undocumented immigrants with the Immigration and Naturalization Service; in 1971 alone the Social Security bureaucrats turned over 15,000 dossiers to immigration officials.[28] Meanwhile, businesses kept expanding the Social Security number's function creep by demanding it as mandatory ID in ever more contexts.

The use of this humble benefits number as "unique personal identifier" was to everyday surveillance as the late discovery of longitude was to navigation. Now disparate informational islands—bank records, employment records, health and even criminal records—could be accurately mapped and linked into a coherent archipelago. With ever-faster computers, increasingly connected through the telephone system, the real distance between these nominally separate dossiers has been diminishing at an accelerating rate for more than thirty years.

In this same period we have been moving just as steadily toward the digitalization of all economic transactions, no matter how minor. This slow migration toward electronic money is both the most convenient and in some ways the most frightening threat to privacy yet. For e-money in the broadest sense is almost always linked to one's identity and creates a traceable record of the time, place, and exact contents of each purchase. In a society where everything has a price tag, the evolution of a cashless economy must also be understood as the rising spectre of the panopticon: life under the threat of total observation. Credit cards, of course, are leading the path forward to a future where money and identification have merged.

7

SURVEILLANCE AND THE SINEWS OF COMMERCE

> This is our destiny: subject to opinion polls, information, publicity, statistics; constantly confronted with the anticipated statistical verification of our behavior, and absorbed by this permanent refraction of our least movements, we are no longer confronted with our own will. We are no longer even alienated, because for that it is necessary for the subject to be divided in itself, confronted with the other, to be contradictory. . . . Each individual is forced despite himself or herself into the undivided coherency of statistics.
>
> —Jean Baudrillard, 1985

> You already have zero privacy. Get over it.
>
> —Scott McNealy,
> CEO of Sun Microsystems, 1999

The records produced by credit cards, bankcards, discount cards, Internet accounts, online shopping, travel receipts, and health insurance all map our lives by creating digital files in corporate databases. The more one shops with credit or prepaid point-of-sale cards, the more one feeds these dossiers. Ubiquitous but fragmented, commercial surveillance helps make us obedient; it create consumers with predictable tastes, borrowers who repay their debts, and personality structures acclimated to cooperation with authority. At the same time, the informational technologies of commerce can be taken up ready-made by the government and police, though we rarely think of mundane receipts and accounts as the building blocks of state power.

CREDIT AND IDENTITY

The origins of the America's commerce-based surveillance begin with the brothers Tappan. During the 1830s, Arthur and Lewis were New York merchants and ardent abolitionists who supplied goods to the booming towns and farms of the hinterland and frontier. To increase profits and capture market share, these otherwise prudent Yankees extended credit over the sprawling, unruly geography of an ever-expanding United States.

Typically, traders servicing the western states and territories would buy goods in northeastern cities, transport them by wagon to riverheads, then travel by flatboat down to the frontier of the Ohio Valley and beyond. Once the goods were sold, the "arks" were disassembled and marketed as lumber, while the traders would travel down the Mississippi to New Orleans and from there head by clipper ship back to Boston, Philadelphia, or New York. Despite the obvious risks—fraud and theft were rampant—much of this trade was conducted on credit. But the Tappan brothers at least took precautions: before fronting dry goods, tools, cloth, or cash "each applicant was questioned individually, usually by Lewis, and no detail reported was ever forgotten."[1] In fact, all the details were written down in huge ledgers, supplemented with correspondence and comments from other sources. The ledgers thus came to act as risk analysis files. Before long the Tappans had a rather large collection of reliable dossiers on scores of merchants, traders, and planters throughout the West and South. Other wholesale merchants began requesting access to the Tappans' intelligence and, for a fee, the brothers obliged.

Further interest in the Tappan ledgers came with the crisis of 1837, a massive and brutal depression. Gentlemen of business who survived this bloodletting emerged more wary of risk and with considerably less coin than before. Demand for the Tappan brothers' information soared, and by 1841 the brothers had turned their private dossiers into the first national credit reporting service, which they called The Mercantile Agency. Using a network of county lawyers and small town magistrates as their "correspondents," the Mercantile Agency "rapidly accumulated a mass of reports on frontier traders, southern retailers, and enterprising, if comparatively small manufacturers throughout the United States." Written in longhand, these reports were organized and bound into huge sheepskin-covered ledgers. Inquiring merchants could thus visit the Tappan offices on the corner of Hanover and Exchange Streets in New York City and review the histories and "ratings" of potential customers. By the early 1850s the Mercantile Agency had branch offices in Boston, Philadelphia, Baltimore, Cincinnati, and New Orleans, and its dossiers contained thousands of pages, updated by thousands of "reporters" and correspondents. Over the years these included men such as a country lawyer named Abraham Lincoln and a young merchant named Ulysses S. Grant. At its headquarters in New York thirty men were employed copying, condensing, and giving out reports. When the Tappans retired in 1849 "the Agency" was in the hands of Benjamin Douglass and his associate Robert Graham Dun. By 1855 the Agency had a serious competitor in the John M. Bradstreet and Sons Improved Mercantile and Law Agency for Cities.[2]

Under the Tappans and their predecessors the Agency's correspondents remained anonymous and their identities were entered in the ledgers as codes or numbers next to their reports. The entries, sometimes updated every few months and at other times updated every year or two, were narrative but concise, often using a set of semi-standardized abbreviations and codes for common words and numbers. Whereas the Agency used handwritten ledgers, Bradstreet was the first to properly index and systematize its reports and publish its ratings. The Agency's earliest, handwritten reports are interesting in that they show emerging standardization while at the same time are replete with idiosyncratic punctuation and subjective commentary. From Delaware County, Ohio, a typical entry:

> Clay & Longwell #sts June 14/73
> Clay is a fine
> Steady young man –can say
> As to his means—Longwell is a farmer- lives about 8 miles from here

> Owns a gd farm—think in his own Name—has some money—is well to do—is a fine man. think he is all right. # Noe. June 16/73 "L" is supposed to be wo [worth]: 8c 10m$ [codes for: 8 hundred, 10 thousand, or $10,800] Clay is a fine young man—Has oof [nothing] but will full heir to 3c4m$ [$4,300] this fall when he becomes of age. #2341 [the correspondent ID][3]

Or this from correspondent number 1854, operating in Caledonia County, Vermont, March 23 1861:

> Daniel Hirm
>
> Hodgden Stone   So. Hardwick. . .
>
> In answer to inquiry
>
> Daniel Hodgden + Hiram Stone furnish the capital +William Hodgeden carries on the tin bus as their agent. That Daniel Hodgden is worth some 15c$ [$1,500] + Stone some more than 15c$ this is all I could learn at present.

Then almost a year later a new entry:

> #1854 Jan 28/62 Stone has a good house had some 2 or 3 m$ [$2,000 or $3,000] when hewent in with Hodgden—so his neighbors say + I think that is so from my acquaintance with him,+ he is a man that will rather fail than lose it. . . [Later in 1862 a short entry] . . . doing quite a bus. [Then in 1864] . . . all right no change.[4]

At other times the entries are not so happy. R.G. Dun even had a standard abbreviation "emb" for "embarrassment." Here is a typical warning:

> . . .has some RE [real estate] in wifes name drinks vy hard & does not attend to
> to bus. is hon but could not ads [advise] any cr.[5]

By 1924 there were, according to the Associated Credit Bureaus, 267 such agencies listed nationwide; in twenty-four years that number had swelled to 1,453; ten years later it was 2,038.[6] In 1933 Dun and Bradstreet merged to form one of the largest credit rating and financial reporting services in the world.

A CREDIT TO THE NATION

The earliest credit cards began fairly informally at the counters of large department stores.[7] In 1914 Western Union also provided metal charge cards to selected customers for "deferred-payment privileges." In the early 1920s, General Petroleum Corporation issued a similar metal card to enable employees to buy gas on credit. Later this service was extended to "select customers." Likewise, AT&T introduced the "Bell System Credit Card" in the 1930s.

But these early forays into a more standardized form of retail credit ended with the outbreak of World War II and the creation of "Regulation W," which was designed to rein in borrowing and consumer spending in order to direct capital toward the war effort. In the peacetime boom that followed, credit expanded again and in 1946 a New York banker developed the so-called Charge-It card—essentially a local bank–issued charge card with limited uses. All these local experiments finally came together in 1950 when Frank X. McNamara of the small Hamilton Credit Company invented a debt-based payment card for use at multiple locations. He got the idea from a customer who took out charge cards with numerous stores and then rented the cards to his acquaintances. McNamara turned this idea into the now famous Diners Club. At first, only 200 customers at twenty-seven Manhattan restaurants in New York City used the card.

By the late 1950s a number of banks were offering lines of revolving credit that could be paid off little by little rather than all at once. Increasingly, local banks were linking up to offer seamless credit card services. The biggest such venture, launched in 1966, involved fourteen US banks and became Interlink, a network for extending retail credit across multiple banking areas. This was of course not just about lending money: Interlink also created a network of informational exchange regarding debtors and their transactions. A few years later another combination of banks, the Western States Bankcard Association, introduced the "MasterCharge program," which eventually become MasterCard. Its rival was the huge BankAmericard program, which later became Visa. As the credit card industry spread, banks wishing to offer such services had to ally themselves with one of these two superpower networks.[8]

This proliferation of plastic was also an extension of new and subtle forms of everyday surveillance that would have been impossible without the widespread use of sophisticated computers. As one pair of authors put it, the new credit cards were

> the keys to a vast economic system. . . . But if the key admits the bearer into the system, it also admits the system into the cardholder's life, allowing merchants, banks, and government to monitor spending habits, travel habits, the types and quantities of purchases, and the promptness or tardiness of payment. With each swipe of the plastic through the little machine on the merchants counter, the cardholder simultaneously exercises and relinquishes a certain amount of freedom.[9]

With the ready availability of magnetic-strip technology and better computers in the early 1970s the information trail produced by credit cards became even more complete and automatic. By 1972 the Associated Credit Bureaus of America were building a fully operational network of interconnected computer databanks that would facilitate almost instant credit and background checks.[10]

THE DEBT BOOM

By the recession of the early 1980s millions of Americans were reeling financially; for many, credit card debt became an economic lifeline, while for others it was the millstone that dragged them under to economic oblivion. And for the rest of the decade paying with plastic grew at a phenomenal rate: "Between 1982 and 1990, the total amount of consumer credit outstanding rose from 620 billion to 950 billion." The average person's debt load increased by 30 percent.[11] Amid this atmosphere the federal government again accelerated the collapse of privacy. In 1983 the Office of Management and Budget launched a debt collection system that for the first time allowed federal agencies to share with private credit bureaus the names of individuals who owed the government money. In exchange the feds received direct computer access to the private credit records of over 100 million Americans.[12] (Even as late as 1977 only 3.4 percent of all household spending was done on credit cards; by 1997 that number had reached 20 percent.[13])

At the same time Visa initiated a "computerized dragnet" to map and locate businesses with higher than average suspect credit card transactions; such a pattern might indicate theft or fraud (that year counterfeit cards alone had cost the industry $42 million). Offending businesses were cut off or required to use electronic authorization. Rational business practice dictated such a move, and evolving technology allowed it. The flow of ever more detailed and routine information to corporate databases was inevitable.[14] The effect was to further discipline and rationalize everyday existence. The "consumer" now constructed in the files of credit agencies as a legal and historically knowable entity was increasingly recruited to self-monitor: corporate omniscience generates consumer accountability.

The retail credit system creates useful information while at the same time demanding transparency in the habits of debt-addicted consumers. As the World Markets Research Centre put it, "This is a long-term trend, reflecting both an overall escalation and a seismic shift from public to private debt. Private borrowing, by both corporations and individuals, has increased from US$ 200 bn in 1992 to over US$ 1 trn per year [in 2002]. . . . Total debt as a percentage of GDP has swelled to mountainous levels, from 150% of GDP in 1982 to nearly 300% today."[15] Such profligacy keeps the world economy in motion, but for lenders it involves massive risk. The rate of people declaring bankruptcy doubled in 2002, with more than 1.5 million Americans filing.[16]

Economic order in such an environment demands increased discipline and surveillance. Enmeshed in the matrix of obligation, responsibility, technology, and one-way financial transparency, the debtor is rendered accountable and therefore productive and governable. Thus credit acts to discipline and regulate the modern subject in even non-economic ways.

CHECKING IN WITH THE AUTHORITIES

By the early 1980s some credit cards allowed customers to withdraw cash from banks by inserting plastic cards at new "automatic teller machines" or, as they were first known, "customer bank communications terminals."[17] From these local experiments emerged numerous regional partnerships that by 1982 had linked up to form the first nationwide ATM network.[18] Soon other industries were following suit, setting up automatic, computerized "customer self-service terminals" for selling gas, airline tickets, and car rentals while merchants began experimenting with "point-of-sale" systems for direct debit, prepaid debit, and credit cards. By the mid–1990s ATM point-of-sale systems using magnetic-strip swipe-card technology began showing up at checkout lines across the country. By the late 1990s the leader in POS technology, Mag-Tek, boasted that its equipment was in use at millions of sites around the world with applications including "PIN-secured ATM cards, credit cards, grocery store checkouts, automated gas pumps and credit-card-payment airplane cellular-based telephones."[19] These millions of new electronic transactions all left digital records of who bought what, where, and when. Easier access to cash and commodities had inadvertently spawned a national web of data collection feeding thousands of gargantuan digital databases. Here was a shift of historic proportions: populations and demographic subgroups and even individuals emerged from the informal darkness to be known, counted, and controlled.

OVERFLOW TECHNOLOGIES

Magnetic-strip-based prepaid debit cards were adopted by mass transit systems, telephone companies, pharmacies, and welfare agencies.[20] Along with magnetic-strip cards came other cards using optically encoded images read by scanners or embedded chips read by computers.[21] The surveillance potential of these high-tech cash surrogates was immediately obvious: along with enabling new types of consumer research thanks to the automatic, electronic records updated with every transfer, the plastic-operated self-service kiosks and ATMs were usually monitored by cameras. Those paying close attention to the *Washington Post* in 1984 might have caught a glimpse of the shift under way: "Mosby was charged after he was identified through a picture taken by a remote camera at an automatic teller machine that showed a man using a bank card belonging to Bruce Glover."[22] By the early 1980s thieves of minor mental capacity were routinely being busted after using stolen ATM or credit cards at machines equipped with surveillance cameras.[23]

The argument here is not that the playing field should be leveled for those who wish to prey on their fellow citizens. The point is more abstract but very serious: with this digital cash came an unplanned, unexamined extension of state power and social discipline.[24]

BARCODES FOR ALL

Amplifying and extending such power further was the simultaneous growth of digital tags—using barcodes and scanners—that give unique and detailed identities to inanimate objects ranging from boxes of ice cream to government documents. First invented in the 1930s, bar codes were in regular use by 1967 when railroads began deployed them for tracking and routing freight cars.[25] The black and white stripes hit the retail world of supermarkets in 1973 amid oil price shocks, recession, military defeat in Vietnam, and massive labor unrest; the year that economic geographer David Harvey marks as the symbolic end of modernism and the rise of a crisis-induced "condition of postmodernity."[26]

By 1983 the national market for scanners and bar codes (or uniform product codes) was worth an estimated $325 million a year and growing at over 30 percent annually.[27] Since then barcodes have been introduced for use on everything from auto parts and live turkeys to hospitals patients and military supplies: virtually all products now carry a barcode.[28] Credit cards and ATMs document who is shopping, where and when, and the addition of barcodes makes transparent exactly *what* is being purchased.

SMART CARDS

If magnetic-strip cards, barcodes, and the like can deposit information—such as a customer's identification number—why not create cards that can also gather and sort information; that is, communicate in two directions? This is the idea of the "smart card"—the ID that carries with it a constantly updated dossier in the form of a microchip. With this technology a single card can store and update information on a person's identification, drivers license status, or medical and credit history. The first cards embedded with silicon chips were created back in 1974 by a French engineer named Roland Moreno.[29] Since then the technology has slowly but surely found use in hospitals, offices, factories, and schools.[30] Austria and Germany already use smart cards as their national healthcare IDs. So far the biggest users of smart cards in the US are peanut farmers. The US Department of Agriculture recently adopted a program to keep track of its peanut quota system by issuing 70,000 smart cards to peanut growers in sixteen states. And to test consumer response to smart cards, Visa International, the largest bankcard issuer in the US, will allow healthcare providers to store and access a patient's medical history through the chips in new state-of-the-art credit cards.[31] In Finland, the forward salient of hip techno innovation, smart card technology has morphed into a subset of personal communications gear: Finns use their Nokia wireless phones to simultaneously order and pay for coffee in cafés, transmitting an electronic request along with the correct amount of e-cash.[32]

Such digital miniaturization exponentially concentrates the amount and quality of consumer data available for analysis and resale. Processing, or "data mining," the accumulated information from smart-card transactions is the next logical step after their introduction.[33] As one specialist who supplies Safeway with high-tech surveillance gear explained upon introducing the store's new ID-tagged discount cards and hidden cameras: "We could monitor how much time an individual spends in the shop and in what order they shopped it. We could learn about any dead-spots in the store as well as what the shopper bought."[34] For example, a woman in San Francisco reported that nine months after buying a home pregnancy test from Safeway she began receiving the company's coupons for diapers and baby food, mailed to her home.[35]

COOKIES AND DATA MINING

On the Internet, commercial surveillance races toward a boundless new horizon of possibilities; now even "window-shopping" can be recorded, stored, and analyzed in a myriad of ways. Bear in mind that credit card numbers and all the information they carry about the owner's age, income, mail-

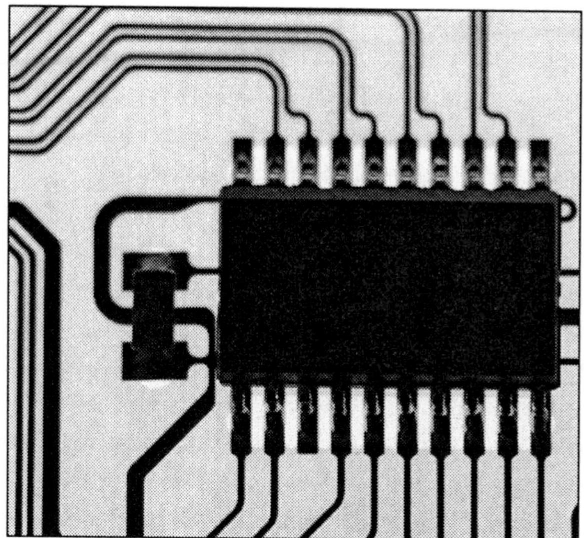

Miniaturized computing to maximize power (credit: Jan Chelminski)

ing address, and habits are ever present in e-commerce. In addition, roughly half of all major websites on the Internet use surreptitiously downloaded programs—called "cookies"—that tag, track, and analyze the movements of every visitor.[36] Originally developed at Netscape in 1994 by a feckless young programmer named Lou Montulli (who maintains that he didn't think about the larger implications of his new piece of code), cookies at first merely identified Internet surfers when they returned to a website for the second or hundredth visit. In other words, cookies were a simple, site-specific form of cyber ID that communicated only with their computer systems of origin.

However, because a cookie is essentially a piece of parasitic code that rides quietly in the guts of one's computer hard drive it has the ability not only to monitor what one does on the cookie's site of origin, like Yahoo or Netscape, but also to report back to its home base with details of all the other sites its host computer has visited. Cookies report on where you've been, when, and for how long. Some cookies are even intelligent enough to count keystrokes, copy whole files, and connect all of this information to the computer owner's user identification, credit card, and passwords. To use Foucault's language, cookie surveillance both "individualizes and totalizes," creating simultaneously unique individual dossiers and broad demographic profiles. Thus the 'net really has become something of a panopticon full of individual cells. Or think of it as a massive laboratory for market research, "a two-way mirror into consumer behavior."[37]

The firms with the most sophisticated cookies are also the ones that most diligently mine their data for sellable products. Take, for example, the case of DoubleClick, a company that builds detailed profiles of Internet users and then sends back demographically tailored advertisements. When users visit any of the 11,000 DoubleClick affiliated websites, a cookie is placed on their hard drives. There it gathers information such as usernames, passwords, and preferences, all of which are later uploaded to DoubleClick's central database. Among the information collected we find "names, e-mail addresses, home and business addresses, telephone numbers, searches performed on the Internet, Web pages or sites visited on the Internet and other communications and information that users would not ordinarily expect advertisers to be able to collect."[38] Many online stores do something similar. Sharper Image, for example, has rigged its website/e-catalogue with a "dynamic browser" that assigns each visitor an ID and watches what he or she does, adjusting the look of its homepage accordingly.[39]

Internet service providers also excavate the deep veins of information created by their customer bases. NetZero, with more than 5.7 million members, has opened its digital files to NFO Worldwide and InsightExpress so that those firms can "access household and individual samples . . . based upon demographics and/or Internet usage." And depending on the level of detail, the data miners can cross-reference "online behavioral data" with offline research.[40] Such data becomes more valuable as ever smarter cookies link the files from a wide range of sources.[41]

A PANTHEON OF TASTES

So why the drive to know consumers so intimately? Marketing theory tells us that American tastes have undergone a sea change since the 1960s. Mass culture has fragmented into a hyper-variegated landscape of niche markets and rapidly evolving microtrends. As a result, commerce requires ever more exact intelligence and ever more routine surveillance.

In many ways the new approach to consumer research began in 1974, just as the economic impact of market saturation and falling profits was hitting hard. That year scientist-turned-entrepreneur Jonathan Robbin created a computer program that correlated data from the US Census with information from credit firms, shopping outlets, and countless other sources—call it a system of commercial profiling. The mass market was now disaggregated into "life style segments" or "clusters" ranked according to the nation's 42,396 zip codes, all of which were sorted by affluence. Thus was born the famous Claritas Cluster System and its absurd yet apt nomenclature of cute nicknames for the various demographic types. There are the "Pools and Patios," "Gray Power," "Shotguns & Pickups," "Young Influentials" and the "Bohemian Mix." The Claritas version of social class as layered niche markets runs from the peak "Blue Blood Estates" down to "Inner Cities." As one *Los Angeles Times* report put it, "Working from the assumption that people tend to live near others who are like them, a zip code, the theory goes, can classify people according to their tastes in everything from politics, to religion, to mustard."[42]

At one level it is easy to laugh at Claritas, but the company addresses the class, race, and the geography of uneven economic development more frankly than most institutions in US society, and its cluster profiles have an uncanny and sad political resonance. For example, at the top:

> 01. Blue Blood Estates – Established executives, professionals, and "old money" heirs that live in America's wealthiest suburbs. They are accustomed to privilege and live luxuriously—one-tenth of this group's members are multimillionaires. The next affluence level is a sharp drop from this pinnacle.

A bit further down comes,

> 05. Kids and Cul-de-Sacs—Similar to Executive Suites and Pools and Patios, Cluster 05 ranks high on all affluence measures. Although married couples and children still dominate this cluster, some married couples without children are moving into Kids and Cul-de-Sacs. These suburban folks lead busy lives centered on family activities.

Further on,

> 10. Bohemian Mix—Dominated by mobile, highly educated singles, Bohemian Mix is an eclectic group of executives, students, artists, and writers who prefer to live in rented high-rises. Very few children are found in this multi-racial cluster.

Jumping down some more levels,

> 47. Inner Cities—Concentrated in America's poorest neighborhoods in large eastern United States cities, these young, African-American single parents live in multi-unit rental complexes. High unemployment and public assistance are prevalent here. When work is available, they have service and blue-collar jobs. They have grade school and high school education levels.

Still further down on all the "affluence measures" is,

> 62. Hard Scrabble—Scratching a living from hard soil describes those who live in our poorest rural areas. Reaching from Appalachia to the Colorado Rockies, and from the Texas border to the Dakota badlands, life is hard for Cluster 62 folks. Mining occupations and chewing tobacco show the highest indices in Hard Scrabble.[43]

By this logic the computer mind of the market feeds us to the demographic blast furnace of merchandizing; out the other side come appropriately targeted ads for clothes, food, and politicians.[44]

DATA MINING FOR POLITICS

Ultimately much commercial investigation is merely annoying. But how might such surveillance and data mining be problematic? Here are a few snapshots: A firm called eHealthDirect.com Inc. allows insurance companies to "benchmark" best practices by analyzing vast collections of medical records to determine which forms of treatments (or nontreat-

Data mining: social control as automatic function. A 1980s mainframe.

ment) result in greater profits.[45] Another "disease management company" called American Healthways claims it can deliver most firms a 20 percent reduction in medical treatment costs by searching pharmacy records for ways to rationalize (which means cutting services). Conversely, two major HMOs have hired various technology firms with "sophisticated computer software" to search patient insurance claims and pharmacy records for individual high-cost cases; HMO staff then intervene in any number of helpful, or very unhelpful, ways. The same technology could conceivably be used to find and fire high-maintenance or unhealthy employees.

Already, six large Massachusetts employers, including Polaroid, Gillette, and Houghton Mifflin, deploy this sort of insurance information to identify health risks—such as congenital heart defects—among their more than 120,000 workers. "We're watching health care costs go out of sight and we know there's waste and inefficiency," explained a Polaroid executive. In a similar vein, the University of California at Berkeley recently settled a $2.2 million lawsuit after illegally testing some 9,000 workers for pregnancy, sexually transmitted diseases, and genetic ailments without the employees' permission or knowledge.[46]

Even property management firms have started using computerized surveillance to vet would-be renters. A firm called SafeRent aggregates credit reports, applicants' monthly income, recent zip code, Social Security number, lease information, applicant demographics, and searches of criminal records. SafeRent also allows users to comment on the behavior of residents—for example, if they have been excessively noisy, messy, or threatening. . . or overly political. Back in the 1980s when such systems were first making news, one prominent target was a Seattle tenant activist named Samira Yunker, who fought a purely political eviction attempt and won but then found herself listed as an "undesirable" tenant. "It's like having a criminal record or being on a blacklist," said Yunker. And since these are private informational systems, the renter has no appeal process.[47] There is also a computer application called Mobile Workforce, "designed to help roving workers track time schedules and collaborate on projects." As is detailed in a later chapter, this is just one of a host of new tools designed to allow bosses to keep tabs on workers in the field.[48]

FOR SALE TO UNCLE SAM

A final word on data mining: once information is commodified and for sale on the open market it is also available to law enforcement agencies. Back in the mid–1980s when government officers were engaged in the digital great leap forward the Selective Service bought a commercial mailing list compiled by a national chain of ice cream parlors. Why? Along with notes on chocolate and vanilla the list contained the names of 167,000 kids who had given their birthdates in the hope of winning free ice cream sundaes. The feds used this information to mail out timely reminders about military draft registration. Not long after that the IRS purchased consumer lists to determine whether citizens leading lavish lifestyles were paying their taxes.[49]

One can imagine how the FBI might wish to cross-reference the subscription list of *Guns & Ammo* with online research from cop-hating Internet chat sites and available psychiatric medical and insurance records, or the membership lists of "extremist" political organizations.

Even before the advent of the short-lived Total Information Awareness System, (now renamed the Terrorist Information Awareness System) government agencies wishing to profile any, or all, adult Americans could turn to Acxiom Corp., a giant information service firm operating out of the Ozark foothills. All day, every day, Acxiom's computers gather and digest the informational trails left by 196 million Americans. The firm's cyber nets haul in data from credit card transactions, magazine subscriptions, telephone bills, real estate records, vehicle registrations, fishing licenses, consumer surveys, and census surveys, to name just a few types of sources. Clients can purchase demographic or individual profiles. According to one report: "Acxiom often can determine whether you own a dog or a cat, enjoy camping or gourmet cooking, read the Bible or lots of other books. It often can pinpoint your occupations, the car you drive, your favorite vacations."[50] In the end, all the fragmented and disparate dossiers of e-commerce and digital bookkeeping are easily united into metafiles, which can be used by both business and the state.

8

CAMERA LAND: SECURITY AESTHETICS AND PUBLIC SPACE

> You had to live—did live, from habit that became instinct—in the assumption that every sound you made was overheard and except in darkness, every movement scrutinized.
>
> — George Orwell, *1984*

Washington, D.C., was the first to go. In 2002, the District's police began constructing a centrally monitored, citywide closed-circuit television surveillance system—the first of its kind in the nation. Eventually, the Metropolitan Police Department (MPD) plans to operate over 700 cameras, watching streets, schools, Metro stations, federal buildings, and even parts of a Georgetown business improvement district. All images are streamed to the MPD's $7 million, "NASA-style" Joint Operations Command Center. Filled with video recorders, computers, and communications gear, this room is staffed by the D.C. police, Secret Service, FBI, and at times other agencies.

Once the full camera system is operative, police will have the ability to read license plates and track cars moving through the city, zoom in on individuals, read newsprint from hundreds of feet away, and send real-time images to the laptops of the department's one thousand patrol cars. Engineers are even working to equip some of the cameras with night vision and possibly biometric facial recognition software.[1]

RULED BY THE LENS

The CCTV camera is the synecdoche of potentially totalitarian state and corporate superintendence. Public space, in turn, is the basic ingredient of democracy. From the Greek polis to the town square to the rough and open culture of contemporary urban streets, public space is a resource, a commons, the crucial platform of popular democratic tradition. How many revolutions, including our own, were catalyzed on the public stage of the street or the commons? Destroying or controlling these public spaces has always been a political tool by which rulers battle restive populations; the nineteenth-century urban planner Baron Haussmann famously redesigned Paris with massive boulevards to allow easy military access to the city's center and to break up working-class slums. Like commercial life, which is now thoroughly tagged, metered, and recorded, so too are the politics of access, mobility, and public space being radically restructured by the new surveillance. The clearest example of this is the proliferation of closed-circuit television.

By the late 1960s CCTV was already coming into regular use as video technology became cheap enough for practical deployment. Early struggles over the politics of surveillance cameras were sometimes ugly.[2] But as the politics of design and public safety received more attention in the 1960s and 1970s, propelled in part by the "target hardening" theories of Oscar Newman, cameras found ever more application.[3]

CCTV has always been bound up with the specific spaces in which it operates. As the American economy has been dramatically restructured since the early 1970s so too has the country's geography. For example, from San Francisco to New York, formerly industrial waterfront transit and shipping depots have been recast as themed historic districts catering to upper-middle-class leisure activities like shopping and dining. As security-sensitive public and semi-public spaces have proliferated, so too has CCTV. Particularly important in this tale are the Rouse-style malls that

For your protection (credit: Jan Chelminski)

dominated suburban, and even urban, development projects in the 1970s and 1980s. To operate profitably, these private, enclosed yet publicly accessible retail spaces required the feeling of safety: call it *security aesthetics*.[4]

Suburban shoppers demand protection and regulation; cameras provide that as effective tools of deterrence, enforcement, and investigation.[5] Perhaps more important, cameras not only watch *but are themselves watched* and thus telegraph the semiotics of "safety." As a typical trade publication dealing with retail security explains: "One 'psych out' technique is the use of overt CCTV, where customers see themselves entering a store on an overhead monitor. Another is the stationing of greeters who personally welcome customers into the store."[6] This public display of surveillance deters theft by producing correct and useful types of fear (fear of authority) while suppressing middle-class fear of the potentially criminal "other." Surveillance is intimately bound up with the security aesthetics of retail space, which is itself predicated on the insider/outsider distinctions and codes of social hierarchy.

The rise and proliferation of convenience stores in the 1970s provided a new set of spaces in which intensive surveillance was feasible, profitable, and in many ways necessary: being a convenience store clerk is one of the most dangerous jobs in America. And the utility of cameras here helped habituate us to more cameras everywhere else. The *Convenience Store News Industry Report* for 1991 estimated that 19 percent of convenience stores and 43 percent of gas stations had cameras in or on their premises.[7] Today most franchised fast-food outlets and convenience stores have cameras. From these nodes of public space on private property the cameras continued to spread as their production and operation became less expensive and more politically acceptable. By the early 1980s some police had started deploying CCTV to watch crime hot spots.[8] And now we have the massive project in Washington, D.C., that amid the smoke and panic of post–9/11 America almost seems reasonable.

RESISTANCE IN CAMERA CITY

As soon as news of the D.C. surveillance network broke, civil libertarians began raising questions. Of particular concern was the system's total lack of any written guidelines or even the window dressing of some sort of community consultation in its development. Public outcry forced D.C. Police Chief Charles H. Ramsey to promise a set of written parameters, but even months later the details of how the cameras would be used remained a mystery.

Despite meetings with police brass, the ACLU still wanted to know: Who would monitor the video? When would the system be complete? How long would tapes be kept and by whom? What agencies would get access to the tapes? And what steps would be taken to prevent video voyeurism or racist and anti-homeless profiling? Nor were the ACLU's concerns merely hypothetical: already police in Detroit and Florida had used CCTV to stalk personal foes, political opponents, and young women.[9]

Other critics went further, arguing that written regulations and police consultations with the ACLU do little more than legitimize a dangerous and unnecessary form of police power. Noting that official guidelines are very frequently violated and can always be changed, Mara Verheyden-Hilliard of the Project on Civil Justice (PCJ) said, "Instead of signing off on this new system we think it needs to be abolished. There's a very strong legal case for the elimination of these cameras. People have the right to traverse the streets and parks of D.C. without being under the scrutiny of Chief Ramsey and the FBI."[10]

Though one does not have a total right to privacy while walking on the street—we accept that being looked at is the price of being in public—people do have a Fourth Amendment protection against unreasonable searches. And it could be argued that when police watch a person with high-powered, interconnected, and intelligent cameras that are linked to criminal history databases they are in effect conducting a warrantless and unconstitutional search.

TARGETING DISSENT

Perhaps the most disturbing features of the D.C. surveillance network are its past political uses. The first people to be watched were thousands of activists protesting at NATO's fiftieth anniversary summit. The surveillance gear was again deployed in April 2000 to monitor activists and control crowds during mass protests against the joint World Bank/International Monetary Fund meeting, and again to watch protesters at the contested inauguration of George W. Bush in January 2001.

"Americans have the right to protest with some level of anonymity but this system and the other uses of surveillance are stripping people of that right," argued Verheyden-Hilliard. "After the inauguration we talked with numerous people who don't normally go to demonstrations—many of them were shocked and really intimidated by the police militarism and intense surveillance." Simply put, surveillance has a politically chilling effect.

Activists know all about that: police surveillance, while always "creepy," was particularly intense in D.C. "There were lots of cameras on the streets but also guys on rooftops. Some were filming, some were snipers—a bullet backing every camera," reported documentary filmmaker Mark Liiv. "They make a really big deal of getting up in your face and letting you know that you're being filmed. . . . If there are all these high-powered cameras on buildings, why are the guys in the street if not to psych us out and breed paranoia?"[11]

The D.C. police have even used their surveillance system to observe the very orderly, rather mainstream Million Family March in October 2000. And along with powerful cameras mounted on buildings the department has equipped its helicopters with wireless surveillance video that also feeds the monitors at the high-tech Command Center. For a more close-up view from within the crowds of demonstrators the MPD has contracted with a private "script-to-screen" video firm called SRB Productions. Advertised as "100% minority and woman-owned," SRB has worked for everyone from the Oprah Winfrey show to the US Navy. As a police hireling the firm conducted surveillance of demonstrations using its commercial television equipment, according to an SRB spokesperson. It also mixed a "best of"–style protest video for the chief's viewing pleasure.[12]

RULE BRITANNIA

To really grasp the future of CCTV, cross the Atlantic to the UK, the country with the highest CCTV density in the world. "The CCTV market in the UK is probably the most developed in Europe and is growing 25% a year," explained one industry expert.[13] By the late 1990s the center of every city and major town in the UK was under the watchful eye of police cameras. A constellation of unique factors explains this culture of supersurveillance. First there is the UK's lack of a written constitution with any explicit protection of privacy built into it. The availability of inexpensive, high-quality cameras also fueled the spread. And finally there was the extreme political climate of the early 1990s.

In those days, the British media was gripped by a moral panic that fixated on the double threat of crime and terrorism. When it was all over the UK was covered in cameras. The cycle started in 1990 when the IRA resumed its "mainland campaign" with a bomb at the London Stock Exchange. More explosions followed. One in April 1992 left London's financial district with three dead, ninety-one injured, and more than $1.2 billion in damage. The next year another massive "dump truck bomb" in the same general area killed one and injured dozens more. Later the IRA bombed central Manchester and launched daylight mortar assaults on Heathrow airport and a cabinet meeting at Number 10 Downing Street. In

Early CCTV command and control center, 1974

response, the police erected a "Ring of Steel" security cordon around central London. In came vehicle barriers, traffic bans, random armed checkpoints, and hundreds of new electronic eyes in the form of CCTV.[14]

Amid this security buildup, two ten-year-old boys abducted and killed a toddler named Jamie Bulger. The kidnapping was caught on grainy surveillance footage and endlessly looped by British television. All of this helped cast video surveillance as the public safety tool du jour. Now the UK has more than 2.5 million cameras; London alone is wired with 150,000.[15] Most famously, London's Newham borough council and the Metropolitan Police installed 300 digital cameras with FaceIt brand biometrics to scan its High Street for deviants. One British academic has even described CCTV as the "fifth utility," along with water, gas, electric power, and telephones.[16]

But contrary to what the boosters say—in the US and in the UK—the record of CCTV is mixed. In London cameras have been correlated with declining crime rates but now crime is on the rise again despite CCTV surveillance. To date no terrorists have been caught via CCTV. However, leading British criminologists have found that CCTV does lead to racial profiling. One large study by Clive Norris and Gary Armstrong found that Black people were twice as likely as whites to be watched for "no obvious reason." [17]

AMERICA ON FILM

Regardless of how large the D.C. surveillance system becomes, cameras are already spreading across the US. The RAND Law Enforcement Technology Survey found that 41 percent of local police departments and 66 percent of state police departments used "fixed-site video surveillance cameras."[18] Another study by the International Association of Chiefs of Police found that 80 percent of US police departments use CCTV, while another 10 percent are planning to do so. A 1998 study by the ACLU of New York counted 2,397 surveillance cameras, some controlled by the police, all "trained on public streets, sidewalks, buildings and parks in Manhattan." When asked for an explanation, then Mayor Giuliani waved the ACLU away, saying, "They raise questions about everything." More disturbing still is the increased use of hidden or disguised CCTV cameras in Gotham.

Tampa, Florida, has installed thirty-six digital cameras equipped with biometric face recognition software. Once captured on video, the digitalized facial patterns of people on the street were to be automatically compared against photos in the department's "wanted," "missing," and "gang registered" databases.[19] Suspicious persons or those labeled deviant because of previous encounters with the law would be closely watched by police and through such pressure encouraged to leave the thoroughfares of Ybor City, Tampa's nightlife district. So far the biometric aspect of this technology has been a total failure, but getting such a system to function is not out of the question.[20]

In Oakland, California, over seventy surveillance cameras watch the civic center, and a force of blazer-clad security personnel ushers away homeless sleepers and skateboarding youth. A duplicate system exists around San Francisco's Yerba Buena Center for the Arts, where the rules include everything from no lying on blankets to no kite flying to no bike riding. Santa Rosa, California, also has cameras watching its Courthouse Square and "Transit Mall" with the explicit intent of discouraging the presence of homeless people and youth. Baltimore has video cameras scanning 106 of its downtown intersections.[21]

Scores of other towns have similar small-scale systems. Worcester, Massachusetts, has CCTV around its parks. Virginia Beach uses CCTV to monitor the pedestrian crowds of its boardwalk.[22] Similar arrangements exist on Mobile's Dauphin Street, where the local Mardi Gras is celebrated. More cameras (paid for with money confiscated during drug busts) watch Mobile Government Plaza, the park near its adjacent convention center, and the traffic corridors that feed into downtown streets. In Los Angeles police are using motion-sensing cameras to fight graffiti. In contrast to cities that opt for hidden cameras, LA's motion-sensitive Flashcam–530s play a recorded announcement as they take a photograph, thus foregrounding the panoptic effect of internalized self-policing. Along with warding off graffiti writers the cameras help police direct municipal "scrub crews" to repaint or "buff" walls that have been tagged.[23]

As technology prices dropped, some American cities started outfitting their traffic arteries with live CCTV for monitoring and managing the flow of vehicles. Minneapolis was in the lead and by 1994 had 142 cameras dispersed along key segments of the freeway system with plans for a total of 180 cameras by the end of 1995. Mounted mostly on tall buildings, some cameras send video signals to the city's Traffic Management Center via microwave while others use fiber-optic or coaxial cable.[24] Seattle now uses a similar system.[25] According to the General Accounting Office, the R&D for this wave of cameras has come in large part from the federal government, which invested $50 million in surveillance technology between 1997 and 2002.[26] Cameras continue to sprout up so fast it's impossible to monitor their proliferation adequately.

LEARNING TO BEHAVE

Schools are another space where everyday surveillance has been spreading. In Huntsville, Texas, school officials deployed cameras in 1985 to deter and catch pot-smoking high school students; the officials also considered using similar tools in the junior high schools.[27] The Reynolds School District in the Portland, Oregon, area installed cameras in 1994 against the wishes of both staff and students.[28] Independence High School in Columbus, Ohio, uses cameras to monitor hallways and outdoor student gathering spots,[29] while the unfortunately named Hempfield High School in Lancaster, Pennsylvania, keeps most of its twenty entrances locked shut; access and egress are gained by way of the central office, where a security camera and two-way mirrors serve as unblinking sentinels. Visitors with legitimate business can show identification, surrender their keys, pin on a guest ID badge, and then enter. Other Lancaster schools use cameras and plainclothes security guards.[30]

Even very safe, well-heeled suburban schools are installing cameras. Jackson High School in a "tiny, upscale community" outside Seattle has 25 security cameras watching everything from the hallways and cafeteria to the football field and parking lot. "Everywhere you go, there's a camera right above you. . . . If you're, like, with your boyfriend or something they're constantly watching you," explained one student. Other schools on Puget Sound also use cameras.[31] In at least one case the ACLU has protested school camera schemes, such as the $840,000 project in Boulder's public schools. But most such systems generate little controversy.[32] An expert from Sandia National Laboratories estimates that 30 percent of high schools and 15 percent of middle schools now use CCTV.[33]

The justification for stripping bare the lives of children and teenagers is captured in the common mantra of "child safety" and school shootings. But in reality schools, for all their faults, are still some of the safest places for juveniles to be.[34] Nor are cameras used only against surly, drug-addled, possibly violent teens—they're increasingly common in grade schools to monitor hallway rowdiness. As one straight-faced press account from North Carolina described: "For Eddie Henderson, principal of East Montgomery Middle School in Biscoe, life is simpler since five surveillance cameras were installed at the school to monitor hall behavior." The principal of this mid-sized school explained that cameras deny students the luxury of "re-making history" when explaining their antics. As another official said, "It will give you the truth instead of across-the-board suspensions when you don't know the true story."[35]

Here we have a perfect, almost caricatured, illustration of Louis Althusser's notion of "interpolation"—which is central to understanding Foucault's interest in the panopticon. Interpolation is that moment in which authority names or hails a subject who in turn answers, thus recognizing and reinforcing his/her relation to the matrix of social power and in so doing gives authority's rules and dictums a real and lived meaning that penetrates and colonizes the subject's own soul. The student is "hailed" by authority claiming privileged access to truth; the student responds and as such is further inserted in the framework of power based on truth.

Behind the overuse of surveillance are two driving forces: the authoritarian cues of a larger society obsessed with crime and terror, and the general bureaucratic compulsion toward continually greater control. If school officials want cameras, then even the slightest provocation will suffice. In Rapid City, South Dakota, surveillance cameras were installed after staff found threatening graffiti in a bathroom.[36] And what are the cameras actually policing? More often than not cameras monitor quite healthy behavior. This is the classic "net widening and mesh thinning" that criminologists have long noted. First the net of police power expands to cover ever more types of allegedly deviant behavior; then deviance is "defined down" so that ever more innocuous behavior is criminalized. Thus the mesh of the net becomes tighter until even minor infractions are met with a formal sanction. For example, the Hemet Unified School District in Southern California has strictly prohibited unsupervised skateboarding. To enforce this absurdly overbearing ban the school has rigged its grounds with surveillance cameras.[37]

School buses are another site for electronically watching the young; in some states up to half of all school districts have cameras in their busses. The busses of McGugan Junior High in Oak Lawn, Illinois, are equipped with cameras that the principal occasionally uses to humiliate students, such as Jimmy Romanao, who temporarily lost his bus privileges after he was caught "grabbing a piece of paper out of his friend's hand" and "using foul language."[38] Occasionally school surveillance gets out of hand even in its own terms. The superintendent of a school district near Pittsburgh was caught stalking several of his subordinates by using computer software searches, a private investigator, and the school's CCTV system.[39]

Let's face it: America is full of borderline, petty despots. They gravitate toward work as police officers, security guards, or supervisory bureaucrats like foremen, welfare caseworkers, and school principals. They have authoritarian personality structures straight from the pages of Marcuse. They thrive on the little sadomasochistic thrills provided by rules, rule breaking, and disciplinary action. They merge their own emotional agendas with the society's larger need for order and discipline along class, racial, and gender lines. They keep us working or keep us within the speed limit or keep us in our "natural" place. The new surveillance brings out the worst in this type, rewarding and nurturing their will to both submit and dominate just as it binds these local overseers to the larger structures of oppression.

But more important, visual superintendence of public space has a corrosive effect on democracy. After all "politics" is not an abstraction. It occurs in real places, like streets, schools, universities, work sites, and urban commons. Though freighted with clichéd overuse, Orwell's warnings in *1984* really are quite instructive. The proliferation of CCTV and similar technologies threaten to reshape our culture and public spaces and therefore our very minds in ways that preclude progressive social change, cultural experimentation, and basic liberty.

9

THE DIGITAL LEASH: MOBILITY AND FREEDOM

> The Loop has electronic sensors embedded every half-mile out there in the pavement itself, each sensor counting the crossing cars every twenty seconds. The Loop has its own mind, a Xerox Sigma V computer which prints out, all day and all night, twenty-second readings on what is and is not moving in each of the Loop's eight lanes.
>
> —Joan Didion, 1976

> There are no free roads.
>
> —Motto of the International Bridge Tunnel and Turnpike Association, 2002

If the mythology of the frontier helps define pop notions of "the American character," then nothing encapsulates American notions of freedom better than the open road. The ability to move unencumbered through space is central to our film, music, literature, and folk culture. From the Oregon Trail to the hell hounds chasing Robert Johnson to *Easy Rider*, we prize one inalienable right above all others: we are free to move.

Within the trope of geographic mobility rides a whole cosmology of real and imagined possibilities: to move away is the American surrogate for rebellion. Physical mobility is the palliative for the frustrations of social immobility; it is the promise of a better horizon; the proverbial backdoor, always open, awaiting one's escape. But no longer. The anonymity of the road is dead. On this front the politics of public space meet the questions of access and travel in a quintessentially American fashion—via the automobile.

FREE TO PASS

However archetypically spooky CCTV cameras might be, they are only one of a myriad of technologies that police public space and physical movement. Consider also the array of technologies for reading identification codes from a distance. Industry types call this gear "automatic electronic identification" (A/ID), or when used on trucks and cars it's "automatic vehicle identification" (AVI).

Some A/ID systems use mounted or handheld receivers that monitor the energy emitted, or reflected, from a "radio frequency" badge or tag. Other systems use magnetic strips that are read when swiped through properly equipped computers. And increasingly A/ID systems use barcodes that can be read up close or from afar by laser-bouncing monitors. As with so many features of the present, rudimentary A/ID technology was introduced in the early 1970s. At first quite expensive and futuristic, the technology was used only for controlling access to executive suites, military labs, and similar hot spots.[1] By the late 1980s, A/ID was managing inventory, baggage, parcels, and livestock as well as controlling passage in and out of restricted, security-sensitive locations.[2]

Increasingly, A/ID relies on an array of microchips often called "inlays" or "embedded circuitry." Typically, such an identification/access card will communicate its serial number to a receiver by means of emitting or reflecting a low-energy radio frequency, or by means of a magnetic-swipe strip or optical barcode.

As such technology grows smaller, lighter, and more flexible, manufacturers are starting to produce "smart labels," and "smart keys," and "smart badges." Inevitably, costs will fall further and many "read-only" barcodes, tags, and badges will be upgraded to communicate like smart cards as parts of "interactive data networks." Once that is achieved, information on people and objects in time and space can be constantly updated and recorded passively and automatically in real time to create a ubiquitous self-generating infrastructure of the dossier.[3] The implications of this for the politics of mobility could be rather intense. In a thoroughly tagged world, geographic maneuver and escape become difficult. Escape from the past or from persecution, the freedom to reinvent, resist, and restart, will all be severely curtailed in the fully digitalized landscape of the possible future.

EVERY VEHICLE, A LEASH

Beginning in 1988 a number of regional transportation authorities began experimenting with automatic toll payment technology based on automatic vehicle identification. One of the first systems to go online was the North Dallas Tollway, using electronic identification technology developed at Los Alamos National Laboratories in the early 1970s for high-security access control.[4] At the same time, similar systems went online in D.C., Illinois, San Diego, and Tulsa; most of these used barcode technology and electronically read tags attached to car windows. Monthly bills were sent out in itemized statements listing the place and time of each toll crossing.[5,6] The total number of drivers involved in these experiments was minimal.

But then Washington, Boston, and New York City's Metropolitan Transportation Authority all joined up to create one giant, integrated e-toll system that would eventually cover the Northeast and mid-Atlantic states as well as parts of Appalachia. The first piece of the system went up in 1989 on New York's Verrazano Bridge, which at the time carried about 58 million vehicles a year between Staten Island and Brooklyn. The initial tags went to some government employees, the fleets of a few local trucking firms, and then anyone else who volunteered. Each vehicle would get a little box bearing a "unique serial number" of up to twenty digits that would be read as it passed through tollbooths. The technical know-how and logistics were handled by the defense contractor Lockheed and communications giant AT&T.[7]

Next, the Lincoln Tunnel was outfitted; again, buses and guinea pig trucking companies were tagged. From this emerged a commitment from the New Jersey Turnpike, the New Jersey State Highway Authority, and the New York State Thruway Authority to create a coordinated, areawide automatic vehicle identification system that came to be known as E-ZPass.[8]

Once the Big Apple was tagging vehicles, everybody else followed suit. By the end of the decade numerous statewide and regional systems existed: California had FasTrak; Illinois, I-Pass; Kansas, K-Tag; Oklahoma, PikePass; Virginia, Smart Tag; in Florida they use the SunPass. In Hong Kong they just call their high-tech toll tags the "Octopus Card." Perhaps when all the systems here are linked together we'll call ours the "Leviathan Card."

By the early 1990s, the E-ZPass system (the largest AVI network in world) operating in and around New York City had pulled in eight states: south to Maryland, Delaware, and West Virginia; north to Massachusetts and soon New Hampshire; and west to Pennsylvania.[9] By the middle of the decade, E-ZPass traffic accounted for an estimated 40 percent "of all toll transactions and 67 percent of all toll revenue in the United States."[10] In 1993 when the New York system went online 60,000 tags were issued. Within five years that number had increased by a factor of ten; Massachusetts alone had almost a quarter of a million vehicles with E-ZPass tags on its roads. Throughout its area of operation there are now well over two million people whose vehicles are tagged with E-ZPass transponders. System administrators expect that two-thirds or all local commuters will eventually be tagged.[11]

As one transportation expert put it: "We should be making our roads smarter, not wider." Thus North Carolina, South Carolina, and Virginia are all toying with the possibility of integrating their electronic toll systems into the E-ZPass network. In other regions a similar process of agglomeration is under way. Such rapid growth is easily explained: electronic tolls offer the advantage of speed. And one could imagine how they might be made even more attractive—for example, by charging higher tolls on those who use more gas and clog the roads by waiting in line to pay *cash*.

How convenient! A fast-moving toll system for almost the entire East Cost and every other patch of metropolitan sprawl. But also, how strange. Each E-ZPass tollbooth is equipped with a computer, connected by fiber-optic cable to a "data center" in Secaucus, New Jersey, run by Chase Manhattan Bank. Each tag produces a precisely itemized monthly E-ZPass statement that reveals "a billing address, a credit-card number, how often a driver is on the road and his or her whereabouts at a certain time."[12] Without much discussion, a system of soft, unstaffed electronic checkpoints has been erected along thousands of miles of highway and at dozens of major urban bridges and tunnels controlling access to some of the nation's most populous cities. If originally pitched to the public as such, would we have hesitated?

In all these examples enrolled drivers register not only financial information but their driver's license numbers and vehicle registrations—bureaucratic details, but quite important. Such identifying information marks the difference between an anonymous prepaid electronic toll system, much like prepaid phone cards, and a system of detailed surveillance that logs the movements of literally millions of drivers.

STRICT CONFIDENCE

Already E-ZPass and the other AVI systems are eroding privacy in unforeseen ways. First of all, E-ZPass is not just a toll system but also a method of ticketing: all tollbooths are mounted with cameras that photograph the license plates and faces of speeders who pass through the gates too quickly or without transponders. Every month about 7,000 Massachusetts drivers appeal against fines for speeding or other electronic toll violations. In fact, New Jersey planned to pay four-fifths of the cost of its $500 million electronic toll system from the fines that system would generate.[13]

More important, it is now routine for toll authorities to share travel records with police. Legal professionals confirm that bridge and toll surveillance is becoming a common evidentiary feature in criminal courts. The first case to open these records was a 1997 homicide investigation in New York; by 2001 a similar ruling permitting the subpoena of electronic toll records had been issued in Massachusetts. And lawyers in California have been able to subpoena the Bay Area's FasTrack records for civil cases. Now, California's transportation authority, CalTrans, argues that its electronic toll files do not contain "personal" information because several people may share a single FasTrak pass and thus the information is *not* covered by California privacy laws.[14] Although E-ZPass records are supposed to be private, an investigator hired by the *Albany Times Union* obtained the travel dossiers of the paper's editors with no difficulty. Such information could help in forcing out-of-court divorce settlements or, when integrated into something like the Pentagon's now shelved Total Information Awareness System, be useful in monitoring political dissidents.[15] Then, of course, there are also the mistakes: one deliveryman faced $1,500 in false tickets thanks to some glitch in the EZ Pass mainframe.[16]

There are other types of traffic surveillance as well. In San Antonio, the city has recruited 60,000 volunteers to attach transponders to their vehicles so the city's fifty-three automated radio frequency readers stationed at strategic points around town can map traffic flows and respond to accidents and bottlenecks with greater speed and accuracy.[17] The most elaborate of all traffic management systems is, quite appropriately, in Houston, home base for so many NASA missions. Officials there have rigged the city's intersections, freeways, and exit ramps with drive-over motion sensors and a network of live video cameras. All of this information is fed by subterranean fiber-optic cable to the so-called "Tran Star Command Center," where hard-working traffic engineers and technicians watch the real-time, color-coded flow of vehicles on a huge, 40-foot-by–10-foot screen map.[18] In the Bay Area a similar system of widespread roadside receivers now reads the FasTrack transponders intended for paying tolls. The information gathered is used to mange traffic jams.[19] Though it sounds bizarre, Washington, D.C., Maryland, and Virginia officials are planning to manage traffic by monitoring the energy emitted from hundreds of thousand of commuter cell phones as they creep along the congested Capital Beltway. Similar surveillance-based traffic management systems are emerging elsewhere.

As for the future, auto industry experts "predict" (read "want") electronic toll collection (ETC) technology to become a standard built-in component of all new vehicles. One of the main institutional champions behind the spread of this toll-taking and car-tracking technology is the International Bridge, Tunnel and Turnpike Association (IBTTA), whose motto ("There are no free roads") began this chapter. The concept of mobile toll payment has now merged with the gasoline credit card. As one fawning story put it, "A little gadget called Speedpass lets you pay for gasoline and snacks from your local Mobil and Exxon station in just seconds." Using the same radio frequency identification technology as electronic toll collection, Speedpass is a plastic keychain tag that is read by an intelligent gas pump. The price of one's gas is then subtracted from an electronic account. McDonald's may also start using the same technology.[20] In other words, there will be even more records tracking our movements through time and space.

INSIDE THE BLACK BOX

Since 1990 General Motors has installed so-called "black box recorders" in over 6 million automobiles. These Sensing and Diagnostic Modules, or SDMs, are the size of a videocassette and record a wide range of information. According to the *New York Times*, the SDM records "not only the force of collisions and the air bag's performance, but also captures five seconds of data before impact. It can determine, for example, whether the driver applied the brakes in the fifth second, third second or last second of a collision. It also records the last five seconds of vehicle speed, engine speed, gas pedal position and whether the driver was wearing a seat belt."[21] As you might expect, one device begets another: Vetronix Corp., now sells a $2,500 "Crash Data Retrieval System" whose intended customers include police departments, insurance companies, and car rental agencies.[22]

An Indian firm is developing a version of the black box called "Nexgenlogger" that can store data on stopping, starting, rate of speed, engine temperature, and other factors for up to 90 days. There is even the possibility of using commercial INMARSAT satellites to track such recorders and monitor their information while in use.[23] In America the possibility of monitoring the minutiae of vehicle behavior is also meeting the spectre of satellite tracking. Leading the way in this are Elite Logistics, described as "a leader in the fast-growing telematics industry" and a firm called Independent Witness Inc. Together they are merging "event data recording technology" with global positioning system tracking so as to reduce "fraudulent and exaggerated insurance claims." Such information (if linked to the Internet, as is being planned) could also allow parents to monitor the movements of their driving adolescent children and allow employers and the police to keep tabs on workers or parolees. "Some people call this big brother; I call it 'dad,'" said one booster.[24] Fans of the technology point out that it protects the innocent. But will lack of this technology or resistance to it be viewed as part of a suspicious profile? And what is "innocent," exactly?

PUBLIC TRANSPORTATION

In New York the old token-operated turnstiles of the subway have given way to a system using magnetic-strip cards, each of which is assigned an ID number. If one uses a credit or ATM card to buy metro cards then the card's ID number is linked to the purchaser's personal and financial information through credit card records.[25] How have New Yorkers reacted to this creepy new technology? They have embraced it with abandon: "The New York Transit Authority reports that the transit card-ATM program has exceeded expectations and is now a permanent fixture of its Metro card-distribution system. The program has doubled in size since it began in 1998, and rider interest in using ATMs to buy transit cards [and] using bank-issued debit cards has not yet peaked," reports *Bank Network News*.[26]

In Los Angeles as well buses are being equipped to take a form of swipe-card payment. (The politics of bus riding are particularly interesting in Los Angeles where the 40,000-member Bus Riders Union has used an assortment of guerrilla tactics such as fare boycotts and civil disobedience.)[27] The same vehicles also have onboard CCTV and are tracked via GPS.[28] The San Francisco Muni system also uses CCTV and bugs its busses with hidden audio mics.[29]

SKY-D

Since the attacks of 9/11 the most intensely controlled mode of transportation is commercial aviation. To limit access to planes the government is working on a smart ID system for frequent flyers called Sky-D, which would use biometrics and/or chip-embedded smart cards. Sky-D would tap into "all available public information—such things as credit ratings, telephone numbers, addresses, driver's license files and voting registrations." Using sophisticated software the program would form this mass of data into a meaningful personal profile of each traveler. The sojourner whose records "show a normal, stable life would be presumed to pose little risk as potential terrorists," but people with "no credit history, no fixed address and no other evidence that they are who they claim to be" would be treated as suspect. Of course, we are assured that the confidentiality of all this data will be maintained.[30] Sky-D, as currently conceived, is by definition a violation of the assumed (though not necessarily legally protected) privacy of the countless databases from which it draws. Along with Sky-D, the National Transportation Aviation Authority is working on "SkyGuard" for tracking and disciplining airline workers. Like Sky-D, this program would use smart cards carrying biometric identifying information.[31] Here again is the logic of the E-ZPass: selling convenience in exchange for personal information.

Currently the Transportation Security Agency is testing a prototype for its new Computer Assisted Passenger Pre-screening System II, or CAPPS II. This commuter program uses government and private information—such as financial and legal records, consumer purchase data, health records, and anything else available—to evaluate individual passengers before they board a flight. As one report explained, the system "will rely heavily on commercial data warehouses containing names, telephone numbers, former addresses, financial details and other information about virtually every adult American." And CAPPS II will "rate passengers using a color code: red for immediate threats, yellow for people with questionable backgrounds and green for the vast majority. The rating will be given to the airlines for decisions on whether a passenger should be allowed to board or be subjected to additional questioning." The system's files would be regularly refreshed with new information that would be stored for up to fifty years, all without a passenger's knowledge. The backbone of this vast electronic passenger-screening network is being built by Lockheed Martin.[32]

More problematic still is a "no-fly list" also created by the Transportation Security Administration using information from the CIA, FBI, State Department, and what was the INS. Ostensibly designed to keep terrorists from boarding and taking down planes, the list has also been used to harass and limit the mobility of peace activists and other dissidents. Along with various radicals from the Bay Area, some twenty activists from Wisconsin were prevented from flying to Washington to meet their congressional delegation; a Green Party activist in Maine was also delayed from flying by the same means.[33] A lawyer from the Center for Constitutional Rights who is routinely subjected to as many as three searches in each airport also suspects that she's on the no-fly list. And versions of the list now circulate via the Internet for use by casinos and major firms like DuPont.[34]

Beyond the specific material harm to a few activists being delayed, what are the deeper implications here? Clearly this "swarming of disciplinary technologies" has a chilling impact and helps deepen a culture of obedient quiescence. The emerging surveillance landscape brings with it very serious political implications: mobility is as integral to democratic politics as is freedom of speech or the right to assembly (which is itself predicated on spatial mobility). The "enclosure" of once relatively anonymous roads by means of cameras and automatic vehicle identification marks a radical transformation in the politics of the built environment that ratchets up the type of spatial control discussed in the previous chapter on CCTV from a local to a regional level. Placing political limits on air travel takes that project to a national and international level.

10

THE NEW TAYLORISM: SURVEILLANCE, WORK, AND DISCIPLINE

In the past man has been first; in the future the system must be first.

— Frederick Winslow Taylor
The Principles of Scientific Management, 1911

Winston must log on to the computerized phone system at the Charles Schwab brokerage firm no later than seven minutes after eight lest a supervisor called a "team lead" harass her. Once her computer is up and running, a message appears announcing yesterday's "productivity scores" in the form of a list ranking, from best to worst, the performance of all thirty technicians at Schwab's tech-support call center. Arranged in clusters of low, see-over cubicles, the technicians work beneath a series of elevated LCD screens upon which are posted their names and minute-by-minute productivity scores.

"You look up and see who's cleared the most calls, who's done the least, whose phone is 'engaged,' whose is 'idle.' It brings out the worst. You want to win. You want to beat your colleagues. And everyone just works constantly," says Winston, here pseudonymously identified with a sobriquet from the pages of Orwell.[1]

Such is life on the new shop floor, where surveillance and constant psychological pressure to work harder are the norm. According to the American Management Association, more than two-thirds of US corporations keep their employees under regular surveillance and that percentage is growing all the time.[2] From the low-tech body and bag searches at retail stores to computerized ordering pads at restaurants to the silent monitoring of e-mail and phone traffic in offices, the American workplace is becoming ever more transparent to employers.

Rather than "freeing workers" and "flattening hierarchies" – as the New Economy hype would have it – computers, databases, and high-speed networks are pushing social relations on the job backward toward a new digital Taylorism where every motion is watched, timed, and controlled by the boss. Along with being invasive and increasing the rate of exploitation, this on-the-job surveillance makes it easier for supervisors to fire and harass contumacious workers. Though it is true that computers have been analyzing and managing modern production since the days of Hollerith and Thomas Watson, the microprocessor revolution of recent decades has brought such superintendence of labor and materiel to a new intensity.

This frontline digital invasion of the workplace hit full force by the early 1980s. In a tone that now sounds quaintly startled, an article from 1984 observed that

> At Northwest Orient Airlines in Minneapolis, the 55 data-entry workers who feed ticketing and payroll information into company computers are expected to type at a speed of between 9,000 and 16,000 keystrokes per hour, with a sophisticated computer system keeping track of speed. Fast workers can win the right to have an hour of 'flexitime' in setting their schedules, but slower ones can lose pay. All workers must maintain a speed at least 75 percent as fast as the three fastest workers, or they can be fired.[3]

Back then, workers, unions, and critical observers accused computer surveillance of increasing "illnesses such as hypertension, heart disease, migraine headaches and stomach maladies" among workers suffering the "technostress" of having "a computer constantly watching and from being evaluated by a sometimes unseen supervisor."[4] Over the last two decades this matrix of digital regulation has become more routine, intense, and ubiquitous. But today's superintendence has its origins in the rise of industrial production and modern management.

Throughout history laborers have been watched and pressured to work hard, be it by slave drivers, landlords, guild masters, or any number of superiors. But only under modern industrial production have the day-to-day, even minute-by-minute realities of work been so thoroughly shaped by surveillance and the attendant politics of knowledge. Even early industrial capitalism used rather traditional methods of task organization. As shown by Sydney Pollard, most mines and mills in the 1870s and 1880s tended to hire skilled laborers, who in turn hired helpers and subordinates of various sorts. In cotton mills, skilled spinners were often in charge of several machines upon which were usually stationed their relatives and children. In mines, excavation was organized by crew bosses called "butties," who subcontracted and supervised gangs of miners working in teams for a shared per-tonnage piece rate. Even women laborers in button factories hired girls to assist them. As Pollard notes, this extensive and old-fashioned subcontracting was not so much a method of management as it was a method of nonmanagement in which owners off-loaded that burden of supervision onto workers.[5]

Such arrangements did not last long, stasis not being the nature of market economies. The drive for growth, profit, and survival in a competitive environment created constant innovation. Old craft-originated labor processes were soon swept away by more efficient methods, and nothing would be as catalyzing in this transformation as the theory of "scientific management."

EMPIRE OF THE STOP WATCH

Frederick Winslow Taylor, the father of scientific management, was an obsessive-compulsive, a neurotic, socially awkward freak who even as a youth counted his steps, analyzed his physical motions, and measured the duration of his various activities—all with an eye toward improving his "efficiency." Due to his diligence, self-discipline, and eccentricities (and to the macrolevel logic of economic competition) his peculiarities have become ours; his neuroses have been standardized and duplicated; his compulsions extended and normalized into the template of modern work and everyday life.

The child of elite and overbearing parents, Taylor was under heavy pressure to perform and achieve from an early age. His father was a lawyer and expected his son to follow in his path. The boy was sent to Exeter, in preparation for Harvard and the bar, but midway through high school Taylor, presumably in rebellion against his father, did the unthinkable: he left the most exclusive prep school in America and got a factory job at the Midvale Steel Works. However, a neurotic compulsive he remained, and after a few months of determination, focus, and hard work the young man had mastered numerous types of machine tasks and was appointed gang boss in the lathe department.

Once in charge of his former colleagues Taylor, inexorably driven toward efficiency, set himself the task of totally restructuring the shop-floor work culture. In other words, he became the biggest rate buster in history. As a lathe operator on the line he had been part of an informal system of work regulation. Years later Taylor, testifying before a House inquiry on the spread and effects of scientific management, described the situation: "We who were the workmen of that shop had the quantity output carefully agreed upon for everything that was turned out in the shop. We limited the output to about, I should think, one-third of what we could very well have done. We felt justified in doing this, owing to the piecework system—that is owing to the necessity for soldiering under the piecework system. . . ."[6] If the lathe operators worked too hard the rate of pay per piece might fall once the bosses saw how much actual labor was needed, so the men dragged their feet, or as Taylor preferred, "soldiered."

To smash this custom Taylor initiated a bitter three-year fight in which he sought to "get a fair day's work" from his former colleagues by increasing the pace of work and output while cutting wages. His descriptions of the struggle are painfully blunt: "We fought on the management's side with all the usual methods, and the workmen fought on their side with all their usual methods." Taylor demanded more work, and when he didn't get it he fired the men who had trained him and worked by his side, hiring and training greenhorns and then firing them as needed.

For their part, the operators resisted collectively and individually, ultimately resorting to systematic sabotage. "Every time I broke a rate or forced one of the new men whom I had trained to work at a reasonable and proper speed," Taylor explained, "some one of the machinists would deliberately break some part of his machine as an object lesson to demonstrate to the management that a fool foreman was driving the men to overload their machines until they broke. Almost every day ingenious accidents were planned."[7]

As for the mechanics' obstinacy, Taylor's descriptions are refreshingly amoral, revealing a realistic, situational ethics rather than the usual moral acrobatics of those who know they are doing wrong: "I did not blame even these laborers in my heart, my sympathy was with them all of the time."[8] Elsewhere Taylor is supposed to have, in fact, admitted to his former friends on the shop floor that he too would resist had he been in their position.[9] But Taylor eventually broke the men of the lathe shop, went on to rationalize most other tasks at Midvale, and wrote up his insights in book called *The Principles of Scientific Management*. Soon, managers throughout the US were embracing his ideas.

At the heart of Taylor's revolution was the politics of knowledge and surveillance. The shop-floor struggle between workers and bosses hinged on the question of information, and management's tools for accessing worker knowledge were methodical observation plus organized record keeping. According to Taylor, the original problem at Midvale was the "ignorance of the management as to what really constitutes a proper day's work for a workingman."[10] The bosses in Taylor's estimation simply did not understand the actual work process and did not know the real amount of labor-power (as opposed to simple labor time) that was actually needed to load pig iron or stoke a blast furnace.

From his stint among the lathe operators, Taylor had "fully realized that, although he was foreman of the shop, the combined knowledge and skill of the workmen who were under him was certainly ten times as great as his own."[11] When Taylor set about reengineering other jobs at Midvale he not only observed the work process but also researched and kept dossiers on the men he sought to break. In short, the key to all his victories was surveillance. His observations made transparent the "hidden transcripts" of worker resistance, exposing their secret, slow-motion withholding of labor-power at the point of production.

This penetration and colonization of work by the supervisory gaze is the essence of scientific management, an otherwise not-so-scientific conspiracy against labor. Nor is surveillance simply the first stage in a reengineering process; constant superintendence is the key to exerting managerial control once a new rate of work has been set. Constant surveillance is the circuitry by which control is transmitted from boardrooms to the hands of workers. As Harry Braverman explains in his deft intellectual demolition of Taylorism, *Labor and Monopoly Capital*, "the pivot upon which all modern management turns [is]: the control of work through control over the *decisions that are made in the course of work*."[12] Recall Foucault's discussion of the panopticon as a model of control in its ideal form, where the effects of power are constant even when its application may be intermittent. Surveillance achieves discipline and creates docile bodies by causing the subjects of observation to police themselves; that is, to make the right decisions by "internalizing the gaze" of their overseer. Being watched, or possibly watched, places a supervisor inside one's head.

These power/knowledge politics are clearly spelled out in Taylor's three principles of scientific management, which (quoting Taylor and using Braverman's analysis) can be summarized as:

One, *surveillance and seizure of knowledge*: "The managers assume . . . the burden of gathering together all of the traditional knowledge which in the past has been possessed by the workmen and then of classifying, tabulating, and reducing this knowledge to rules, laws and formulae. . . ."

Two, *separation of mental and physical tasks*: "All possible brain work should be removed from the shop and centered in the planning or laying-out department. . . ."

Three, *control of labor through knowledge*: "The work of every workman is fully planned out by management at least one day in advance, and each man receives in most cases complete written instructions, describing in detail the task which he is to accomplish, as well as the means to be used in doing the work."[13]

The impact of this triple maneuver is to deskill work, thus making workers more interchangeable, docile, and cheaper. But the process also *exposes* the labor process and laborer in a useful and organized fashion.

Others followed Taylor: Hugo Münsterberg, Elton Mayo, and Henry Ford all emphasized the further automation, de-skilling, and fragmentation of tasks, but they all built upon the basic power tectonics of scientific management. As Braverman points out, "[I]f Taylorism does not exist as a separate school today, that is because, apart from the bad odor of the name, it is no longer the property of a faction, since its fundamental teachings have become the bedrock of all work design."[14] While it would be unfair and incorrect to say that all of management theory has involved the deliberate degradation and simplification of labor processes (there are also processes of re-skilling evident on many of the "reengineered" shop floors) it is true that transparency and the flow of power as mediated by surveillance are inherent to management, even in jobs that cannot be much disaggregated into easy-to-master tasks.

THE DIGITAL SHOP FLOOR

Back at the Charles Schwab tech-support center Taylor's name is virtually unknown but his political soul is ever present, embedded in the very machines that Winston and her colleagues work upon. The combination of software and hardware that keeps tabs on Winston is a customer relationship management (CRM) system made by Aspect, the market leader in supplying corporate America with high-tech "customer relations portals." With 3 percent of the country's workforce employed at call centers, Aspect's market is huge. Along with ranking workers against each other in real time, Aspect's system allows managers to listen in on calls, search for keywords, and archive all e-mail and voice traffic for later analysis. This data can then be aggregated or disaggregated in almost any fashion. As one Aspect manger put it, the company's technology can "drill down" into stored data to retrieve a single year-old call just as easily as it can search a massive database for keystroke or call-time patterns that might indicate theft, drug use, or unauthorized breaks.[15]

But most important, Aspect's gear allows Schwab managers to create an intricate and invasive corporate culture of measuring, ranking, and intimidation. In fact, Schwab's disciplinary rituals read like examples straight from Foucault. Take, for example, "Normalization," a three-day quarterly retreat in which managers collectively evaluate their subordinates and then publish a list of who gets bonuses and who gets discipline. Inevitably, this choreographed "bench marking" of "best practices" raises the productivity bar ever higher. "A year ago we had three minutes after each call to write up what happened. That was called 'wrap.' Now there's no wrap time; we have to write notes as we handle calls," says Winston. The point of such regimes is not to find the measure of "a fair day's work" but rather to drive workers to their very limit, to extract from each hour of wages paid the maximum possible amount of labor power.

Not only is surveillance deployed through high technology, but even spatial arrangements and field of vision play a part in Schwab's office-level surveillance: the technicians are visually exposed to each other and management, just as their scores are displayed. This surveillance at the level of floor plan is perhaps the most obvious and basic form of pressuring the white- and pink-collar proletariat.[16] As for the one-way transparency of workplace information technology, it is built into federal law: legally all communications occurring on corporate-owned computers and phone systems are automatically open to monitoring by employers. Some states impose mild restrictions on workplace eavesdropping, and many firms give new employees obscure warnings in the fine print, but few workers get more than that.

INTERNET AS PLAYGROUND, NETWORK AS SHACKLE

Nothing has advanced surveillance on the job like the Internet. With an estimated 122 million Americans having some sort of online connection at their worksite, the web is both a place to waste time and an infrastructure for tracking and disciplining workplace laggards. As for the Internet's almost infinite distractions, consider this: one reputable research group found that 30 to 40 percent of all workplace web surfing is not job related.[17] And foremost among the web's attractions—surprise, surprise—is pornography. According to the *Boston Herald*, one sex industry survey discovered that 70 percent of all online pornography traffic takes place between 9 a.m. and 5 p.m. Even merely risqué Internet content can hurt corporate profits.[18] Several years ago Victoria's Secret held a live, online, 45-minute lingerie show on a spring Friday afternoon—the *perfect* time for the office-bound workers of America to take a quick break, log on, and watch ladies walk around in underwear. What ensued was an informal, apolitical, but massive nationwide work stoppage: one estimate figured that the show cost American employers a total of $120 million in lost time.[19]

Contrary to the hype of the Internet's early boom, this supposed productivity panacea in fact requires constant policing. Large corporations are routinely firing employees by the dozens for "inappropriate Internet use" such as porn surfing, gambling, online video game playing, chat-room socializing, shopping, and job hunting.[20] Ironically, one of the many distractions offered by the Internet is surveillance itself. Since 1997 hundreds of private day-care centers have equipped themselves with web cameras that allow anxious parents to watch real-time images of junior from the comfort of their desktops. And for those with private babysitters there's always the home-installed, web-enabled "nanny cam" for less than a hundred bucks.[21]

In response to such problems many corporations with vast, almost anonymous communications networks are loading up on computer programs that were until recently the sole domain of the Pentagon. In fact, the Privacy Foundation discovered that one-third of all American workers who use the Internet or e-mail on the job are under "constant surveillance."[22] More often than not, this surveillance is automatic. Raytheon, for example, offers a $65,000 software package called SilentRunner; instead of simply searching for suspicious keywords this program uses complex algorithms to study relationships between people and computers for patterns that might indicate fraud, insider trading, or espionage. Once found, these networks of relationships can be displayed in three-dimensional on-screen graphics, giving investigators enhanced powers of analysis. One added feature: the program is "passive," meaning that it's almost impossible to detect.[23] As one top technology magazine noted in a review, "SilentRunner 3.0 puts a surprising amount of power at an administrator's fingertips. It can yield great insight into how and when information is transferred across a network."[24]

Such technology isn't just for catching laggards and thieves; high-tech surveillance can also be used to break worker organizing or even informal forms of shop-floor resistance. "Workers, disgruntled or not, leave open back doors and work around security measures for convenience," comments another trade review of SilentRunner.[25] More elaborate yet is the emerging field of "computer forensics," which involves teams of in-house corporate sleuths who surreptitiously copy employees' hard drives and analyze the content for signs of errant behavior. As the chief of Microsoft's corporate security explained, "People don't always tell the truth, but their computers usually do."[26]

Indeed, the veracity of computers is so stubborn it can survive even the efforts of users to erase incriminating information. In the service of truth and paymaster, digital investigators now use Encase, a supercharged software application that copies drives, excavates deleted files, and scans for naughty content like padded expenses or talk of unions. Research that once took weeks at the hands of highly trained experts can now take mere hours and be executed by someone with only a week of preparation. Encase's earliest users back in 1998 included the Secret Service, US Customs Service, and the LAPD, but within two years the firm's base market had shifted toward large corporate players like Disney, Bank of America, Coca-Cola, and Philip Morris.[27] Note the accelerating rate at which the best federal spying tools are passed off for routine use by the private sector.

THOUGHT POLICE ON THE JOB

The AFL-CIO estimates that 50,000 people a year are *illegally* fired because of union activity. The role electronic surveillance plays in this can only be guessed at. But here are a few illustrative examples: Ken Hamidi, once an Intel employee, ran an e-mail forum of current and former Intel workers to discuss the grim side of programming and engineering at the vanguard of the New Economy. Intel objected and tried to block any Hamidi communication that was sent to Intel employee accounts. Allegedly the firm even pressured Hamidi's Internet service provider to delete Intel-employee responses to Hamidi. Finally a California court ruled that Hamidi's e-mails, when sent to Intel's servers, constituted "unlawful trespass."[28]

Even more audacious was Northwest Airlines' attempt to seize the personal—that is, privately purchased, home-based, non-business-related—hard drives of several employees who were also union activists.

The organizers, struggling to win a new contract, had used their e-mail and home computers to orchestrate a mass "sickout" in which flight attendants and ground staff all called in sick simultaneously rather than formally calling a strike. The action's intent was to ground the carrier's planes during the lucrative Christmas season so as to force through a better contract. It worked. No flight attendants meant no flights. Northwest was compelled to cancel 317 of its fullest, most profitable trips between December 30, 1999, and January 2, 2000.

Enraged, company executives struck back in kind, suing the union for waging an illegal strike. To prove their case they subpoenaed the hard drives of rank-and-file leaders. Their demand was granted by a federal judge, but a contract was signed before the hard drives were handed over.[29] The totalitarian resonance of these two examples should not be overlooked: the very right of workers to communicate freely is under attack.

RETAILING DISCIPLINE

Offices and call centers aren't the only worksites being scrutinized by the digital gaze; increasingly retail stores and even restaurants are wired in a similar fashion. Step into Calzone's, a crowded middlebrow San Francisco eatery specializing in overpriced pasta with reheated sauce. Though trying hard to achieve an aura of sophistication and quality, Calzone's and its four sister restaurants turn a profit thanks in part to rigorously Taylorized operations that rely on the latest in handheld high-tech.

Rather than taking orders on paper pads the wait staff here use the Pokky System, a network of mini mobile computers that beam information back to the bar and kitchen via radio waves. The back-of-the-house staff receives the transmissions from a little printer that spits out paper tickets.[30] The technology means less walking but also less talking, arguing, flirting, and complaining among servers, bussers, cooks, and bartenders.

"Pokky allowed us to cut our labor costs by at least a third," says Calzone's manager.[31] His sentiments are echoed by restaurateurs everywhere. One, whose praise is posted on the Pokky website, writes that the device "has literally dropped my labor costs back to pre-minimum wage increase days." The system also automates inventory and sales analysis since data in the Pokky System's main computers can be searched for interesting patterns, such as what's selling and who's selling and what's disappearing without being sold. Not all workers enjoy the changes.

"You just end up working really, really hard," says Julia, a former waitress at a Pokky-enabled restaurant who—like Winston—prefers to use a name lifted from Orwell. "There was never a break. Compared to other restaurants, I handled about twice as many tables as normal." Management counters that more tables equals more tips, but Julia says that after sharing tips with the bussers and food runners the pay didn't make up for excessive hustle or the hectic ten- and twelve-hour shifts.[32]

Julia had other, more subversive complaints as well: "Trying to organize a union there would be impossible. We worked so hard that we hardly knew each other." And, on a perhaps less noble but possibly more practical front, there was the question of "re-expropriating the expropriators." Pokky's electronic inventory means no free meals or drinks, no comping an appetizer to a table because of a spilled drink or to get a better tip. No slack, unless, of course, a digital sabot gets stuck in Pokky's wireless gears.

"I finally learned how to crash the system," says Julia. "Then we'd switch back to paper and I would steal entire bills. Service an $80 table and just pocket the cash." As for justification, Julia—something of a nihilistic Marxist—explains: "The boss and his wife were filthy rich; they forced us to work fifty-hour weeks. They'd both spend all their money on cocaine and face-lifts. So fuck 'em."

Like it or not, there are many Julias on the front lines of low-wage America. And when correlated with poor pay, on-the-job theft begs deeper questions: whose actions are worse, the exploitative boss or the broke and pilfering worker? Regardless of one's position on this sort of informal struggle, retail-level spying cannot simply be dismissed as employer paranoia. Thus, about 2,000 restaurants nationwide use some sort of handheld Pokky-style POS system. Jamba Juice Co., with 300 outlets, is testing a similar device, Amerauth Technology Systems' UltraPad 2700. And many businesses use stationary versions of the same technology.[33] For example, National Wholesale Liquidators just purchased a new point-of-sale system for tracking "data transfer" and "debit/credit processing." The company expects to save $2 million annually by reducing labor costs 35 percent and cutting down pilferage.[34]

Increasingly, "loss prevention" in the retail realm—also known as thwarting theft—involves digitalized video and special pattern-sensitive software, which was originally developed for use in casinos. Loronix, one of the lead companies in this field, combines digital closed-circuit TV with computerized POS technology in a unified system that feeds all data into a master computer that is able to archive and correlate every keystroke and image. This information can then be searched automatically for unusual patterns. Perhaps a cash register has 5 percent more returns than average; this might be a sign of the purloining. To check, just review the corresponding video. Likewise, the computer can search endless hours of video for suspicious visual patterns: a cashier putting his hands in his pockets and then looking over his shoulder. What might that indicate? The original casino version of this technology looked for dealers who even for a second moved their hands under the table, a probable sign of stealing chips.[35]

Retail environments also use some decidedly low-tech surveillance, such as "spotters" or "mystery shoppers" who frequent an establishment and then file evaluative reports with corporate headquarters. Taco Bell—which also uses a vast high-tech, centrally wired, Loronix system—has 150 full-time mystery shoppers who stalk the corporation's 7,500 outlets looking for rude employee, slow service, and free refills. This national snitch force visits each restaurant once or twice a month, filing their analyses by handheld computers directly up-linked to Taco Bell's nerve center in Irvine, California. Taco Bell, despite its size, is actually just a piece of the behemoth Yum! Brands Inc., which also includes KFC and Pizza Hut, brands that also use mystery shoppers and point-of-sale surveillance methods.[36] Even little eateries like Calzone's use mystery shoppers.

One industry expert, quoted in *Nation's Restaurant News*, estimated that a full 90 percent of American restaurant chains use mystery shoppers, nor are these the only industries to do so.[37] Hudson United Bancorp, a growing "community banking franchise" that fancies itself the McDonald's of finance, deploys mystery shoppers to track "sales per banker per day."[38] Industry insiders estimate that mystery shopping, now a $400 million to $600 million business, has boomed over the past decade in part due to increased consolidation in the retail business. "If you own a thousand stores, you can't be at every store all the time," explained a founding member of the Mystery Shopping Providers Association.[39]

AT THE BEDSIDE

As healthcare has become increasingly profit-driven over the last twenty years the pressure on frontline health providers has increased exponentially. To extract more labor from fewer staff, medical managers are borrowing practices from other industries. A growing number of nurses and orderlies are now required to wear computerized "radio-wave" ID badges that transmit their location on the ward to a computerized map monitored by a shift supervisor. These systems include new bedside call lights and intercoms that are monitored from a central location. With increased transparency and decreased staffing, nurses and medical technicians find themselves under ever greater pressure to move from bed to bed, dispensing more service and more labor power per hour.

"It's nonstop work. Our patients are very sick. They're in acute condition and need a lot of physical and psychological care," says exhausted oncology nurse Mary Alice Martinez. But with a radio badge system made by Hill Rom the patient-to-nurse ratio at the Mid-Peninsula Medical Center in Burlingame, California, where Martinez works, has increased from around six patients per nurse to eight. Such "efficiency" has reduced caregiving to its purely technical functions; visits with patients—known as "psycho-social interventions"—are squeezed out of the process in the interest of pressing down costs.[40]

HIGHWAY AS PANOPTICON

Even work on the open road is subject to the new superintendence. The pecuniary logic of the corporate bean counters is extended, by the magic of the technological gaze, to every road and street in the nation. More and more American trucking firms have equipped their vehicles with various high-tech tracking tags.

The most common technology is based on the Global Positioning System. These cell phone–sized transmitters automatically beam the coordinates of their location to twenty-four earth-orbiting, Pentagon-owned-and-maintained satellites. Thanks to GPS, big trucking firms like JB Hunt can create up-to-the-minute maps pinpointing the exact location of each truck and trailer in their vast fleets. Most trucking companies contract for GPS services from specialists like OmniTracs, a division of Qualcomm, or HighwayMaster Communications of Dallas. According to *Forbes*, commercial GPS is an $8 billion-a-year business and growing.

With two-thirds of all freight in the US now hauled by truck, it is no wonder that business is interested in knowing more—*much more*—about where truckers are and what they are doing. As *Fleet Equipment* magazine explains, "Computer software programs and global positioning satellites (GPS) systems have given fleets a way to route, reroute and track vehicles, loads and drivers to make the most of their rolling assets."[41] Kenworth, the truck maker, is even beginning to build into its rigs a GPS-based "telematics tracking system" designed to "allow fleet dispatchers to track drivers throughout North America. The dispatcher receives information on the driver's identity, adherence to a predetermined and authorized route, vehicle weight, and other data." The firm's futuristic concept truck, the T800, even includes biometric fingerprint pads for verifying driver IDs.[42] In other words, no switching vehicles with your buddy so you can drop by to see mom in Amarillo or surprise your main squeeze in Fort Wayne.

Vendors of trucking surveillance gear are clear that one of the technology's big advantages is controlling drivers and getting them to work harder. "Maximize profits, increase efficiency and minimize downtime . . ." chimes the brochure of a CCTV firm specializing in outfitting trucks, parking lots, warehouses, and loading docks. The copy goes on to explain how extensive use of video surveillance can keep drivers moving and hold them accountable for damage that might otherwise be billed to employers due to confusion. "If drivers had 'switched' as a favor to each other then management can be informed and take action to prevent future occurrences."[43]

These are significant developments. One of the attractions of long-haul trucking has always been the job's independence. There are more than sentimental notions involved here: truckers have at times played an important role within the American labor movement. Throughout the 1970s truckers staged numerous nationwide strikes that at times bettered conditions for workers in their industry and for labor as a whole.[44]

BIG BROWN AND THE NEW STOP WATCH

At United Parcel Service digital on-the-job surveillance joins old-fashioned Taylorism in its most dramatic form. A common feature on the landscape, UPS, the nation's third largest employer, is also a massively dynamic yet overlooked technological innovator. Known among its workers as "Big Brown," "Uncle Brown," or the "Brown Machine," the firm handles 7 percent of US GDP, has over 350,000 workers worldwide, and was described by one analyst as among "the most technologically sophisticated companies doing any kind of business anywhere."[45]

Always a rigorously ordered firm with a penchant for time-motion studies, UPS was started in 1907 by James Casey as a small local delivery firm in Seattle. By the 1920s Casey's firm had merged with a few competitors and expanded to Oakland and Los Angeles, and just a few months before the crash of 1929 the firm opened United Air Express, which flew packages up and down the West Coast and as far east as El Paso. Despite the depression of the 1930s UPS continued innovating with technologies such as mechanized package sorting and conveyor belts. During this era an authoritarian corporate culture began to flourish, and all UPS vehicles were painted Pullman brown "because it was neat, dignified, and professional."[46] So too were the company's strict work rules, written up in a tome called the *UPS Policy Book*. Along with practical instructions on package handling these pages offer up a plethora of "Caseyism" epigraphs, such as "You can't be a big man unless you have shown competence as a small man."[47]

Much of the firm's rigorous work rules and intense surveillance culture flowed from the personality of Casey, who in his austerity (despite phenomenal wealth) and business-oriented single-mindedness was almost a caricature of the Calvinist captain of industry. Supposedly, Casey was "so consumed by the package delivery business that he rarely spoke of anything else." [48]

By the 1930s, UPS headquarters had relocated to Manhattan. There the publicity-shy bachelor Casey worked long hours in a barren office, lived in "an unadorned two-room suite at the Waldorf Towers, and was known in his spare time to wander through Manhattan department stores, invariably ending up in the room where workers wrapped the packages for delivery. He liked watching."[49]

UPS was using "scientific management" as early as most other big American firms, and eventually its work rules were crystallized into a set of procedures called "the Methods." Today the Methods run about fifty pages and describe basic procedures, all designed to minimize excess motion, speed work, and keep the drivers moving. For example the Methods instruct: "Buckle the seat belt while inserting the ignition key. . . . Engage the starter with one hand while releasing the parking brake with the other." That sounds fair enough, except that drivers who pause between actions are subject to discipline. In the past the company relied on as many as 2,000 industrial engineers whose job was to watch and measure work practices in the interest of constant refinement and reduction of motion. The same holds true today: drivers guilty of wasteful and excessive movements are fined and disciplined by supervisors, who watch the loading docks and even travel delivery routes in search of errants.

But the firm's culture of observation, measurement, and control took a quantum leap forward with arrival of cheap digital computing. Starting in the 1980s UPS managers began a massive, almost awe-inspiring high-tech makeover. Their first move was purchasing two leading technology firms to develop and test specialized package tracking equipment. By the early 1990s UPS was busy creating the first nationwide integrated wireless network, a task that involved creating a partnership between four major telecommunications firms and their seventy-five junior partners. Big Brown needed this ethereal web to facilitate its latest technology.[50]

At the heart of the new system is the "Delivery Information Acquisition Device" known to all as a "DIAD board." Carried by drivers at all times, this computerized clipboard combines the functions of a time clock, GPS tag, and two-way, text-based pager. At best the DIAD enhances flexibility and efficiency, while at worst it is an electronic leash that keeps UPS drivers working at a furious pace.

Simply stated, the DIAD is the Pokky system on steroids. Work starts when a driver logs on to the DIAD with his or her personal ID. Using cell-phone technology, the DIAD board logs the number, sequence, and duration of stops, clocks the speed of each task, notes the driver's location, and communicates all this to a receiver in the truck, which then automatically relays all data to the local dispatch center and from there to a huge UPS computer (one of the world's largest) in Paramus, New Jersey, where information is archived and kept for at least eighteen months. Similarly, long-haul drivers at UPS are monitored by a device called IVIS, which records and transmits the truck's location and speed, the driver's work patterns, and the minute details of engine performance ranging from temperature to average miles per gallon.

So what is all this surveillance for? "It's to grow the business and provide better service," says Pat Canavan, UPS vice president for package project management. When asked about cutting labor costs, company spokesperson Joan Schnorburt explains: "The union has been involved in the process at every step of the way. This is about creating more jobs through growth." All this is true, but perhaps not the whole story. Some of the more political elements in the Teamsters, particularly activists with the Teamsters for a Democratic Union (TDU) see another dimension to the Brave New technologies. "The holy grail, for management, is to scab a UPS strike," says Charles Richardson, a researcher who has analyzed UPS on behalf of the International Brotherhood of Teamsters. Richardson argues that the technological leap forward at UPS is ultimately about "stealing knowledge" and making smart machinery that can be operated by not-so-smart scabs. Currently, work at UPS is too complicated and time-sensitive for replacement workers to handle. Thus during the 1997 strike the company shut down operations rather than hire temps.[51]

Short of scabbing, UPS technology can already be used to fight union activism. Steve Henderson, a UPS driver in West Virginia, alleges that surveillance was used to harass and target him because he is a TDU member and was active in the 1997 strike. Along with scrutinizing every detail from his DIAD reports and subjecting him to "on the job supervision" ride-alongs in which line managers with clipboard in hand scrutinize every single move he made, "Uncle Brown" also sent spies out to secretly videotape Henderson while out on his route. They finally busted him taking an unauthorized 18-minute bathroom break at Hardy's, Henderson says he was sick, but UPS fired him for "stealing time."[52] "They're out ta getcha, man," says Henderson, who eventually won his job back with union help. "Only thing to do is watch out and stay organized."

Drivers and linemen at Southern New England Telephone report similar harassment involving the overuse of GPS reports after they won a strike. One CWA organizer reports that rank-and-file union activists have been given what he thinks are punitively unfair surveillance-based evaluations at Verizon. Another commonly reported pressure tactic is for managers to merely show resistive workers their GPS printouts.[53] Inevitably these reports contain proof of some deficiency or technical violation: when every move made by every worker is tracked all the time, and when work rules attempt to regulate even the minutiae of the labor process, then pretty much everyone will be in technical violation of the rules at some point.

So too at BellSouth, where managers have installed GPS tags on 14,000 of the company's trucks and union activists say they are harassed by a gratuitous focus on efficiency and the details of their GPS reports. Many workers see it as a simple speedup, since they are now held to impossible-to-meet deadlines. "I feel like they got their eye on me all the time," said one cable repairman. "I can't slow down anywhere anymore. . . . They're nitpicking us to death. . . . I love my job. [But] I don't need any more stress." Managers at BellSouth assure workers that only the guilty have something to fear. As one executive explained, "If they are loyal, dedicated employees . . . this [GPS] unit should be of no concern to them."[54]

Some unions have managed to come to agreements in which management limits its use of electronic surveillance while others have used digital records *against* employers. One Teamster official said he had used UPS DIAD records to prove that drivers were *not* taking their legally allotted lunch breaks and thus giving the company labor for free, a fact that helped leverage some minor concessions from local management.

SEEING BEYOND MAMMONISM?

Ultimately the question of workplace surveillance extends beyond the question of abuses by this or that firm. Nor is the issue simply one of trust and worker morale. Rather, the spreading superintendence of workers points to deeper problems of greed and accumulation as principles of social organization. Of course an economy based on competition and investment for private gain will seek to extract ever more value from workers. And whatever other function automated keyboards, telephones, or GPS tags serve they will also be used by managers to increase leverage over labor.

This drive for control may be all the more imperative because, as one theorist of the Information Society put it, capital's propagation of telecommunications "stimulates capacities that threaten to escape its command and overspill into rivulets [that are] irrelevant, or even subversive, of profit."[55]

Only regulation, legal limitations on surveillance technology, and a popularly enforced reverse transparency in which corporations are subject to the gaze of critics will keep the tendency toward total observation in check. Nor is there, for this or any other social problem, a "solution" as in a commonsense policy "fix." Society is a battlefield of competing, overlapping, and criss-crossing interests; regulations that would check the disciplinary gaze of the employer class can serve only as rules, or boundaries, to contain and shape what might otherwise be a very unfair contest.

11

THE BENEVOLENT GAZE: DOSSIERS AND THE HELPING PROFESSIONS

Save me from the people who would save me from myself. . .

— *Gang of Four*

The deepest need of the poor is not coal, nor food, nor clothing, but the thoughtful care of a wise, sympathizing friend, who will visit them in their homes, study their individual problems and devise with them ways and means.

— "Friendly Visiting"
Pamphlet of the Charity Organization of Baltimore City
March 1889

Just as work is subject to intense surveillance, so is unemployment and the impoverished life of irregular work. By the late nineteenth century one of the most total systems of everyday surveillance had emerged, not in the name of punishment or profit, but in name of "benevolent assistance to the poor." So central have the "helping professions" been in developing routine forms of surveillance that no history of this sort would be complete without an examination of social work and its moralistic precursor, the "scientific charity movement" (SCM).

In America, "helping" the poor has always been bound up with policing and punishing them. This in turn has always hinged on a compulsion to "know the poor" by defining, categorizing, and ultimately blaming them for their own plight. In a society that denies the true causes of poverty—low wages and structural unemployment—the poor necessarily show up as objects of mystery to be examined, measured, interrogated, and indexed, or as James C. Scott would put it, made "legible."[1] In a society that hides the real mechanics of exploitation and sees all social phenomena through the lens of individualism, it is assumed that the poor—their genetics, their habits, or their culture—*must* be the true cause of poverty. And political technologies of surveillance have always been most readily applied on socially weak populations, such as the impoverished.

Just as photography was developed as a political tool within the larger matrix of managing prisoners and then spread outward to other populations, so has aiding and watching the poor served as a laboratory for testing new political tools, such as chronological case histories, interagency information sharing, computer matching, and electronic cash.

FROM ALMS-GIVING TO THE SCIENCE OF CHARITY

The end of the eighteenth century and the first half of the nineteenth century was a time of great institution building. Hospitals, orphanages, penitentiaries, asylums, and reform schools all emerged as major institutions in this era; and all of them were, in essence, new tools for containing and knowing society's outsiders: the mad, the criminal, the poor. The rise of these institutions was a "great enclosure" that sought to contain and manage the bodies of those rendered unusable in the emerging industrial order. Central to these projects was the founding myth of *transformation:* the wandering madman would be healed; the criminal set straight and made penitent; and paupers educated, disciplined, and made productive.

The great institutions would know their subjects and thereby change social dross into useful components of the social order.[2]

Colonial methods of controlling the poor had been rougher, less politically ambitious. Typical strategies included driving away destitute wanderers, giving the local poor basic "outdoor relief," or auctioning off able-bodied paupers to work for wealthy farmers. None of this involved much observation and record keeping, but the advent of the poorhouse changed that. This new institution would simultaneously contain, feed, and "reform" the poor, while its rigorous discipline "would suppress intemperance, the primary cause of poverty, and inculcate the habit of steady work," thus saving the poor from themselves.[3] "The first almshouse opened in Boston in 1740. By 1884 there were about six hundred in New England."[4]

Central to this reconstitution of the poor was their division into a taxonomy of types, clustered around a basic distinction between the deserving and undeserving poor. Michael Katz, the great social historian of American poverty, quotes an early example from the Quincy Report of 1821:

> 1. The impotent poor: in which denomination are included all, who are wholly incapable of work, through old age, infancy, sickness or corporal debility. 2. The able poor; in which denomination are included all, who are capable of work, of some nature, or other; but differing in degree of their capacity, and in the kind of work, of which they are capable.[5]

The poorhouse sought to save the former and transform the latter. Inevitably the mission failed: poverty persisted, even growing worse with the boom and bust cycles of the market, the decline of traditional rural economies, and the rapid spread of minimally planned urbanization. Organized alms-giving continued—mostly in the form of "outdoor relief"—and the financial cost for local governments soared while the political instability and violence associated with deprivation—"mobbing," thievery, and disease—increased.

Just as the early nineteenth century was the age of institution building, so too was it the age of associations: American society at that time was full of local and regional associations, populated by civic-minded middle-class activists (upstanding Protestant burhgers and well-to-do farmers, or more often their wives). These volunteer committees tended to be religious and addressed themselves to mobilizing rudimentary public sanitation and education campaigns. They organized for the abolition of slavery, to coordinate supplies and triage during disasters and epidemics; and most of all for the suppression of vice: drunkenness, gambling, ignorance, crime, and prostitution. More routinely, these largely female-populated civic committees also handled the distribution of basic charity to the multitude ranks of paupers, since most poor were not contained in the great reformatories of the workhouses and continued to circulate freely.

And just as the poorhouse kept rudimentary records on its inmates, so to did the genteel soldiers of benevolence, working through alms-giving charity associations, conduct simple investigations into the habits of the poor. Known as "friendly visiting," charity workers made a practice of dropping by to check up on poor families to whom they had provided food and coal. At first friendly visiting began as a form of instruction or cultural aid designed to give the poor "immediate positive moral influence." Religious sermonizing and Bible study were often part of the visiting; though the arcane vernacular and verse of the Bible soon gave way to more accessible, popularly pitched religious tracts.[6] (In fact, a whole publishing industry grew up around the production of these texts, the televangelism of yore.)

As the charitable associations grew more numerous, organized, and professional, their efforts to vet the "deserving" poor from the able-bodied "undeserving" became ever more systematic and the function of friendly visiting shifted from spiritual proselytizing to pseudo-scientific surveillance. By the 1840s visitors were keeping written records on both individuals and types.[7]

INVENTING TEXTUAL AUTHORITY

By the 1870s the culture of Protestant volunteerism had morphed into a less-religious and more medical force calling itself the "scientific charity movement." Its goal, like the poorhouse before it, was to reform the poor and thereby end poverty; it too would fail. But not before building the methodological infrastructure of modern social work with its case files, home visits, individual budgets, client evaluations, treatment recommendations, etc.[8]

Like the poorhouses and religious groups before them, the increasingly organized scientific charity movement sought to contain the costs of relief by reshaping the interior lives of the poor, and "home visiting" remained one of its most powerful tools. An early exemplar of the movement—the Baltimore Association for the Improvement of the Condition of the Poor—explained the logic of visiting as follows:

> Our agents are instructed to ascertain the character and conditions of the needy, and to graduate their relief in amount and kind according to their necessities, in a both moral and physical point of view. Always keeping in mind that the principle object of this Society is not alms giving, but that it seeks chiefly to prevent and remove the causes which produce poverty.[9]

Another charity movement handbook revealed the centrality of surveillance in listing the five things that the new alms-giving movement had to do. They were:

1. Act only upon knowledge got by thorough investigation.
2. Relieve worthy need promptly, fittingly, and tenderly.
3. Prevent unwise alms to the unworthy.
4. Raise into independence every needy person, where this is possible.
5. Make sure that no children grow up to be paupers.[10]

Through surveillance the movement sought to instill among the impoverished a Protestant ethic of hard work and self-discipline that fit perfectly with the cultural demands of the new industrial economy.[11] Other charity movement how-to pamphlets make the same point. For example: "Homeless men should receive neither money nor food at the door. Such aid only increases the number of drunken and vicious loafers who live in voluntary idleness. All homeless men, not withstanding their tales to the contrary, can get meals, lodging and bath in exchange for work at the Friendly Inn. . . ."[12]

Throughout the movement's literature the primacy of moral instruction over material support rears its head again and again, even as regards children: "The fact is, however, that the alms giving to little children is more hurtful than any other form of indiscriminate giving. Money so expended perpetuates the brutal selfishness which makes a helpless child a decoy and catch penny for the vicious, and destroys in the child all hope of manliness or womanliness."[13] Ultimately, concludes Katz, the "task charity organizers set themselves was to teach the poor that they had no rights."[14]

In the name of vetting cheats and instructing discipline, the charity movement transformed "friendly visiting" into a formal strategy of surveillance, investigation, and categorization. As the superb work of Karen Tice notes, the mission was now "fact-gathering, classification, microscopic inspection, bureaucratic consolidation, and exhaustive documentation. Archiving the lives of the poor and deviant became a hallmark of the movement's practice."[15]

At first, case records were "meager, terse, and haphazard," often relying on "diarylike entries of interventions taken by social workers along with their quick diagnoses of clients." Some agencies used a simple ledger format with quick one-liners next to the client's name, such as "below the mental standard," "is ignorant," "is profane," or "girl has no shame."[16] But as the narrative and interpretive case histories grew in length they also become more detailed and standardized. Tice finds that by the 1920s writing case records had "become a primary disciplinary obligation."[17]

To guide interventions and give a quick case overview most charity organizations created "face cards" that mapped or indexed the key players in a case. These served to help the visitor cover all "component parts of the record," and thus gather as much information as possible on as many fronts as possible. Usually these cards listed an adult couple, their children, the place and dates of birth, and current and past addresses; all adult relatives; all current and previous employers; and all "other interested parties" such as local churches, hospitals, sanatoriums, the courts, other social work agencies, and even neighbors.

The final form of these ongoing investigations was the chronological narrative case history. Here the scientific charity movement borrowed heavily from the emerging discipline of sociology, particularly the Chicago School variety, which emphasized ethnographic methods and analytic nar-

Visible Index, 1915. An experiment in easy-access file cards

rative. For social workers, biographical case histories operated at two levels and served two purposes: Each individual case history helped lay bare the life of the impoverished home, exposing the needy within as either deserving or slothful and undeserving. These excavations then served to shape and calibrate the forms of benevolent interventions. Perhaps a family would be directed toward work, or given less assistance in light of previously hidden aid from other sources, or perhaps the burden of caring for children would be "lifted" and the children removed to a special home.

Meanwhile, at the aggregate level case histories as a whole served to legitimize the emerging profession of scientific charity and social work among the poor.[18] For the women who mostly built and guided the movement this was of utmost concern. Their efforts—whether noble or base and manipulative—were often disrespected and sidelined by the patriarchal policing actions of male-dominated professions like medicine, the bar, business, and government. As one writer reminded social workers in 1929, the Census Bureau still classified their trade as "semiprofessional," in the same league as "mediums, fortune tellers, and chiropractors."[19] At times it almost seems that the quest for wider social and professional legitimating was a bigger concern for the charity bureaucrat than was poverty itself. Indeed, the annals of these organizations overflow with self-involved studies, reports, and programs on how and why "visitors" were to construct more professional paperwork and thereby a whole profession. Here is a typical reference from such a document: "It is a matter of importance that the style of our records should be above criticism. This applies to good English, spelling, punctuation, paragraphing and all things which go to make up a readable and attractively told history. The responsibility for this rests on three people: The stenographer, the visitor, and the secretary."[20]

Tice describes such maneuvers a bid for "textual authority." And clearly, texts have authority, authorities have texts, and the road to greater social recognition among the better classes is paved with certifying paper—in this case records, files, investigative notes, "diagnoses," and "interventions." We see in the history of social work a deliberate attempt to create the mechanism for constructing and wielding "truth claims." The raw material for all this professional self-invention was, of course, the lived world of the poor.

The same bureaucrat, cited above, explained: "There should be no technical differences in the recording of the histories of the various types of cases, such as widow, sickness, unemployment. . . . It should be stated definitively [in the case history]: why the family came to our attention; how they came whether referred or by personal application; the condition of each member at application, including financial, physical, moral and religious, mental and industrial; the condition of the home, including sanitation, cleanliness and privacy; the social history and standards chronologically; wages of each member; budget."[21]

Thus case histories have entries like: "Jan. 15, '20. . . . Found family living in basement of apartment house. One room lighted by high, small window. . . . Place dirty and cluttered; odor damp and close." Or "Was able to earn $4 or $5 dollars a week. . . . Believes that food comes to about $10 a week. . . ."[22]

The drive toward the dual goal of respect for charity workers and discipline for the poor led social workers to imbue their dossiers and record keeping with a quasi-medical, quasi-legal style and vocabulary. If we were to deploy the optics of Pierre Bourdieu, we could describe such efforts as a conscious attempt to create the "field" of social work. Again, from the report cited above, the Charity bureaucrat explains this political alchemy as based on the almost occult powers of surveillance: "The clients, after this preliminary review must now take their positions as 'cases'—no longer simply persons in trouble but family units in direct relationship to the [benevolent] society."[23]

TRANSMITTING DISCIPLINE

How did these investigations discipline the poor? At the level of its manifest function, surveillance was intended to "diagnose" paupers into precise categories, each needing precise treatments. At the level of its latent function this close, textually based superintendence of the poor was about ritual degradation mixed with material threat: routine inspection humiliated the poor and misbehavior meant an end to aid. Consider this from the summary overview of what was deemed a resistant and difficult case:

> Mrs. H. had always been a spineless and inefficient person, unwilling to take any steps against her husband, or to follow the advice, either of the society or the Hospital Social Service Department, which was taking a continuous interest in the family. These characteristics continued after her husband's death, and it was only by the exercise of force that the district was enabled to get complete examinations made of her and the children. The children were found free from disease, but Mrs. H. was found to be tuberculous, and was induced, under pressure, to allow the district to place the children through the department of public charities and her self to enter Otisville sanatorium. Her furniture was placed in storage by the district, with the promise to re-establish her home if she would remain at Otisville until cured.[24]

Here we have benevolence cheek-to-jowl with punitive regulation. Lest we think such interventions were rare, there were tens of thousands of such actions in every major city.

MULTIPLYING POWER WITH NETWORKED FILES

Not only were charity agencies numerous and their investigations even more so, but agencies also shared files and cross-fertilized each other's dossiers to create dense networks of interagency linkages. These contacts are evident throughout typical case histories, where correspondence with and telephone calls to or from other agencies are frequently noted, summarized, or directly quoted. For example: "Jan' 16 '20 Letter to supt. City Hospital: We are interested in the family of Andrew Mayo of 953 Amber St. who is now a patient in your hospital. This is the second illness and stay at the hospital since October 1919. We believe he was discharged the first time in November. Will you kindly send us diagnosis and prognosis of both illnesses? Is there tubercular involvement? Can you give us any idea as to when Mr. Mayo will be able to go back to work?"[25]

Or this: "Dec 1, '19 Letter as follows to Supt. of Workhouse: We are writing to you in connection with a new prisoner, Will or Alexander Barlow, who was committed by the Lower Court to the work house for 19 days. . . . He has had an extremely dissolute sexual life since he was a young boy. He has also had from time to time desire to go off tramping the country. When he is on one of these tramps, he looks and acts like a regular hobo, and is utterly disregardful and unmindful of his wife and three children." And from the same case: "Dec. 2,'19 Letter to SACRED HART CHURCH giving report to date."[26]

The purpose of such exchanges was to share surveillance and build dossiers. Thus a typical entry from a "visitor" of the New York Charity Organization Society: "Feb. 25, '20. 'Phoned SPCC [Society for the Prevention of Cruelty to Children] family was reported in 1914; man drinking, home not good, both man and woman accused of neglect. . . ." This information received was then duly relayed on: "Letter to Miss Pond, Warwick Hospital, giving full summary of family and of Agnes."[27]

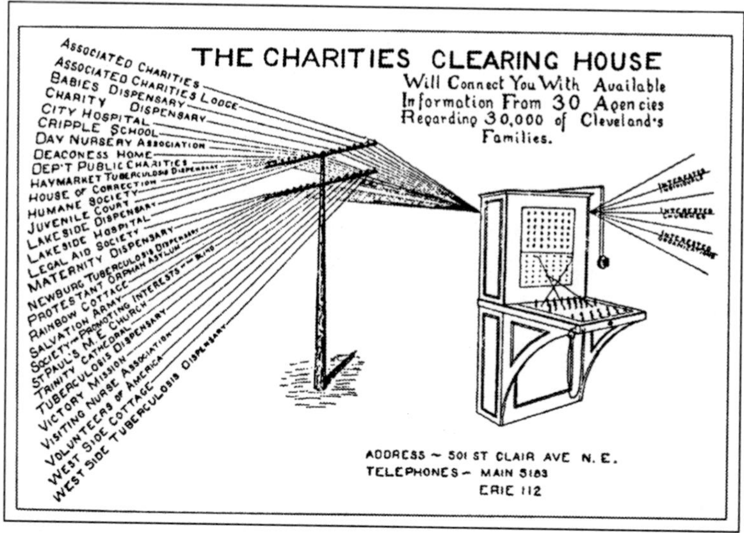

Charities Clearing House (1922). Connecting, collecting, and redistributing dossiers on the poor.

In fact, such interagency communication was so common that in many cities charity agencies established formal clearinghouses or exchanges where dossiers were traded and cross-referenced. In Cleveland the Charities Clearing House boasted that it would connect relief organizations and investigators "with Available Information from 30 Agencies Regarding 30,000 of Cleveland's Families."[28] The number of files involved in these exchanges were huge: the New York Charity Organization Society kept files on 170,000 individuals; while in Chicago the charity exchange managed dossiers on 555,000 families.[29]

As Tice notes, "Although dubbed 'confidential,' such case material was circulated widely, not only to charitable agencies and interested organizations but also to prospective employers, landlords, banks and the police. . . . In 1916 the Boston Children's Aid Society suggested a 'black list' and registry for alcoholics. . . "[30] One charity professional even created a weekly published list of known traveling mendicants who now "found themselves confronted by advance knowledge of themselves. To be told the history of their lives and schemes for years past, and given twenty-four hours to leave town or be arrested was very disquieting."[31] By 1919 charity movement professionals had organized the National Association of Social Service Exchanges, and interagency trafficking in documents became a job function in itself.[32]

THE NEW RELIEF

With the collapse of the world economy during the Great Depression, the federal government was forced to create an infrastructure of public welfare provision. Most of it was connected to types of work but not all. Among the new programs was Aid to Dependent Children (which later became AFDC and then TANIF). State- and county-managed "mothers pension programs" and "widows and orphans funds" were broke, so the New Deal stepped in. Though less punitive than traditional relief, the new program soon led to a recrudescence of the old investigative methods in the form of home visiting or as office interrogations, "the assumption remained that a public assistance client was in need of counseling and rehabilitation and had fewer privacy rights than others."[33]

The postwar economic boom was likewise marked by aggressive rhetorical assaults on the "underclass" as morally impoverished. "Victims blaming reache[d] an entirely new pitch" and this justified harder forms of social work intervention in the name of curing, uplifting, and coaching the poor, the delinquent, and the deranged.[34]

Fast forward to the 1960s. To drive people from the welfare rolls, officials have devised what Frances Fox Piven and Richard Cloward call "rituals of degradation." The most important of these hinged on highly gendered forms of surveillance that fixated on the symbolic politics of female sexuality. In a cryptic but powerful and racist fashion, officials described the poor (particularly the brown-skinned poor) as "overpopulating," a naturalistic, thus dehumanizing term. Follow the slippage of the semiotic chain back, and controlling poverty means controlling population, which means controlling women's sexuality, desire, and ultimately freedom. Or more concretely: to qualify for and maintain income support, single mothers on Aid to Families with Dependent Children (AFDC) where forced to submit to prying interviews about their sex lives with questions such as: "When did you last menstruate?" Poor women were also forced to submit to routine home inspections, where everything was examined for signs of a "spousal equivalent"—a man in the house. Even children were interrogated with questions like "Do any men visit your mother?" More aggressive yet were the unannounced, warrantless nighttime raids in which poor mothers were searched for signs of vice and "immorality." In fact, until 1968 Alabama made it illegal to receive aid *and* have relations with a man.[35] At least one court ruled that welfare recipients had no right to privacy, while fourteen states held them ineligible to vote.[36]

All of this plus the informal power of stigma and intimidation gave welfare caseworkers surveillance powers beyond those of any police department. And these powers were channeled into a capillary-level war against the spirit and minds of poor women: who were to be reduced to a self-hating subcaste. For example, Piven and Cloward unearthed the following exchange from an administrative hearing on the excesses of AFDC surveillance. Here a welfare investigator answers questions for an administrative judge:

> Q. How often were you refused admission to the recipients' home?
>
> A. Very, very seldom. Less than 1 per cent.
>
> Q. After identifying yourself and requesting permission to inspect the recipient's home, did you ever say that he or she had the right to refuse entry?
>
> A. Never.
>
> Q. Why not?
>
> A. It was always my understanding that they had to open up their premises to inspection if they wanted welfare.
>
> Q. What did you do then?
>
> A. My partner and I then went through the house as fast as possible. [Investigators always worked in pairs.]
>
> Q. How long did that usually take?
>
> A. Five to seven minutes.
>
> Q. Why did you hurry so?
>
> A. The object was to go as far as you could before the client objected. Usually we'd split up. One of us would keep the client busy talking and the other would move quickly through the rooms and closets. . . . Sometimes we'd split up before entering a house, one of us going to the front door and the other going to the back.
>
> Q. Why was that?

A. If there was a man in the house, he'd leave by any means available —windows, fire escape, or out the back door.[37]

Easily recognized is the basic "moral" function of "friendly visiting among the poor"—here stripped of its benevolent and spiritual trappings. This is the logical evolution of a political form that was always fundamentally about the social control.

HARD RIGHT

The Reagan Revolution, radically remade the policing of welfare at the level of both ideology and technology. First, the return to its ideological foundations:

Driving the Reagan administration's discursive and financial assaults on the poor was a small clique of neoconservative ideologues such as Charles Murray, George Gilder, and Lawrence Mead. Mead argued "the main problem with welfare is its *permissiveness*, not its size."[38] Unlike many of his colleagues, Mead performed no awkward intellectual backflips to make all the pieces of his theory fit. He acknowledges that many forms of work are emotionally and financially unrewarding. In Mead's view, "there are good grounds to think that work, at least 'dirty' low-wage jobs, can no longer be left solely to the initiative of those who labor." And in a chapter called, "Why Work Must Be Enforced," Mead layed out his vision: "Low-wage work apparently must be mandated, just as a draft has sometimes been necessary to staff the military. . . . Government need not make the desired behavior worthwhile to people. It simply threatens punishment. . . ."[39]

Thus did Mead call for shifting the debate around poverty from the lexicon of "equality" to that of "citizenship." In summing up his desire for a new regime of exclusion Mead concluded: "The question is no longer what the worst-off members of the community should receive. Now the question is who should be a bona fide member of the community in the first place." And to "address the puzzling reluctance of the poor to do more to help themselves . . . social policy must focus on motivation and order rather than opportunity or equality."[40]

It is this generalized view—rehashed, repackaged, and always pitched as new—that served (and still serves) as the footing of the New Right's twenty-five-year-long assault on the poor. Now, add to this hatred of the poor, the new capacities of the cybernetic state and welfare surveillance become truly impressive.

THE DIGITAL NANNY STATE HATES YOU

It began, as it so often does, in the name of controlling immigrants. With the arrival of Reagan, his recession, and then brutal austerity, pundits began fulminating anew about the hordes of cheating immigrants who were allegedly sopping up welfare dollars. In response, the federal government launched a huge financial and political drive to compel states to digitize all their social service and welfare records. This was an expensive proposition, and by 1985 only three states—California, Colorado, and Illinois—had fully converted to computerized files and linked into the computerized information systems of the INS. In keeping with the theme of efficiency, this new network went by the catchy acronym SAVE (Systematic Alien Verification for Entitlement).[41]

Soon the campaign to computerize in the name of combating fraud went beyond immigrants. In February 1986 the government promulgated regulations that practically forced all states to establish computerized "income verification programs." This was SAVE writ large and it was now expanded to police both new immigrants and citizens alike. Thanks to digital files and telecommunications, social workers could now "check a welfare applicant's finances by examining state unemployment insurance wage and benefit records; Social Security wage records; and some Internal Revenue Service records." This was the first time the IRS began sharing information on individual taxpayers' unearned income from bank accounts, stocks, and elsewhere.

What was most dramatic about the big linkup of 1986 was that the federal government had no legal authority to force states to computerize (or share their) records but as a still classic article in the *Washington Post Magazine* reported: "The White House's Office of Management and Budget has written its 'income verification programs' so stringently that it will be difficult and expensive for states to meet the Sept. 30 deadline without using a computer." Taking their cue from the feds, most states gave "social workers direct access to state wage information, property records, motor vehicle records and public school enrollment records. Some states [also computerized] birth, marriage, divorce and death records," all in the name of reducing costs by fighting the menace of welfare fraud. Some states with particularly permissive laws even allowed social service investigators to tap into bank records, credit, and hospital records. Thus the *Washington Post Magazine* concluded, "In effect, the federal government is creating a de facto national data bank through state governments."[42]

But in many ways this mid–1980s mass migration to computers was just the culmination of a long slow process of erosion. A 1983 report by the House Government Operations Committee had concluded that for many years few federal bureaucracies were actually paying much attention to the Privacy Act of 1974. Passed in the wake of Watergate, that law, if read generously, prohibited the government from collecting and swapping information about citizens without their consent.

As early as 1977 the (now defunct) Department of Health, Education and Welfare, had started using automatic computer-based record-matching techniques to circumvent the Privacy Act. In the name of busting welfare cheats the so-called "Project Match" involved federal investigators programming a computer to compare two huge sets of federal records: a list of welfare recipients and a list of federal employees in twenty-one states that had high numbers of both. "In a matter of days, the computer had pulled together the names of everyone on both lists." Not surprisingly there were a few employees of the federal government who were also illegally collecting welfare. In the end, the number of offenders was so few and the sums involved so small that disgusted federal judges refused to send any of the petty hustlers to jail. In the eyes of many, the whole operation had been a blatant violation of the Privacy Act. But the Carter administration got around this by arguing that the informational exchange was just "interdepartmental assistance" in the form of "routine information" sharing rather than a Privacy Act governed "record transfers."[43]

By 1982, the White House had ordered the IRS to use its computerized records to aid the Selective Service in tracking down young men who had not registered for the draft. It was the type of computer dragnet that would have caused a massive outcry in the early 1970s, but now it was barely even news.

WAY PAST 1984

By the late 1980s computer record-matching was being joined by technologically forward-thinking experiments of an even more totalizing design. In 1987, for example, Philadelphia began eliminating paper benefit checks for more than 100,000 welfare recipients and substituting computer-verified photo identification cards.[44] Around the same time the Los Angeles County Department of Public Social Services began using electronic fingerprint identification.[45] Soon a half-dozen other localities were experimenting with high-tech antifraud/antipoor policies. In Camden, New Jersey, welfare recipients switched from welfare checks and food stamps to government-issued ATM cards. In Newark and throughout New Jersey, recipients were being fingerprinted and cross-referenced against the databases of New York State.[46]

A welfare recipient in Ohio described the regime as follows. "Well, they want to know everything. I mean everything. How many people you got living with you and that's nobody's business. How much rent you pay. How much utilities you pay and if you can't pay it then that's tough luck. They put everything on that big screen and anybody and everybody can look right there on that big screen and say, 'oh look at this.'"[47]

By 1993 the federal government, now led by Democrats determined to "reinvent government" had proposed a nationwide Electronic Benefits Transfer System "to disburse such benefits as social security; railroad retirement; federal civilian retirement; military pensions; food stamps; Aid to Families With Dependent Children (AFDC); and Women, Infants and Children (WIC) in all states."

By the end of the century welfare recipients in more than forty states had switched from checks to computerized smart cards. Now authorities had chronologically and geographically indexed and itemized records of all welfare transactions: a brave new version of knowing the poor has arrived. As investigative journalist Christopher D. Cook discovered, electronic benefits transfer (EBT) is also a huge and profitable business: "Citicorp has captured a remarkable 65 percent of the EBT market." Other big players include Lockheed Martin and Deluxe Electronic Payment Systems. These firms make millions by giving welfare recipients only a handful of free transactions each month; once these are used up recipients are charged between one and two dollars per debt.[48]

Along with a switch to EBT many cities and counties have also started using fingerprinting as a means of supervising the poor—searching their ranks for cheats, scofflaws, and serious fugitives. Often, even local forms of workfare, general assistance, and access to homeless shelters involve fingerprinting.[49]

These seemingly technocratic projects—launched in the name of "savings" and "efficacy"—in many cases save little or no money, or even cost more money than the older programs.[50] And regardless of any real economic savings that might accrue, the theatrics of making the pauper class "legible" is fundamentally about demonizing poor people. Sociologist John Gilliom summed it up well: "Strip away the bureaucratic language of fraud control, regulatory enforcement, consent forms, and the like, and we see a simple pattern in which a government agency is using broadly targeted and ongoing surveillance in an effort to force a dependant population to live at an intolerable level of poverty."[51]

12

THE EYE OF JUSTICE

"The whole dossier continues to circulate, as the regular official routine demands, passing on to the higher Courts, being referred to the lower ones again, and thus swinging backwards and forwards with greater or smaller oscillations, longer or shorter delays. . . . No document is ever lost, the Court never forgets anything. One day—quite unexpectedly—some judge will take up the documents."

"And the case begins all over again?" asked K. almost incredulously.

"Certainly," said the painter.

—Franz Kafka
The Trial

It's about getting into their minds.

—Parole Officer,
Dallas, Texas

Listen closely to the bureaucrats at the California Department of Corrections and a strange geography of power emerges. Rather than focusing solely on prisons and prisoners, the officialdom speaks of "the system" containing a "total CDC population" of nearly 290,000. About 60 percent of this population is "under the custodial control of the Department." The remainder are "serving the rest of their sentences in the community" as parolees—members of a semi-free subcaste.[1] In the mind of the prison bureaucrat the prison regime does not stop at the gate; "the system" extends into the streets and the line between the convict inside and civilian outside becomes blurry.

An estimated 6.6 million Americans live under the control of the criminal justice system: either in jail, in prison, or on parole or probation (which is usually a county-level program used for low-level offenders in lieu of incarceration). The majority of this population—oscillating back and forth between courts, jails, prison, and parole—are poor and dark-skinned.[2] The massive fourfold increase in incarceration over the last two and a half decades has translated into an increased flow of politically marked, criminalized bodies through the circuitry of social control. After all, prison is just one node within a larger system that extends from urban ghettos to the courts and jails to mental hospitals and homeless shelters and halfway houses. One frequently overlooked space in this circuitry of social control is "the community," where parolees and probationer serve "street time" as the "unjailed" legal zombies of the court system.

Parole and probation are not just simple functions of prison. Instead, each component in the system amplifies and feeds the others. As the criminal law has become more punitive the surveillance and policing mechanisms of parole have grown more intense. Just as the total number of ex-cons hitting the streets has increased, so has the proportion of that group that is sent back to prison. And within the subset of those who "fail" parole, a greater proportion than ever is sent back to the joint for simple "technical violations" like missing a meeting with a parole agent or failing a "whiz quiz"—that is, showing traces of drugs in their urine.[3] The Government Accounting Office found that "the number of federal and state inmates released to communities increased more than threefold" from 1980 to 1998. In that same period, "the number of offenders reincarcerated for violating parole or other release conditions rose more than sevenfold." Furthermore, such "reincarcerations represent an increasing proportion of all prison admissions—for instance, reincarceration of violators of parole or other release conditions represented 17 percent of all prison admissions in 1980 but increased to 35 percent of admissions in 1998."[4]

Thus we see prison as increasingly self-sufficient, generating its own population. The propellant in this process is the continually expanding infrastructure of routine identification and surveillance. By this means, prison extends its social power outward into the free world, feeding itself and creating a subcaste of permanent convicts.

DOING "STREET TIME"

Consider again the system in California; it is extreme, but therefore indicative of possible future trends in other states. In 1990 the demographic "echo" of the big lockup binge began to bounce back to the streets. That year the number of felons paroled to San Diego County suddenly jumped by 20 percent.[5] A similar surge happened elsewhere, and as the number of parolees grew the nature of parole changed radically. To control these waves of the unjailed, California is divided into four parole regions policed by roughly 2,000 armed parole agents who are backed up by the CDC's Special Services Unit, an elite tier of mobile prison guards doing antigang investigations on both sides of the prison wall. Always ready to cooperate with these forces are local and state police.[6] By 1999, the year the Golden State's twenty-five-year increase in incarceration rates began to level off, roughly the same number of people entered prison as exited. From a population of 154,000 inmates, 124,000 were paroled. On average, 70 to 80 percent of these people will be "violated"—that is, sent back to prison because they violated a condition of parole.[7] A recent Bureau of Justice Statistics report concluded that 67.5 percent of those released from prison in 1994 were rearrested within three years, an 8 percent increase from ten years earlier.[8]

Eighty percent of parolees are unemployed, and about the same number are addicted to drugs or alcohol.[9] They tend to end up in the poorest neighborhoods of the state's cities: Los Angeles County is home to 41,000 of these former prisoners—that's more than the number of teachers in the LA Unified School District.

Because parolees are still under the control of the CDC, their movements, associations, and day-to-day behavior are all strictly supervised. For parolees the regular gossamer-thin Fourth Amendment protections against unreasonable search and seizure are suspended; former cons are compelled to submit to any and all requests for a police search. Any violation of parole rules—possession of a small knife, drinking a beer, missing an appointment, dirty urine—can mean a ticket back to the Big House. Surrounded by poverty, drugs, and other veterans from inside, the parolee awaits an almost inevitable return to prison.[10]

Stalking the unjailed is a small army of parole agents. Once seen as quasi social workers, both parole and probation services have in the last twenty-five years become adjuncts to the police; armed and in many cases uniformed, tactically trained, and involved in prestige operations like paramilitary antidrug raids and gang sweeps.[11] Unlike regular cops, parole and probation offices can act as judges in the field, sending their already convicted prey straight back to prison.[12] Increasingly, reducing recidivism is no longer even the official function of parole and probation programs. Instead, the mission is surveillance and incarceration. One of California's top probation officers, interviewed by criminologist Jerome Skolnick, kept a plaque on his wall bearing an inscription that captured his profession's new esprit de corps: "Trail'em, Surveil'em, Nail'em, and Jail'em."[13] Toward that end agents routinely drop in on parolees and probationers to "toss" their homes for contraband, just as prison guards routinely search convicts cells. Likewise, police investigators focus on parolees, scooping them by the dozen to mine for intelligence.[14]

ELECTRONIC SHACKLES

"I want him to think that I'm always there, that I'm always watching," says an agent with Texas's "Super-Intensive Supervision Program," the Lone Star State's version of zero-tolerance parole. In this startup program around 1,600 of the state's most dangerous former cons wear electronic ankle bands that communicate with a command center in the state capital. It's the latest in the high-tech social control of the dangerous. While one agent watches the parolee's movements on a computer terminal, another keeps tabs from the field. Any infraction of the parolee's schedule of work, official interviews, home inspections, and curfew means a year back in the state pen. "I'm still a prisoner," laments one of the system's wards. "I'm a prisoner in my own home."[15]

When such complaints come from convicted pedophiles one hardly cares, but like so many other criminal justice innovations and "reforms" intensive parole only begins with "the worst of the worst" and from there it inevitably expands to include others. In many states home detention and electronic monitoring were introduced as alternatives to incarceration but now operate in *addition* to prison.[16] And as technology improves, becomes cheaper, and accumulates we might see a radical proliferation of these soft forms of incarceration.

Witness the evolution of those famous electronic ankle monitors: At first such technology usually employed a simple FM transmitter (worn on the ankle or wrist) that communicated to a monitor, which in turn communicated through the telephone, at appointed times, to the authorities.[17] Today, new home detention devises use satellite-based GPS tracking, once a phenomenally expensive Pentagon technology.

"It's 'Star Wars.' You can literally watch where kids go and you can set up parameters where they can't go," explained one New Jersey probation official. With GPS tags, the guardians of order can now supervise the real-time movements of their wards. If the parolee wanders into a forbidden "hot zone," alarms sound on a central computer, a digital record of the transgression is logged, and if necessary an immediate response can be made.

Nationwide there are an estimated 2,000 people in twenty-eight states wearing GPS tags and many more wearing the traditional FM shackles, or using touch-tone telephones to check in with police computers from their sofabed lockdown.[18] Typically, GPS supervision works as follows: the parolee wears an electronic anklet that communicates with a portable, three-pound tracking unit "about the size of a child's lunch box." This gadget in turn communicates with at least three of the twenty-four Navstar satellites of the GPS system, triangulating its own exact latitude and longitude. By way of an internal cell phone, the tracking unit on the ground calls in its coordinates to the computers of the parole and probation officials. If the anklet strays more than 100 feet from the three-pound tracking box/transmitter, an alarm is triggered on the parole agent's computer.

By mapping in real-time and extreme detail, GPS monitoring allows for radical transparency at the same time that its flexibility permits relative freedom of movement for the parolee. As one press report put it, "The system is so precise that [parole officer] McCullough can see that an offender is traveling 67 mph on Interstate 80."[19] This combination means that the use of GPS is not limited to house arrest, as were FM transmitters, and this allows expanded use of electronic monitoring. In Florida, corrections officials say their 600-unit program will likely expand to include all 150,000 of the state's felony probationers.[20] Such GPS proliferation was much buoyed by a recent $100 million in parole-oriented grants from the Justice Department; and according to the frightening boasts of the technology's boosters, GPS tagging could "eventually monitor millions of offenders, even small-time burglars and juvenile vandals."[21]

As for the inevitable "function creep" and "defining down of deviance," a New Jersey program using a system called ComTrak already monitors low- to no-risk juveniles in a manner that allows "the state to program places, or zones, where juveniles can't go, where they can, and when they can be there. Officials can develop a schedule that accounts for a youth's movements—from school to work to community service and back home by curfew."[22] Here "the street" starts edging toward penal colony. Orange County, California, is even experimenting with GPS-enabled wristbands in combination with periodic polygraph tests.[23]

FREEDOM FROM FEAR?

Fueling the rise of the intensive parole is the myth of computer-delivered super-safety. But, as officials in Texas learned, there are limits to the power of surveillance. For example, one of their parolees sexually assaulted a six-year-old boy while wearing a GPS tracking bracelet. In Baltimore, three separate teenage offenders, in apparent imitation of each other, smashed off their ankle bracelets before each committed murder.[24] Or there's the rather humorous case of Angelo "Electro Man" Burnett, who was arrested in his front yard selling crack, an electronic monitor strapped securely to his ankle.[25]

Failures aside, electronic monitoring enhances state power in two ways: It disciplines subjects by forcing the probationers, parolees, and their associates to internalize the police gaze. At the same time, transparency plus strict rules guarantee parole failure and thus more people are sent back to prison.

THE GANG DATABASE

During the late 1980s, before terrorism eclipsed communism as official enemy number one, the media and political class became almost delusionally obsessed with gangs. The moral panic did have some basis in truth; after all, deindustrialization, increased economic inequality, and the ready money of the new and chaotic crack cocaine trade did create an explosion of gang warfare in cities both large and small.

A major byproduct of the "the war on gangs" has been the creation of huge computerized gang databases designed to identify and track gang members, suspected gang members, and their associates. The first of these started during the mid–1980s in Los Angeles. By 1986 the LAPD and Sheriff's Department, bitter rivals for decades, were finally beginning to share their "street gang intelligence" dossiers. Backing the project was the California Office of Criminal Justice Planning, a state agency set up in the 1970s with federal money from the Law Enforcement Assistance Administration.[26] LAPD Chief Daryl F. Gates praised the system because it would give cops "instant access" to huge digital vaults of intelligence for "identifying, prosecuting and removing from the community hardcore gang members committed to violence."[27]

Not long after this, the Ventura County Sheriff's Department set up an antidrug/gang task force, offering new dossiers on gangbangers. Soon, Orange County did the same.[28] In Portland, Oregon, the National Guard aided police in setting up a special computerized youth gang database; likewise in Omaha, where the police got help from outside specialists. All these systems sought to log and analyze information such as nicknames, vehicle types, and geographical patterns.[29] Like their counterparts around the country, Omaha antigang officers kept photographs of active and suspected gangsters.[30]

From these efforts emerged the outlines of various regional networks of gang databases to service the fast-proliferating elite police antigang units.[31] As the crack epidemic raged the volume of names and dossiers grew. In LA, the county's "mammoth" database, called Gang Reporting Evaluation and Tracking (GREAT), contained profiles on an estimated 1,000 gangs and 150,000 gang members and was described by police as one of [their] "most effective tools." Like most other gang databases, GREAT contained names, aliases, Social Security numbers, Department of Corrections ID numbers, physical descriptions, and in many cases photographs of suspected gangbangers and their tattoos. When the Los Angeles rebellion and its nationwide auxiliary riots erupted in late April 1992, LA District Attorney Ira Reiner announced that GREAT contained fully 47 percent of the county's young Black men. Many of these "gang members" had never been arrested and were identified simply on the basis of appearance: baggy pants, red or blue clothes.[32]

Soon even the nearby affluent suburb of Simi Valley had joined GREAT.[33,34]

By the fall of 1997, the state of California began converting GREAT into a statewide system called CALGANG. The basis of the new system would be a software package called GangNet, designed and managed by a firm named for Orion the Hunter. Because CALGANG/GangNet is a standardized, point-and-click, open architecture, Internet-based software system and links together the files of all participating law enforcement agencies, it is both easy to use and prone to growth. From any locality, police can contact the system's master node in Sacramento and retrieve or add information to a statewide metafile. Because the technology is just software and requires no special hardware, it can be run from the laptops that equip most new police cruisers.

As *Government Technology* magazine put it, "The system cross-references from keywords, much the same way one might use a standard Web browser, only now the keywords will include a physical description and dragon tattoo. Maybe the officer gets 50 matches, so he adds the stutter and a BMW. Suddenly, he has narrowed his search down to a half-dozen known gang members who meet the criteria."[35] GangNet can even allow police to create "electronic photo lineups" to show to witnesses at crime scenes.

In the medium-sized California city of Fresno police using CALGANG/GangNet add between 300 and 400 *new* names to their dossiers every three months.[36] In California this translates into more prison time for more young people. Thanks to the "Street Terrorism Enforcement and Prevention Act" of 1988, "any person who actively participates in any crimi-

Tools of the trade (credit: Jan Chelminski)

nal street gang" can be punished with a year in jail. And in California a gang is simply defined as three or more people involved in ongoing criminal activity, such as graffiti tagging. Being identified in police computers as a gang member can also lead to "sentencing enhancements" of two to three years for each separate charge.[37]

THE BIG LINKUP

Since its inception in 1967 the National Crime Information Center (NCIC), managed by the FBI, has been collecting and coordinating information from all local police agencies in the US. NCIC files list everything from wanted fugitives and missing persons to arrest histories, stolen weapons, stolen vehicles, and, since 1995, "Violent Gangs/Terrorists."[38]

Similar to the NCIC is the federal Office of Justice Programs' Regional Information Sharing Systems (RISS), which assists nearly 5,000 federal, state, and local criminal justice agencies in tracking gangs and other known and alleged criminals. The project works with six preexisting regional systems for the regular exchange of criminal information.[39] And with each new crisis state criminal justice bureaucracies grow in parasitic reaction, demanding better technology, new laws, more staff, more money, and more surveillance. This was true in the response to the LA riots (the trigger for the 1994 crime bill) as it was, on a smaller scale, with Cincinnati riots of 2002, which led to the creation of a new Ohio-wide gang database.[40]

THE GUILTY FUTURE

Intelligence dossiers can have an effect similar to hard drugs: when the initial high wears off, the authorities start "jonesing" for more. So it was that police in Wilmington, Delaware, began compiling a database—not of gangbangers or their associates—but of people who authorities believed *might break the law sometime in the future*. Within two months special "jump out squads" had begun files on over 200 people, almost all of whom were Black or Latino.

Just to be perfectly clear: the subjects of the new database were not arrested for crimes or even considered suspects. Instead they were simply people—usually poor Black people—whom the cops had stopped, frisked, interrogated, photographed, and then opened a file because the subject had been found in so-called "hot spots" known for violence and drug dealing.[41]

The function of the database is to map identity, cross-referencing people with places, and thus to allow police to create geographically specific short lists of "potential" suspects when crimes occur. As one critic from the ACLU explained: "So if they've stopped you three times on Eighth and Washington, and a crime occurs on Eighth and Washington, they've got your name and they know you were stopped three times."[42] When the whole scheme became the focus of international outcry, the mayor dismissed complaints as "asinine and intellectually bankrupt."[43]

CONTROLLING IMMIGRANTS

Another important development of recent years is the buildup in the political machinery for identifying and tracking immigrants. Particularly powerful in this project is the computer system called IDENT, in which digitalized "biometric" photographs and fingerprints—not the descriptions of images used by GangNet—can be searched for matches among millions of other such images. IDENT was a project of the INS, but now that agency has been broken into thirds—the Bureau of Citizenship and Immigration Services; the Bureau of Immigration and Customs Enforcement; and the Bureau of Customs and Border Patrol—and the IDENT system is now used throughout the new Department of Homeland Security to identify and track immigrants both at the borders and inside the United States.[44]

This image-to-image system was designed to catch previously deported immigrants who reentered using false documents. Started as an experiment in 1994, the system had 227 terminals around the country by 1998 and its "Lookout Database" contained the computerized prints and mug shots of nearly 2 million people.[45] Despite its awesome power, IDENT suffered a few failures in its early years (for example, a famous serial killer slipped through). In fact, the system was falling out of favor with many lawmakers until 9/11 renewed the steady march toward a high-tech containment system for controlling and intimidating immigrants.[46] And the shock of the terrorist attacks finally forced the dissolution of longstanding rivalries between numerous federal agencies: the FBI gave the INS 81,000 names of "criminal aliens" wanted by federal, state, and local law enforcement agencies, while the INS gave the Bureau details on 314,000 undocumented immigrants wanted for visa violations. Congress in turn provided an additional $3 million to connect IDENT to the INS's 2,300 desktop computers at airports, border crossings, and county jails.[47]

It is no coincidence that IDENT—the most powerful and advanced computer surveillance system in the country—was developed for use on poor, disenfranchised migrants. As sociologist David Lyon points out, the introduction of new surveillance technologies often starts by targeting society's weakest, most marginalized groups, and then through function creep spreads in toward the mainstream.[48]

As part of its "integrated interior enforcement," the INS also operates a nonbiometric database called the Law Enforcement Support Center (LESC) for assisting police agencies in their various wars on undocumented immigrants. Located in Burlington, Vermont, the system "provides a 24/7 link between federal, state, and local officers and the databases maintained by the INS" and functions as the cyberhub of a vast national network.[49] As LESC improves and expands, police in the field will be able to instantaneously check a person's immigration status "even when the crime or infraction isn't worth taking the person into custody . . . like, on running a red light."[50]

Here we see a virtual panopticon tailor-made for the new American working class: "Immigrants will fear the law more intensely knowing that INS/police intelligence systems are automatic, infallible and instantaneous. The electronic dragnet will force internalization of the INS gaze, causing immigrants to keep to themselves, stay out of sight, and steer clear of politics. And the INS optics will work even when—perhaps best when—one's hand is not on the high-tech fingerprint pad. The IDENT/LESC files will reside not just in digital vaults but in the minds of millions of migrants, forced to live as virtual outlaws."[51]

DNA: THE FIRST TO BE MARKED

In 1987 an American rapist, Tommy Lee Andrews, was convicted of a brutal sexual assault on a woman with Alzheimer's. The sole evidence against him, due to the victim's faulty memory, was the deoxyribonucleic acid (DNA) he left behind. It was a historic first.

About two years before this, British scientists had found a way to, more or less, identify individuals by the patterns of their DNA.[52] No sooner was this possible than California and Washington State hatched plans to create the world's first computerized DNA identification databases. In 1991 the US military established the largest genetic-identification project yet—a DNA database on all 1.5 million-service members.[53] These samples are gathered in the name of identifying the dead (the same argument used for fingerprinting sailors almost a hundred years earlier) but the samples will be kept for fifty years—far longer than most service personnel will be under arms. Thereafter, several states began establishing DNA databases by taking samples from convicted murderers and sex offenders.[54]

By 1990 the FBI was building its own database and accepting DNA samples from states for processing and storage. Thus the Bureau set out to built the genetic parallel of the NCIC. At first linking only fourteen state and local laboratories with the feds, the project was soon boosted by the

DNA Identification Act of 1994, which formalized FBI authority to establish a national DNA index. By the end of the decade, all states were collecting DNA and most were participating in what the FBI now called CODIS, the Combined DNA Indexing System.[55]

Though DNA is relatively accurate in identifying individuals, processing of samples can be subject to the same sloppy forensic work as any other type of evidence. Recall the shambles of the FBI lab, in general, or the vicious lies of Oklahoma City Police Department chemist Joyce Gilchrist, who spent years taking public money to simply *invent* evidence; her apparent motive being laziness, stupidity, and a strange bureaucratized blood lust.[56] As for the Bureau's DNA methods, they're so shoddy that courts in Arizona and Illinois won't admit its lab's work as evidence. Just one example of this junk science: the FBI database of DNA samples used for creating the statistical profile of an average Caucasian relies solely on samples from the Bureau's own agents.[57]

While the state's deployment of DNA marks a new certainty in the science of identification, the political impact of that certainty has had a profoundly destabilizing effect on the immediate legitimacy of American criminal justice. In fact, as I write these words news arrives of the 110th person exonerated because of DNA testing. In this case, a Black man with mental disabilities had been forced to confess to a crime he did not commit nor, it seems, know anything about. Such DNA-based upsets of verdicts have raised even more questions about the politics of state-sponsored execution.[58]

But the exculpatory services of properly analyzed deoxyribonucleic acid do not alleviate the civil libertarians' concerns. For one, DNA is better at excluding an individual from the narrow band in which genetic identification could take place than it is at definitively identifying a suspect *as an individual.* In others words, placing individuals in large groups of types is easier than identifying individuals within those groups. Nonetheless, some police have already launched genetic dragnets to search databanks for "cold hits." In 1998 German police investigating the murder of an eleven-year-old girl conducted a mass genetic manhunt in the area where the crime occurred; 16,400 men were swabbed and the killer was found.[59] Just deserts for the perp, but where will such sweeps stop? Will increasingly minor and politically debatable crimes be addressed by similar methods?

More realistically, DNA is problematic because it is not merely a better fingerprint. Unlike papillary ridges, DNA carries within it a world of information. As one contrarian from the ACLU told Congress, "The DNA samples that are being held by state and local governments can provide insights into the most personal family relationships and the most intimate workings of the human body, including the likelihood of the occurrence of over 4,000 types of genetic conditions and diseases." And despite the overwhelming case against sociobiology there is the concern that "there are many who will claim that there are genetic markers for aggression, substance addiction, criminal tendencies and sexual orientation."[60]

On these grounds skeptics like the Council for Responsible Genetics worry that DNA databanks could launch a new eugenics. One can imagine Wilmington, Delaware, police profiling taken to a new level: the genetically "pre-criminal" sorted safely from the "normal."

UNLEASH THE NEW RED SQUADS

In the name of fighting terror, cops and the FBI are seeking new powers to keep regular dossiers on anyone, no matter how law-abiding. The feds, for example, have subpoenaed records from all scuba shops. The purpose is to identify every person who has taken diving lessons during the last three years in case any of them might fit a terrorist profile. Almost all dive shops complied, giving over information on several million people. Only one upscale shop, Reef Seekers of Beverly Hills, refused.

At the local level, metropolitan police forces are seeking and receiving the right to spy on even the lawful activities of citizens who engage in political activity. The most aggressive such effort occurred in New York, where police lawyers have overturned a court-ordered restriction called the Handschu agreement, a ruling from the mid–1980s that made such unprovoked spying illegal. The NYPD's intelligence commissioner, former CIA operations director David Cohen, maintains that the old agreement "dangerously limits" the NYPD in the post 9/11world." A similar restriction was recently overturned in Chicago. While cops in Seattle, Baltimore, St. Louis, Portland, and Norfolk, Virginia, are also looking for latitude. As the *Village Voice* pointed out, these few now-endangered restrictions on police spying were born as a result of many departments' blatant and aggressive red squads, which sought to snoop on and disrupt legitimate political activism.[61]

13

VOYEURISM AND SECURITY CULTURE

> He who fights with monsters might take care lest he thereby become a monster. If you gaze too long into the abyss, the abyss will look back into you.
>
> —Friedrich Nietzsche
> *Beyond Good and Evil*, Section 146

In the wake of the terrorist attacks of September 11, 2001, many media pundits declared that *everything had changed.* As one mawkish tagline for an article put it, "We grew up in a hurry, but have much to learn. A nation longs for normalcy—in a world forever changed."[1] The same claptrap was echoed far and wide. From Gannett's wires came this: "The worst nightmares of national security officials came true Tuesday, and the nation forever will be changed in terms of culture, society, politics, priorities and freedom of movement."[2] Elsewhere: "Everyone is affected. Everything has changed. There may not have been much innocence left in the America of the 21st century, but whatever we had left was extinguished on Tuesday. . . . We are all vulnerable, we are all exposed."[3] Even a year later, during the highly confected public anniversary of 9/11, Fox titled its TV special "The

Day America Changed," while the CBS extravaganza opted for the equally distinct "The Day That Changed America." But was it true?

In reality, the erosion of civil liberties, the increase in surveillance, the everyday culture of fear and xenophobia had all become central to American political culture long before 9/11. So too were the aggressive, totalitarian-style policies of the federal government as embodied in the Patriot Act or the strangely Teutonic-sounding "Department of Homeland Security."

Likewise, the innocent casualties of 9/11, gruesome and horrifying, were not particularly aberrant but just unusually situated. This time the dead were Americans, not faceless foreigners. The Slovenian theorist Slavoj Zizek had it right when he greeted America on the proverbial morning after with a blunt, "Welcome to the desert of the real." His point was that the world is a brutal, vicious place and that America is part of it and deeply implicated in its worst aspects. As he put it, "The towers symbolized, ultimately, the stark separation between the digitized First World and the Third World's 'desert of the real.'"[4] The point was not to justify the crimes of 9/11, but simply to shake Americans from their political somnambulance.

If something did change after the attacks, it was the increased legitimation of obedience and the surging levels of popular consent for fear-mongering, surveillance-based statecraft. Postattack polls showed that more Americans than ever were willing to trade civil liberties for safety.[5] But even this real shift in opinion is often exaggerated. A recent Pew Research Center survey found that in the aftermath of September 11 "only a third of Americans worried that the government's new anti-terrorism laws would excessively restrict" civil liberties. Almost a year later roughly half of all respondents were now worried that new laws might "undermine civil liberties."[6]

Overall, 9/11 looks less like a seismic shift from freedom to tyranny and more like an aggressive and opportunistic acceleration of this country's long slow decline into the soft cage. So, before unpacking Homeland Security and the Patriot Act, we must address America's preexisting culture of fear and its popular obsession with surveillance. Particularly prominent in this are private home security, ignore the spectacle of voyeurism and paranoia exemplified by "reality-based" television.

KEEPING IT REAL

They range from the staged game shows like *Survivor* and *Big Brother* and the emotional food fights of *Jerry Springer* to the ride-along morality plays of *LAPD*, *Cops*, *True Stories of the Highway Patrol*, and *Bounty Hunter* and the surveillance-footage-based specials and hybrids like *Busted on the Job* and *Cheaters*. But all these reality shows trade on motifs of truth, confession, exposure, accountability, and surveillance. All pander to our voyeurism and other base appetites. Watching such shows is fascinating and can be emotionally charged; we identify with the victims, fearing capture by the law, exposure, heartbreak, and humiliation. Yet we also revel in the schadenfreude of watching "real" suffering on tell-all daytime TV, just as we enjoy the authoritarian aesthetics of police culture: the cop's private language of cryptic radio codes and the dramatic brutality of their order-maintenance campaigns in the ghetto. All of this either uses surveillance footage or the "truth exposing" aesthetics of surveillance.

Some of the better writing on reality television highlights the genre's two driving factors; low production costs and the alienation of its audience. In this vein Mark Crispin Miller notes "the degradation of experience by technology."[7] We might add to this the alienation and degradation of experience by the fetishistic culture of consumerism. In the worst cases, this is a world where much of experience is reduced to purchasing the symbols of experience. One owns an "all terrain vehicle" but drives it only on suburban streets. In a market economy all things are equivalent and exchangeable with all others, and thus all commodities (things and services) are at one level reduced to and ruled by their simple abstract essence: *economic value*. Lived experience on this plane, where hard, cold cash rules, can become just as abstracted as value itself. We become like the commodities that surround and circulate through us, mere representations of some other function.[8]

Reality television, particularly the shows that foreground surveillance and purport to expose true, unfabricated events and emotions, brings us back to earth, back to our guts. It spikes our lives with momentary and illusionary flashes of *the real*. This is as true for talk shows like *Jerry Springer* as it is for docu-tainment shows like *Cops* or reality contests like *Fear Factor*.

On the other hand, one could argue that this voyeurism, to which the cathode-ray bread and circus panders, is hardly new, nor can we blame it

Screen shot: Dashboard camera puts the viewer in the driver's seat (credit: Jan Chelminski)

all on the effects of market economics and industrial production. After all, some of the earliest printed tracts in Europe were gallows confessions and bawdy illustrated poems. Thus, we might say that modern media, from Gutenberg to the Internet, have *always* been driven in part by that widespread human attraction to the catharsis of knowing the corporal; of seeing and experiencing violence and sex; of having experience reduced to the rules of the body. But now this merges with the hyper-mediated American culture where, as Eco pointed out, there is a "furious hyperreality" always demanding the "complete fake . . . the fusion of the copy and original."[9] That's exactly what reality TV does.

POWER, KNOWLEDGE, AND BUBBLEGUM

The ultimate reality-based hybrid in which the themes of voyeurism and surveillance from all the other entertainment templates merge is that truly amazing wallow in the mud called *Cheaters*. Billing itself as "real reality-TV," this is the show that stakes out and busts philandering husbands and unfaithful wives. Its methods mix police-style tactics, ride-along footage, and high-tech surveillance with Springeresque pseudo-moralism and raw confrontation. This is all topped off with Oprah-derived pop-psych confessions and vague references to healing. In short, *Cheaters* is totally depraved and, in small doses, thus awesomely entertaining.

The show starts with an epigraph reading: "This program is both dedicated to the faithful and presented to the falsehearted to encourage their renewal of temperance and virtue. . . ." The star and the center of the action is the private investigator-cum-therapist-cum-preacher Tommy Grand. Big and always clad in black, Grand is backed up by a camera/muscle crew of equally imposing men all decked out in inky dark fatigues and t-shirts with "security" emblazoned on the back. Each show follows a series of two or three fast-moving "cases," most of which end with a raid on the cheating spouse. And for veracity and drama, all this is captured on shaky handheld cameras.

We start by seeing "the case" outlined when the aggrieved lover or spouse parlays with Grand. We then see an "investigation," in which Tommy's small army of private dicks videotape and photograph anything suspicious, trailing the "cheaters" to out-of-the-way restaurants and no-tell motels. To create a legalistic, semi-official mood, we get the requisite shots of Tommy and crew timing the length of each illicit rendezvous. All this "evidence" is collated in a chronological case file, which Tommy eventually shares with the aggrieved client.

Once the case is made, Tommy switches from his role as tough-guy gumshoe to just-in-time bereavement counselor as he drops the bomb, showing the client the tape containing proof of infidelity. As the shattered, grim-faced spouse watches, Grand offers sanctimonious lines like "I'm here to be here for you." After the necessary tight shots on the cuckolded husband or heart-broken girlfriend, Tommy, still in therapist mode, "checks in." "Are you sure you want to confront them?"

Then in what seems like an instant we're off with the huge coplike crew, all beefy and bristling with cameras, boom mics, and cables. Now Tommy slides into his third incarnation: moral fundamentalist. Before one typical showdown Tommy explains: "Betrayed and deceived, Glenn's compulsion is to confront his love and seek any justifiable explanation for her

Babylonian ways." At the end of the show one is invited to report suspected infidelity by writing to *Cheaters* at 4516 Lovers Lane, Dallas, Texas.[10]

The *Cheaters* template, a potpourri of all the best of all the rest, resembles similar shows with its authoritarian normalization and justification of surveillance. Here surveillance merely exposes preexisting moral shortcomings. The implication is clear: the honest have nothing to fear, and the guilty have only themselves to blame. This is precisely the logic that makes the soft cage of massive routine surveillance appear reasonable.

RUN, RUN, RUN

Even more sinister and probably just as enticing (but for the moment in permanent hiatus) is the surveillance-based reality game show that was to have been produced by Ben Affleck called *The Runner*. This show would have involved a nationwide manhunt in which viewers would—in the hopes of bagging the $1 million prize—help corner and catch a contestant who is "on the run." This snitch-nation-as-treasure-hunt idea was iced after September 11—sometimes reality overtakes even reality TV.[11]

But why turn to fabricated manhunts when we have "real" ones? *America's Most Wanted* is television's answer to the wanted poster. Along with *Cops* it helped create the reality format upon which Fox rode to glory, forcing all other networks to imitate. Begun in 1988 the show has been hosted ever since by the square-jawed, all-American-looking John Walsh. Walsh's qualification are this: in 1981 his six-year-old son Adam disappeared from a Florida shopping mall only to have his severed head appear two weeks later.[12] With that Walsh became an official crime victim. Next came a made-for-TV movie about the case and from the fame that brought, Walsh was appointed executive director of the new, Reagan-sponsored National Center for Missing and Exploited Children. By 1988 Walsh had been recruited to host the brand-new Fox network "docudrama" called *America's Most Wanted*.

Unlike anything before it, the show sought to track down real fugitives by broadcasting the real facts straight from police files. It was massively successful at capturing both criminals and audience eyeballs, and

Screen shot: Takedown (credit: Jan Chelminski)

ever since it has been recruiting the citizens-soldiers of fear-nation, that parallel America of permanent simmering panic.

Early on the show's producer described its mission in strangely revealing terms: "It's literally impossible for a fugitive to hide if enough people know he's wanted. . . . A criminal on the run encounters dozens of people every day. We're excited that we can use all we know about television to produce these valuable witnesses."[13] The operative word here is "produce." Viewers are hailed as witnesses of a "real" crime and called upon to respond as such and join the state in a nationwide policing project.

America's Most Wanted requires verisimilitude and thus requires large slabs of fictionalized reenactments, which are often staged at the actual crime scenes. This aspect of "producing witnesses" has also been noted to produce new trauma as the original witnesses find themselves suddenly cast as extras in replays of mayhem. For example, early in the show's life news broke of the production company spending over $15,000 to recreate a massive drug hit in a D.C. housing project in which, according to police, a squad of Jamaican Yardies sent down from New York had smashed into an apartment and killed all the occupants.

To get the scene just right *America's Most Wanted* rented the same apartment "with half-smoked marijuana cigarettes still in plain view and bloodstains on the carpets," bought furniture similar to the original, and hired nearly twenty-five actors who "played the victims, the neighbors and a four-member Jamaican hit squad." Outside scenes, in which the gunmen fled down three flights of stairs and through a walkway to a parking lot, took more than five hours to film. "But," as the *Washington Post* reported, "what upset some neighbors was the nightlong reenactment of the killings inside the three-bedroom apartment which began at 5 p.m. Saturday and lasted until past 6 a.m. Sunday."[14]

Already traumatized witnesses described the scenes in harrowing detail: "It just wasn't right; it wasn't fair. They had people hollering with Jamaican accents, ordering people to get on the floor, not to move, and then you heard gunfire. They were firing blanks all night."[15] The executive producer explained such elaborate efforts as necessary so that "tipsters won't send police after the actors."[16]

THE SPECTACLE OF FEAR

So what is the larger cultural and political impact of such surveillance- and fear-based shows? One writer invoked Walter Benjamin and Terry Eagleton to portray the television voyeur as the new *flâneur*—though, instead of strolling through the city anonymously "possessing unpossessed and seeing unseen" he or she now surfs the digital entrails of the information society, skipping from online webcams to *Cops* to *Bounty Hunters* to the eligible *Bachelor* and his many suitors (read contestants).[17] If this is true, surveillance-based entertainment is just one more coat of glitz on the already amazing spectacle of modern American life.

But there seems to be more than mental Novocain at work here. Reality TV is highly political. One study found that regular viewers of cop-oriented reality TV are likely to overestimate the rate of violent crime, particularly among African Americans. The racial disparity here is reflected in or produced by such programs' tendency to cast white police against Black and Latino "perps." Another study linked enjoyment of law-and-order reality TV to authoritarian personality traits—such as veneration of authority and regulation—and higher self-reported levels of racial prejudice.[18] In this light, reality TV begins to reveal itself as part of a general field in which fear is created, shaped, and mobilized to build a capillary level, even intuitive, consent for police power, state authority, and the repression of populations deemed undesirable or dangerous—the poor, dark-skinned, foreign, and politically suspect.

FROM CASTLE TO BUNKER

Voyeurism has a close cousin: the security cult of the home in which many middle-class and well-to-do Americans, operating as if they lived in crime-plagued ghettos, equip their homes with state-of-the-art surveillance and security gear ranging from driveway gates and electric fences to automatic doors, CCTV, and superwired motion sensors. Add to this the mass market for home drug-testing kits, microchip identification implants for pets, voluntary DNA registration with the police, and electronic tracking tags for possessions, online nanny cams for watching babysitters, and one begins to see a landscape that is both nominally "free" yet under constant and oppressive regulation. A brief description of this new private surveillance infrastructure should help clarify how, even before 9/11, our culture was structured around pervasive fear.

The real growth of home security—that is, the routine surveillance of the home by the home—paralleled the massive restructuring of the American economy during the 1980s and 1990s. As income distribution polarized and the state ramped up its incarceration binge, on the home front observation and "defensible spaces" became the name of the game.

In beginning of the 1980s, only around 3 percent of homes were wired with proper alarm systems, but the proliferation of cable television changed that by opening up cheaper means for security firms to monitor home alarms.[19] As crime rates nose-dived in the late 1990s the home security business hit its stride : some 20 percent of houses were fully hooked up with professionally monitored security systems that electronically watched doors, windows, and internal hallways for signs of forced entry. And as with all commodities competition, innovation, and economies of scale caused home security prices to fall 50 percent between 1979 and 1989.[20] In this time of growth, the business of securing private abodes went from a highly competitive industry of small firms to a business controlled by a few national and even international behemoths. Among them we find Protection One, ADT, Security Link, WestTech, and Brinks. These companies maintain huge central monitoring stations that function much like the dispatch centers in large police departments, with backup power, redundant communication, and computer systems and trained operators to contact local police and private security units in the field.[21]

During the 1990s the home security industry grew at an annual rate of 10 percent, topping out at a $14 billion-a-year-business at the end of the decade. One economist found that "houses valued at over $300,000 have a home security system installed 39 percent of the time, compared with only 9 percent for houses valued at less than $100,000." Never mind that poor households are "60 percent more likely to be burglarized than the rich households."[22]

As a home security system becomes more elaborate and multifaceted it requires a brain, or control panel, to manage information coming from the perimeter of a home and its key vulnerability points. Now the best of these nerve centers can be hidden from sight under fake panels or in closets just as easily as they can be accessed remotely, via the web, if the system is hooked into a home PC and the phone lines. One Boston-area "gadget freak" and proud owner of a "smart house" even has his alarm system jacked into the stereo, television, and lighting system, explaining that "it's like having an invisible sentry on guard all the time."[23]

Once ensconced in the "safe" home, the resident becomes his or her own warden, supervising the intricate technical functions of room-by-room surveillance. This is the ultimate totem to fear: cocooning oneself in a chrysalis of motion sensors, magnetic contact strips on doors, breakage alarms on windows, tiny night-vision surveillance cameras transmitting live video from the yard to one's bedside-control station. These fetish objects of security should be understood as votive candles to the middle-class folk-gods of fear.

THE STATE IN MINIATURE

As the suburban abode becomes increasingly fortified with its digital security arsenal, it transmogrifies into a miniature command and control center that can "project power" outward into the public realm. Consider the "GPS Personal Locator for Children," described by boosters as a "brightly colored device, which looks like an oversized watch." This gadget contains a tiny GPS unit that can be tracked from your home or office desktop. As the developer, Wherify Wireless, explains, the "GPS Personal Locator helps keep loved ones safe by combining Wherify's patented technology and the US Department of Defense's multi-billion dollar Global Positioning System (GPS) satellites—plus the largest 100% digital nationwide PCS wireless network. So relax. Now you can have peace of mind 24 hours a day while your child is the high-tech envy of the neighborhood."

Wherify's kiddie shackle also features: a 9–1–1 emergency response, a safety lock to prevent unwanted removal, a built-in pager, and self-setting watch.[24] And now the firm is working on a new GPS tag for teens that will "contain additional functions, such as paging, a cell phone, or the ability to get sports scores." When asked if he would have liked such a device when he was a teen, the company's CEO explained, "If I were a teenage girl, I would probably wear one."[25]

The same equipment has a myriad of other planned and existing uses. As Wherify's fear-pandering web copy explains, "Last year, the estimated total value of vehicles stolen nationwide was 7 billion dollars. . . . Of the 4 million Americans with Alzheimer's disease 60% will wander. . . . Every year 359,000 children are kidnapped. . . . There are approximately 59 million dogs and 58 million cats in the US."[26] In other words, the possibilities for GPS tracking are endless; track your teenage daughter and the car she's driving and the dog she's taking to the beach. But at roughly $300 a pop, plus monthly fees of around $30, GPS services from any firm are as yet fairly expensive.[27]

This use of digital surveillance gear at home marks the third phase in the proliferation of technology from the military to industry to the consumer. For example, state-of-the-art vehicle and fleet management technology, which started as Pentagon know-how and was then sold for corporate use, has now reached the scale of the home. One firm, ProTrack, promises the ability to track your car—in "real time"—from your desktop. This individually retailed package of hardware and software services has most of the features used in professional fleet management: a panic button, encryption, and the ability to store and later download data from the vehicle to the supervising computer.[28]

What, then, is the retrenchment of the home all about? The geographer Cindi Katz links it to the paramilitary restructuring of care-giving; she sees individual strategies of "hyper vigilance" as the logical analogue to massive state and corporate disinvestment in the sphere of social services: "The heightened mobility of capital investment has also led various public authorities to reduce or abate corporate taxes, which, among other things, has reduced public monies available for social welfare. Responsibility for social reproduction has shifted increasingly to private domains where it is accomplished through household labor—still largely women's—or purchased." In this context of engineered scarcity and individual survival, "security" begins to stand in for "care."

At the same time, the return of domestic service as a commercial industry, which Katz notes is created for and by class inequality, demands supervisory surveillance as a form of labor management. If rich women hire poor women to watch the children, who will watch the help? Look no further than the booming "nanny cam" industry. These wireless minicameras, aggressively advertised on the Internet in the late 1990s and early 2000s, can be hidden away and monitored remotely from mommy or daddy's office desktop. As Katz puts it, "In the privatized state, parents become spies. They spy on their nannies and on other domestic workers."[29]

This same type of camera also serves as the platform for whole webcam communities in which thousands of people broadcast their lives on the Internet. As a cultural phenomenon this type of live webcast is imbued loneliness, fame lust, sexual titillation, and simple irony. One webcaster explained why he broadcasts live footage from his bedroom for many hours a day as follows: "Sometimes it's fun. Sometimes it's exciting, but it has something to do with knowing I have a small audience of people watching me. I like getting random messages from 'Sally in the UK' telling me that she likes my cats, or that 'Juan en España' has taken the liberty to e-mail me a naked picture of himself. It's a good diversion from my projects and daily papers I'm writing from school, and the variety or responses I get to it are amazing."[30]

ALWAYS ROOM TO PANIC

If the home is becoming a compound from which to project a miniature private sovereignty over property and dependents, it is also still a place of refuge. But what if the castle-bunker is overrun in a "home invasion"? This popular renaming of burglary also reflects the reconception of the home as sovereign ministate, detached and opposed to a larger, hostile society. What then will be the fallback position? The "panic room" or "safe room," of course.

These impregnable and hidden security spaces were made famous by the Jodie Foster movie *Panic Room*, in which a lone mother has to deal with a gang of home-wrecking thugs. After 9/11, leading builders of panic rooms reported a 35 percent to 40 percent bounce in orders. Starting at $20,000 and soaring upward from there, these hidden little shrines to the twin gods of fear and safety usually feature steel-plated, bulletproof walls, electromagnetic locks, filtered ventilation, stockpiled pepper spray firearms, and dedicated phone lines to the local police and of course the de rigueur centralized monitor for the home's CCTV surveillance system. Once strictly for the rich and extremely paranoid, panic rooms became fairly popular among California millionaires during the stock bubble of the late 1990s.[31] But, as one leading builder of safe rooms has confessed, "very few" of his customers have ever needed their hidden fortresses.[32]

Using the ideas of sociologist Robert K. Merton, one could say that panic rooms have both a *manifest* and a *latent* function.[33] While the manifest function of these domestic garrisons is physical safety from home invasion, the latent function is to amplify the larger political culture's story of ubiquitous threats and individual solutions. Thus the panic room is to the current miasma of crime and terror what the pathetic backyard suburban bomb shelter was to the Cold War nightmare of atomic annihilation: a symbolic defense, an expensive mojo that appears to ward off fear while actually summoning it in a constant, everyday form.

Overall, the fetishism of home security, while clearly being about actual security and target-hardening, is also a cargo cult of individual defense against social disintegration of the sort described by Katz. Here, essentially imaginary, or magical, forms of agency are acted out in the face of massive and nebulous threats. Just as the millenarian methods of the Polynesian cargo cults involved props of power—vines and tin-can "radios" transmitting imaginary messages to the gods in the hope of bringing about a new realm and supernatural waves of "cargo" (commodities) from them—so too is the cult of home security ultimately as much about imaginary individual resolutions to inescapable social crises as it is about real safety.[34]

BLOWBACK ON THE HOME FRONT

"I am sorry . . . I won't do it anymore. Please, no," cries the developmentally disabled boy accused of stealing a hotdog from the larder of his foster parents. It doesn't matter; the man in the grainy surveillance footage continues beating the kid's bare buttocks with a cudgel and occasionally punching the youth in the head. Off screen a woman scolds: "He's lying when he says he is not going to do it anymore."

Frank and Marylynnette Barney learned about home surveillance blowback the hard way. While they were beating and psychologically torturing their new foster child a neighbor was checking his new wireless home surveillance system. Much to this vigilant homeowner's surprise he saw not his pool, patio, or bedroom but Frank and Marylynnette, churchgoing professionals from around the corner, torturing a disabled child. The neighbor's security system was receiving signals from a hidden minicam that the Barneys were using to spy on their prisoner. Shocked and sickened by the scene the anonymous neighbor pressed record. After he'd logged six grueling hours of sadism he handed the tape off to an attorney, who handed it off to the police, who immediately raided the Barney's suburban home where they found a bruised and battered child, blood stains in the boy's bedroom and on the basement walls, and reams of paper upon which the boy had been forced to write, thousands of times over, "I will not disrespect my mother. I will not steal food from this house."[35]

The moral of the story? Be careful where the camera is pointed. When the news of nanny-cam vulnerability first broke the spin was, as always, about a threat from outside the home. Exposing the crimes inside the home; the child rapes, the drunken verbal abuse, the sordid emotional neglect of children, the war between spouses—all this was forgotten. But here again we find a totally rational argument for surveillance. Why not expose awful creeps and monsters like the Barneys? Why not expose the pederasts?

True, there are many cases when one can applaud the outcome of surveillance. But these cases can become a dangerous justification for an extensive, societywide system that is, as such, unexamined. The moral outrage that real crime elicits must not prevent us from thinking. Recall that bit of Nietzsche: "Morality is the best of all devices for leading mankind by the nose." A similar logic informs the post-9/11 "antiterror" crack down. White House and Justice Department officials inform us that extraordinary times require extraordinary measures and that "everything has changed." It's good versus evil. No middle ground. No thinking.

Such simplicity is dangerous.

14

FEAR AS INSTITUTION: 9/11 AND SURVEILLANCE TRIUMPHANT

> Experience should teach us to be most on our guard to protect liberty when the Government's purposes are beneficent. Men born to freedom are naturally alert to repel invasion of their liberty by evil-minded rulers. The greatest dangers to liberty lurk in insidious encroachment by men of zeal, well meaning but without understanding.
>
> — Supreme Court Justice Louis Brandeis, *Olmstead v. United States* (1928)

> There are reminders to all Americans that they need to watch what they say, watch what they do. . . .
>
> — Ari Fleischer, White House spokesman, 2001
>
> This comment was later removed from the official transcript.

Ultimately, 9/11 did not create a technical or legal rupture in the developing infrastructure of everyday superintendence. It did, however, radically accelerate momentum towards the soft cage of a surveillance society, just as it gave the culture of fear a rejuvenating jolt. In many ways the frightening thing about the postattack crackdown has been how much of everyday life was prefabricated to fit neatly into a new and larger project of intensified state observation and repression. In this we see again that the problem with routine surveillance is not that any single instance is so abhorrent, especially when viewed in isolation, but rather that the cumulative overall effect of such measures is corrosive of popular democratic rights and traditions.

PATRIOTS GALORE

As the smoke of the attacks cleared there emerged in Congress a hastily discussed yet massive schedule of domestic repression: the Uniting and Strengthening America by Providing Appropriate Tools Required to Intercept and Obstruct Terrorism (USA Patriot) Act. This hyperbolically named legislation introduced a sweeping arsenal of new federal powers. Put simply, the Patriot Act liberalized use of the federal government's four main tools of surveillance: wiretaps, search warrants, subpoenas, and pen/trap orders (which allow investigators to log and map all the telephone numbers called by a suspect). It was the Attorney General's ultimate wish list. But in other ways it was just a mopping-up operation that legalized already existing and ongoing, yet illegal, forms of investigation.

Proof of this point came almost exactly a year after the attacks when several major papers ran the story of an internal FBI memo from 2000 that detailed the Bureau's routine and widespread violations of privacy laws. Among the memo's many revelations: field agents were improperly tapping and recording phones, illegally videotaping suspects and, without warrants, intercepting and analyzing e-mails with the data-mining software application formerly known as Carnivore. Furthermore, the memo rooted these transgressions in the pathological permissiveness of the 1978 Foreign Intelligence Surveillance Act (FISA). Under this law agents were permitted easy access to warrants if they could show that there was an substantial "foreign intelligence" angle to their work; the warrants would be granted by a special FISA court. It turned out that the leeway of FISA was being used as cover for otherwise illegal investigations.

Despite the exposé of FBI lawlessness, Ashcroft's Patriot Act had as one of its key features a further reduction in FISA's already low standard of proof. Now, even in cases that are entirely criminal in nature, agents can get automatic "administrative" FISA warrants (as opposed to real warrants from potentially hostile judges). As long as the agents assert that there is some foreign intelligence angle to the cases, they receive search warrants on demand. In 2000 alone the docile, highly secretive FISA bench approved 1,012 warrants.[1] And since 9/11 FBI demands for FISA warrants have become so insistent that even the secret FISA court has publicly admonished the FBI for misrepresenting facts on more than 75 occasions. This, from a court that civil libertarians ridiculed as an FBI rubberstamp and that approved *all but one* of the warrant requests put before it in the previous *twenty-four years*.[2]

The key distinction to keep in mind about FISA is that the standard of proof in criminal cases is supposed to be much higher than for intelligence cases, the assumption being that criminal cases can lead to prosecution and imprisonment of citizens and thus must be conducted in a restrained and fair fashion. Foreign intelligence, on the other hand, is merely about collecting information on a foreign power, domestic prosecution is not its goal. Since there is less risk of wrongful conviction from foreign intelligence investigations, requests for search warrants in such cases are held to a lower standard of proof.

The Patriot Act also allows federal investigators to "shop" for judges nationally when seeking warrants. Instead of being forced to possibly face a liberal judge, agents can now pick the judge of their choice from whichever circuit court they please and that warrant can be used in any part of the country. The raft of new laws also allows for nationwide roving wiretaps. In the past the feds were supposed to get a warrant for each telephone line they tapped. Now one easy warrant allows them to tap all the phones that a single subject might use. Such a warrant could thus cover a person's home phone, work phone, and cell phone, as well as the lines of their friends, family, work associates, and social acquaintances.[3]

Other Patriot Act provisions expand the government's automatic access to information stored and generated by Internet service providers. This is done by retooling the parameters of what are called pen registration tap-and-trace warrants. Traditionally such administrative warrants were granted when cops wanted to generate a simple list of all the numbers that had been called from and that had called a particular phone. Because it was deemed that no "content" was revealed by such a list the standard of proof for a tap-and-trace warrant was very low; agents had only to "certify" or assert that they had a good reason for needing the information—in other words, they didn't have to prove probable cause. After the Patriot Act, the same low standard holds true for gleaning information about web surfing and e-mailing. But web addresses and e-mail subject lines, unlike simple phone numbers, all contain revealing content.[4] If you visit the website of a radical environmental group this fact will likely be clear from the web address alone.

Gone too are the firewalls that once prevented the various intelligence agencies from sharing information. Crucially the Patriot Act creates a new massively expanded definition of what a terrorist is. Now anyone who breaks the law so as to impact policy or change public opinion and does so in a way that might endanger human life (including their own) can be investigated and prosecuted as a terrorist.[5] An analysis of the USA Patriot Act could go on for many pages. The point for our purposes is that it liberalizes the legal environment in which federal cops will be gathering and processing the routine informational detritus of the digital age.

TOTAL INFORMATION AWARENESS: THE LOGICAL NEXT STEP

The most explicit and dramatic connection between government spying and the infrastructure of everyday surveillance was the Total Information Awareness (TIA) project of the Pentagon's Defense Advanced Research Projects Agency (DARPA). Begun in January 2002 and defunded in March 2003, DARPA's Information Awareness Office stated that it would "imagine, develop, apply, integrate, demonstrate, and transition information technologies, components, and prototype closed-loop information systems that will counter asymmetric threats by achieving total information awareness that is useful for preemption, national security warning, and national security decision making."[6]

Much like the Transportation Security Agency's airline-oriented CAPPS II, the TIA office was working on a plan to pull together all the disparate records of everyday life. From the digital trails of credit cards, electronic tolls, banking transactions, health records, and library use it sought to create one "virtual, grand database" that could be data-mined for interesting and incriminating patterns.[7] The program was also tasked with inventing "new algorithms for mining, combining, and refining" this information.[8] Connected to this was another DARPA program called Human ID that would mathematically map biometric information from video cameras and other image sources and then use this to track images of people across and through different databases. This would allow the government to identify people with just a photo and to automatically track people as they travel in public space. A rather perturbed-sounding *Fortune* magazine described DARPA's efforts this way: "Every telephone call you make, every credit card transaction, all your e-mail and instant messages, all your medical records, your magazine subscriptions, your police record, driver's license records, gun purchases, travel records, banking records—all would be fed into a hopper and sifted by the TIA spy software."[9]

This complaint from the *Washington Post* was typical: "the potential for abuse is enormous."[10] One could add that the system was abusive by its very nature, that its intended function was to destroy privacy and subordinate the population, above and beyond any "mistakes" that might be made. Heading up this project was the politically radioactive retired Rear Admiral John Poindexter, who was infamously convicted on five felony counts of lying to Congress and destroying official documents during the Iran/Contra Affair (he was later acquitted on technicalities).[11]

Another important and developing part of the same general project was the administration's "National Strategy to Secure Cyberspace"—essentially an attempt (still in the planning stages) to centralize the worldwide web. Currently the purview of the President's Critical Infrastructure Protection Board, this cyber enclosure would require *all* Internet service providers to help build a centralized system for tracking and filtering online traffic. One data industry specialist compared the system to the FBI's Internet surveillance and data-mining program called Carnivore, but added that "it's 10 times worse."[12] Eventually the TIA office of DARPA had its funding cut, thanks to popular outcry against the project. But many of these functions continue in modified form under other names.

FRIEND/ENEMY KULTURKAMPF

Perhaps the most revealing surveillance idea from the Bush team was the failed Terrorism Information and Prevention System (TIPS) program, which sought to turn one in every twenty-four Americans into a snitch. The idea was to recruit meter readers, UPS drivers, and letter carriers to report on "suspicious activities" they witnessed while inside homes. Floated as a serious proposal by Attorney General John Ashcroft in the summer of 2002, TIPS was quickly ripped to pieces by everyone from the mainstream press to the post office, delivery firms, and utility companies it was to rely on. By late fall TIPS had died in its crib. But the program is an important political artifact because of the twisted fundamentals it reveals.

On Planet Ashcroft, society appears as a hub-and-spoke system where citizens mistrust each other, share no popular solidarity, and place all trust in unlimited state and corporate power. Furthermore, this system plays out along the lines of race. Recall Eunice Stone, at best a malicious busy-body, at worst a stone-cold bigot, who called in the Florida police when she overheard three Middle Eastern–looking medical students at a restaurant talking about dates in September. Mrs. Stone insisted they were joking about imminent terrorist attacks. After a huge paramilitary police bust that shut down Alligator Alley, the "terrorists" turned out to be totally innocent, rather square and apolitical medical students who had been talking about how they could return their rental car to Kansas and still get to their residencies in Georgia on time.[13]

This willingness to snitch on anyone who looks remotely Arab is also reflected in polls. A *Newsweek* survey conducted immediately in the wake of 9/11 found that 32 percent of Americans favored putting Arabs under "special surveillance" like that used against Japanese-Americans during World War II.[14] A *San Jose Mercury News* poll had 66 percent of respondents favoring "heightened surveillance of Middle Eastern immigrants."[15]

GET THE IMMIGRANTS, AGAIN

So how do such sentiments translate into policy? Jump back to the autumn of 2002, when men from an ever-growing list of countries are required to report for "special registration" requiring them to be photographed, fingerprinted, and interviewed. In Southern California, *la migra* detains hundreds of law-abiding immigrants, many of whom have only minor technical problems with their paperwork. In Los Angeles the mass arrests are so numerous that officials run out of plastic handcuffs and start shipping the estimated 400 to 900 detainees out to more permanent holding facilities.[16] Fear and outrage grip the Arab, Persian, and South Asian communities; soon hundreds of law-abiding Pakistani immigrants are rushing to the Canadian boarder seeking political asylum.

"I feel sorrow for this society," says a Mr. Pirazdeh, an Iranian political refugee held in an Immigration detention facility in San Pedro. "I still believe this society and this country is based on freedom." Pirazdeh was on the verge of getting his residency papers when he was jailed and threatened with deportation.[17] It was all part of ramping up the cumbersome machinery of the new National Security Entry-Exit Registration System, a futuristic version of the methods first used on the Chinese that will now allow the Department of Homeland Security to better monitor all foreign visitors and immigrants.[18]

To begin with, the new Immigration program required all residents from Iran, Iraq, Libya, Sudan, and Syria who are not permanent residents or naturalized citizens to register their fingerprints and photos with the local immigration authorities. Next to be called in were all male visa holders over the age of sixteen from thirteen other countries, including Afghanistan, Eritrea, Lebanon, North Korea, and Yemen. Foreign students are also to be tracked with a new and totalizing vigor, thanks to the Student and Exchange Visitor Information System (SEVIS). As the State Department explained, in the newspeak of compassionate xenophobia, "The new system is designed to better maintain accurate records of aliens inside the nation, at the same time it supports a policy of openness toward people from other nations." The DHS will attempt to maintain "updated information on approximately one million non-immigrant foreign students and exchange visitors" every year.

Thanks to the Internet, universities and colleges will be compelled to do most of the bureaucratic policing and update the feds electronically as necessary. In their new role as the eyes and ears of homeland security overkill, educational institutions will be required to report if a foreign student fails to enroll, drops out, has poor grades, changes his or her address or name or field of study. Such data will be electronically transmitted to the immigration cops at the DHS and to the Department of State. "When a student falls out of status, INS will be informed and able to take appropriate action." The goal of all this is more data mining, enabling "the INS to better identify trends and patterns to assist in planning and analyzing risks."[19] Ultimately such security strategies amount to hunting fleas with a sledgehammer. Terrorists are captured when their networks are infiltrated, not when whole populations are harassed.

While the immigration officials were getting SEVIS up and running the FBI was shaking down schools for voluntary information transfers. According to the law, universities are free to give limited personal student information to law enforcement agencies without a court order. Department of Education guidelines allow all of the following to be handed over to law enforcement: name, address, e-mail address, telephone number, field of study, the weight and height of athletes, and the date and place of birth. However, investigators still need a subpoena to get student ID numbers, Social Security numbers, or information on a student's ethnicity, race, citizenship, and gender.[20]

IN THE SERVICE OF ORDER

Here again the central question arises: what harm is caused by the proliferation of everyday surveillance? How will carrying a smart-card ID through an environment of swipe scanners, meters, cameras, sensors, and databanks hurt us? Is it just that a few innocent people, like the immigrants discussed above, will be pushed around? That's bad, but is there even more a stake?

Justice Louis Brandeis framed the issue of surveillance in terms of individual quality of life. Recall his famous dissenting opinion in *Olmstead* on the use of police wiretaps, in which he vaunted "man's spiritual nature . . . his feelings" and "his intellect . . ." and saw the Constitution as protecting "Americans in their beliefs, their thoughts, their emotions and their sensations."[21]

Brandeis offers a definition and defense of privacy as eloquent as any before or since, but are these purely individual, experiential parameters enough? What about the political life of the collective? And what about the dangerous implications of privacy? Is not the case for privacy also an argument for lawlessness? Are we protecting the "privacy" to run red lights, steal, abuse children, or kill with airplanes? Put differently, what does one have to fear from total surveillance as long as one obeys all laws? Indeed, total surveillance and total accountability plus total obedience add up to business as usual for the "good citizen."

Already we see signs of this type of ultratrusting, superobedient postmodern subject emerging from within the regime of routine observation and regulation. The *Christian Science Monitor* reports:

> Polls show that kids have been the least surprised by new security measures since they're the most used to having ID cards examined, luggage searched, and jokes screened by authorities. Today's kids trust and confide in authorities, set up Web cams in their rooms, and keep in constant electronic contact with parents and friends. For better or worse, privacy isn't a big issue among teens, and challenges to civil liberties are less of a worry than to older people.[22]

In other words, the structure of feeling is being transformed by increasingly ubiquitous surveillance. Liberty and autonomy are being replaced by obedience and trust in authority.

Underlying this question of obedience is the implicit assumption that state, corporate, and parental powers are infallible. Thus the heart of the matter emerges: are the rules and laws of this society all rational, benevolent, and just? If they are not, and if many of them serve to reproduce racism, stupidity, exploitation, environmental devastation, and general brutality, then should we not resist them?

CIVIL LIBERTIES AND RESISTANCE

Perhaps a view from the past might help reframe the issue. Milton Mayer, once a well-known essayist, described a similar escalation of surveillance, rules, and obedience in the gathering storm of German fascism. He interviewed a German philologist who described the process in terms that might sound familiar:

> What happened was the gradual habituation of the people, little by little, to be governed by surprise, to receiving decisions deliberated in secret; to believe that the situation was so complicated that the government had to act on information which the people could not understand, or so dangerous that, even if people could understand it, it could not be released because of national security. . . . This separation of government from the people, this widening of the gap, took place so gradually and insensibly, each step disguised (perhaps not even intentionally) as a temporary emergency measure or associated with true patriotic allegiance or with real social purposes. And all the crises and reforms (real reforms too) so occupied the people that they did not see the slow motion underneath, of the whole process of government growing remoter and remoter. . . . Each step was so small, so inconsequential, so well explained or, on occasion, "regretted." That, unless one were to detach from the whole process from the beginning, unless one understood what the whole thing was in principle, what all these "little measures" that no "patriotic German" could resist must some day lead to, one no more saw it developing from day to day than a farmer in his field sees the corn growing. . . .
>
> Believe me this is true. Each act, each occasion is worse than the last, but only a little worse. You wait for the next and the next. You wait for one shocking occasion, thinking that others, when such a shock comes, will join you in resisting somehow. . . .
>
> Suddenly it all comes down, all at once. You see what you are, what you have done, or, more accurately, what you haven't done (for that was all that was required of most of us: that we did nothing).. . . You remember everything now, and your heart breaks. Too late. You are compromised beyond repair.[23]

Now, consider again the question of civil liberties: what *are* they for? As far back as the early Greek philosophers we can find notions of "natural law" that transcend the legality of any given state. We find the recurring idea that the law is not the sum total of morality and that at times there must be transgressions against legal norms. Sophocles, for example, has Antigone explain why she willfully disobeyed the king's orders: "Nor deemed I that thy decrees were of such force, that a mortal could override the unwritten and unfailing statutes of heaven. For their life is not of today or yesterday, but for all time, and no man knows when they were first put forth."[24]

Connected to this is the idea that the state's power over individuals may be simultaneously necessary and dangerous. Thus John Locke's argument for legislative government and against the divine right of kings made a similar case *for* limitations on state power and what is essentially the right to commit illegalities. To his critics who saw dissolving government as a sin Locke answered:

> But if they, who say it lays a foundation for rebellion, mean that it may occasion civil wars, or intestine broils, to tell the people they are absolved from obedience when illegal attempts are made upon their liberties or properties, and may oppose the unlawful violence of those who were their magistrates, when they invade their properties contrary to the trust put in them; and that therefore this doctrine is not to be allowed, being so destructive to the peace of the world: they may as well say, upon the same ground, that honest men may not oppose robbers or pirates, because this may occasion disorder or bloodshed. . . . The end of government is the good of mankind; and which is best for mankind, that the people should be always exposed to the boundless will of tyranny, or that the rulers should be sometimes liable to be opposed, when they grow exorbitant in the use of their power, and employ it for the destruction, and not the preservation of the properties of their people?[25]

Admittedly, Locke preferred orderly legislative change to open contest and rebellion, but the philosophical door to illegality is open. The ultimate capstone in this tradition of recognizing an implicit right to illegality is of course the US Declaration of Independence.[26] The key passage, once again:

> We hold these truths to be self-evident, that all men are created equal, that they are endowed by their Creator with certain unalienable rights, that among these are life, liberty and the pursuit of happiness. That to secure these rights, governments are instituted among men, deriving their just powers from the consent of the governed. That whenever any

> form of government becomes destructive to these ends, it is the right of the people to alter or to abolish it, and to institute new government, laying its foundation on such principles and organizing its powers in such form, as to them shall seem most likely to effect their safety and happiness. Prudence, indeed, will dictate that governments long established should not be changed for light and transient causes; and accordingly all experience hath shown that mankind are more disposed to suffer, while evils are sufferable, than to right themselves by abolishing the forms to which they are accustomed. But when a long train of abuses and usurpations, pursuing invariably the same object evinces a design to reduce them under absolute despotism, it is their right, it is their duty, to throw off such government, and to provide new guards for their future security.

The message here is nothing less than an in-your-face proclamation of state fallibility and an assertion of the people's *right* to commit illegalities. It is from this recognition in part that the Bill of Rights, the first ten amendments to the Constitution, emerges with its potentially meaningful containment of state power. We are given protection against "unreasonable search and seizure" and "security in our personal effects" precisely because the state and the social hierarchies served by the law are neither infallible nor the perfection of morality. Read together with the Declaration of Independence, the Bill of Rights and the civil liberties it enshrines begin to reveal themselves not just as protection for the innocent who might be wronged by the excess of the law, but also as an ambiguous protection for types of political guilt. There is in the tradition of natural law a space for rebellion.

It is no coincidence then that the women who met at Seneca Falls in 1848 to declare their "natural rights" and their implicit right to commit illegal acts first quoted verbatim the Declaration of Independence before then setting forth the following challenge to existing law:

> Resolved, That such laws as conflict, in any way with the true and substantial happiness of woman, are contrary to the great precept of nature and of no validity, for his is "superior in obligation to any other."
>
> Resolved, That all laws which prevent woman from occupying such a station in society as her conscience shall dictate, or which place her

in a position inferior to that of man, are contrary to the great precept of nature, and therefore of no force or authority.[27]

The same subtextual recognition of the right to commit illegalities compelled Henry David Thoreau to write *Resistance to Civil Government*. That book's most libertine lines also recapitulate the essences of the Declaration:

> All men recognize the right of revolution; that is, the right to refuse allegiance to, and to resist, the government, when its tyranny or its inefficiency are great and unendurable. . . . Unjust laws exist: shall we be content to obey them, or shall we endeavor to amend them, and obey them until we have succeeded, or shall we transgress them at once?[28]

Mahatma Gandhi and Martin Luther King Jr. both invoked the same obedience to higher laws in defending their disobedience vis-à-vis specific laws. In that light one might ask: would the civil rights movement have been as effective if the world of the 1950s and early 1960s had been as wired with surveillance gear as today's America? If J. Edgar Hoover had something like Total Information Awareness, would his agents have used it, as they did all the other means available to them, to harass civil rights activists, reds, poor peoples' organizations, unionists, and peaceniks? Most certainly.

Much of the history of social progress—from winning the eight-hour workday to women's suffrage to desegregation—was achieved in large part because citizens organized political movements that involved illegal forms of protests. Privacy and civil liberties were essential tools in all these cases. Illegal protests created a nuisance value that served the less powerful as a disposable political resource. The logic was always simple: Agree to a civilized work regime and the strikes and sabotage will stop. Let the ladies vote and they'll stop getting arrested. Desegregate public facilities, and the siege of to sit-ins, boycotts, and blockades will stop. Or today: Stop raping old-growth forests and the rugged tree sitters will come down out of their redwoods. At times when government is truly "remote" and unresponsive, disruptive and sometimes illegal protest is the only resource people have.

Similarly, the right to illegality is revealed in the fact that often the only way to get a constitutional test of a law is to violate the statute in question. Viewed from this angle the spectre of a totally transparent society in which obedience and self-policing are the ideal is a threat to the basic preconditions of oppositional politics and social progress.

What would it take to wind back the "thousand things" that make up the soft cage? Clearly there must be prohibitions against ever-expanding surveillance, but only popular pressure will cause the state to build new firewalls of privacy. Only sustained protest will compel regulators to tell corporations, police, schools, hospitals, and other institutions that there are limits. As a society, we want to say: Here you may not go. Here you may not record. Here you may not track and identify people. Here you may not trade and analyze information and build dossiers. There are risks in social anonymity, but the risks of omniscient and omnipotent state and corporate power are far worse.

NOTES

CHAPTER 1: LIFE IN THE GLASS BOX

1. One of the latest erosions of privacy came quietly in the summer of 2002 when Bush overturned Clinton administration rules to allow marketers, and therefore anyone with cash, to access medical records *without* patient consent. See Robert Pea, "Bush Rolls Back Rules on Privacy of Medical Data," *New York Times*, August 10, 2002.

2. Amy Cameron, "Homing Device: How Your Cell Phone Tracks Your Movements," *Maclean's*, February 19, 2001; Ephraim Schwartz, "FBI Phone Tapping and Locating Cell Phones Making 911 Calls: Is It Privacy or Paranoia?" *InfoWorld*, January 15, 2001; Marcia Savage and Amanda Stirpe, "Under Surveillance: Location-Based Wireless Technology Raises Privacy Concerns for Solution Providers," *Computer Reseller News*, December 4, 2000; Charlie Schmidt "The Road Ahead," *MIT's Technology Review* 104, no. 6 (July 2001); "Car Use Down, Public Transit Use Up in San Francisco Bay Area," Associated Press, April 17, 2001.

3. Riochard Boureaux, "Palestinians' Phone Boycott Is Call to Arms," *Los Angeles Times*, July 7, 2001.

4. See chapter 9, "Structure of Feeling," in Raymond Williams, *Marxism and Literature* (Oxford: Oxford University Press, 1978).

5. Kathryn Balint, "Looking After You: Technology Takes Surveillance to a New Level," *San Diego Union-Tribune*, November 5, 2000.

6. Statement of Alan Davidson, associate director, Center for Democracy and Technology, "Cybercrime: Protecting Public Safety and Personal Privacy," before

the Subcommittee on Crime of the House Judiciary Committee, congressional testimony by Federal Document Clearing House, June 12, 2001.

7. Ian Pattison, "Smart Cards: Chipping into Greater Customer Loyalty," *Guardian* (London), July 31, 1999; Bryan Brumley, "Europe Fertile Ground for Smart Card Expansion," Associated Press, December 18, 2000.

8. Jennifer O'Connell, "Smart Cards Threat to Privacy," *Sunday Business Post* (London), April 25, 1999.

9. David Lyon, *The Electronic Eye: The Rise of Surveillance Society* (Minneapolis: University of Minnesota Press, 1994).

10. Ronald Rosenberg, "Citgo to Use Avitar Drug Tests; Job Applicants to Undergo New Saliva-Based Exam," *Boston Globe*, October 12, 2000.

11. Brian Thevenot, "School Drug Testing Praised; Principal Applauds Voluntary Program," *New Orleans Times-Picayune*, December 7, 2000.

12. Sue Anne Pressley, "Puff or Play?" *Newark Star-Ledger*, November 26, 2000.

13. "Banks Say Thumbprints Stamp Out Fraud," *Cleveland Plain Dealer*, October 12, 2000.

14. Randy Kennedy, "At Kennedy, Testing a Truism: The Eyes Don't Lie," *New York Times*, November, 2002; David Mack, "Apartment Security System Gives Residents Palm Reading," *Chicago Sun-Times*, October 22, 1995.

15. Athima Chansanchai, "Tell-Tale Hearts?" *Village Voice*, June 1, 1999.

16. Tina Moore, "Fingerprint System Replaces Lunch Money in Pa. Schools," *Washington Post*, February 25, 2001.

17. "Talk of the Nation," National Public Radio, July 27, 1999.

18. See http://news.mpr.org/features/199911/15_newsroom_privacy/theprice.html.

19. "Nice Work for the Aviation Industry," *Airports International*, October 1, 2000; Phelim McAleer, "'Fool-Proof' Security Cameras Put the Innocent in the Frame," *Sunday Times* (London), July 18, 1999.

20. "High-Tech Security on Tampa Streets," Associated Press, July 1, 2001; Amy Herdy, "Eye on Ybor: Police Cameras Go Spy-Tech," *St. Petersburg Times*, June 30, 2001. Interestingly, it is the right wing that leads opposition to surveillance; see David McGuire, "Rep. Armey Blasts Tampa over Face-Recognition System," *Newsbytes News Network*, July 2, 2001. Visionics, the US firm that outfitted Tampa, first worked its magic back in 1998 on the streets of London's borough of Newham: S.A. Mathieson, "Online: In Sight of the Law," *Guardian* (London), March 1, 2001.

21. Balint, "Looking After You"; Andrea Combers, "Tiny Tracker," *San Francisco Examiner*, December, 13, 2000; or consider this: "A new service, ParkWatch,

can help family members keep tabs on one another. Parents and kids wear wireless wristwatches with individual ID numbers. The watches are rented for $3 a day and tracked by antennas around the park. Simply drop by a kiosk and have your watch scanned to pinpoint where anyone in your family is," Lisa McLaughlin, "Personal Time/Your Family," *Time*, October 23, 2000.

22. Beatrice Garcia, "Medical Chips Implanted," *Miami Herald*, May 11, 2002; "Applied Digital on the Brink," *Miami Herald*, February 24, 2003; Deborah Circelli, "America Meeting the 'Chipsons,'" *Palm Beach Post*, March 25, 2002.

23. Fred Vogelstein, "Cons, Don't Leave Home Without It" *US News & World Report*, July 21, 1997.

24. Davidson, "Cybercrime."

25. William Schwabe, Lois M. Davis, Brian A. Jackson, MR–1349-OSTP/NIJ, 2001, Rand and International Association of Chiefs of Police; Joe Salkowski, "Child-Care Web Cams Put Focus on Trust," *Chicago Tribune*, July 23, 2001.

26. For an excellent discussion of these issues, see Jeffery Rosen, "Why Internet Privacy Matters," *New York Times Magazine*, April 30, 2000.

27. *Roy Olmstead v. United States of America*, 277 US 438 (1928).

28. "We have a long-standing policy of cooperation with law enforcement," said AOL spokesman Rich D'Amato; Calvin Woodward, "Police on the Internet Trail; Online Data Can Be Used in Probes," *Richmond Times-Dispatch*, May 28, 1999.

29. It is worth noting that much of Foucault's work recapitulates the arguments of Weber, though in different form and with profound and unique additions. For hints of what we might call the "bio-power" of files and record keeping, see Max Weber, "Bureaucracy," in H.H. Gerth and C. Wright Mills, eds., *From Max Weber: Essays in Sociology* (New York: Oxford University Press, 1958).

30. Michel Foucault, *Discipline and Punish: The Birth of the Prison* (New York: Vintage, 1979), pp. 3, 1.

31. Michel Foucault, "Right of Death and Power over Life," from *The History of Sexuality, Vol. 1*, excerpted in Paul Rabinow, ed., *The Foucault Reader* (New York: Pantheon, 1984), p. 259.

32. Foucault, *Discipline and Punish*, p. 6.

33. Ibid., p. 138.

34. Ibid., p. 30.

35. Peter Linebaugh and Marcus Rediker, *The Many-Headed Hydra: Sailors, Slaves, Commoners, and the Hidden History of the Revolutionary Atlantic* (Boston: Beacon, 2000).

CHAPTER 2: ANTEBELLUM ID

1. Michael Sherman, *Virginia Gazette*, November 21, 1745, cited in Gerald W. Mullin, *Flight and Rebellion: Slave Resistance in Eighteenth-Century Virginia* (New York: Oxford University Press, 1972), p. 40. Recent scholarship has emphasized the complex and varied forms of slavery in the American South. Indeed, conditions ranged from the stereotypically large and despotic plantation to the small family farm where slaves lived with their "owners" in twisted approximations of familial domesticity. True order was maintained not just by terror, brainwashing, and isolation, but also by co-optation and accommodation. Nonetheless, the dominant feature of slavery was terror from above and resistance from below.

2. Orlando Patterson, *Slavery and Social Death* (Cambridge, Mass.: Harvard University Press, 1982); Erving Goffman, *Asylums: Essays on the Social Situation of Mental Patients and Other Inmates* (London: Penguin Books, 1961). More generally, see Ira Berlin, *Many Thousand Gone: The First Two Centuries of Slavery in North America* (Cambridge, Mass.: Harvard University Press, 1998).

3. *Identification* as part of surveillance and *identity* as a component in creating human subjectivity are different issues but they are nonetheless intertwined. It is difficult to fully dehumanize a people and simultaneously fully register, identify, and police them as individuals. And so it was that the planters were caught between the obfuscating effects of their worldview and the real threats posed by restive slaves. It was within this political interstice that identity/identification became a contested terrain upon which African Americans waged race/class struggle from below.

4. To understand surveillance in the old South—that is, the world of the plantation dictatorship—it is useful to imagine the world from the paranoid yet rational perspective of the planter class. In some parts of the Deep South such as the Mississippi Delta, whites, and rich whites even more so most of all, were totally surrounded and out-numbered by African American and African slaves whom they frequently abused and always exploited. Slavery provided the planter class with an aristocratic lifestyle, which could be dressed up in the patrician's mind as natural as well as noble and chivalrous. But by the 1780s that world was under attack as northern states began to restrict and outlaw slavery and European nations began cracking down on slave trading. These external pressures plus slave rebellions such as the Haitian revolution, Gabriel's plot, Denmark Veseyie's uprising, and Nat Turner's justified but brutal rampage turned the South into an armed camp, a siege society consumed by race hate, defined by everyday violence, and ever more obsessed with the ideological sanctity of the slave project. In this society, surveillance emerged as a crucial technology of power.

5. Mullin, *Flight and Rebellion*, pp. 21–22.

6. Peter Kolchin, *American Slavery: 1619–1877* (New York: Hill and Wang, 1993), p.102.

7. Mullin, *Flight and Rebellion*, p. 61.

8. Ibid.,

9. Louis Hughes, *Thirty Years a Slave, From Bondage to Freedom* (Milwaukee: South Side Printing Company, 1897), p. 20.

10. Kolchin, *American Slavery*, p. 7

11. Mullin, *Flight and Rebellion*, p. 65.

12. The free and enslaved Black men (primarily) who worked the river boats of the South were a particular source of trouble for the planter class. See Thomas C Buchanan, "Rascals on the Antebellum Mississippi: African American Steamboat Workers and the St. Louis Hanging of 1841," *Journal of Social History* 34, no. 4 (2001). Or, see Thomas C. Buchanan, "The Slave Mississippi: African-American Steamboat Workers, Networks of Resistance, and the Commercial World of the Western Rivers, 1811–1880" (Ph.D. Diss., Carnegie Mellon University, 1998).

13. Francis Fedric, *Slave Life in Virginia and Kentucky; or, Fifty Years of Slavery in the Southern States of America* (London: Wertheim, Macintosh, and Hunt, 1863), p. 29.

14. Allen Parker, *Recollections of Slavery Times* (Worcester, Mass: Chas. W. Burbank & Co., 1895).

15. Salley E. Hadden, *Slave Patrols: Law and Violence in Virginia and the Carolinas* (Cambridge, Mass.: Harvard University Press, 2001).

16. Austin Steward, *Twenty-Two Years a Slave, and Forty Years a Freeman; Embracing a Correspondence of Several Years, While President of Wilberforce Colony, London, Canada West* (Rochester, N.Y.: William Alling, 1857), p. 27.

17. Ibid., pp. 37–38.

18. Hadden, *Slave Patrols*, pp. 11–12, 15–18, 27.

19. Quoted in ibid., p. 16.

20. Slave Pass, 1852, Samuel Grove, Elliott Papers, Missouri Historical Society, St. Louis, Mo.

21. Herbert Gutman, *The Black Family in Slavery and Freedom: 1750–1890* (New York: Pantheon, 1976); Bonnie Thornton Dill, "Our Mother's Grief: Racial Ethnic Women and the Maintenance of Families," *Journal of Family History*, no. 13 (1988): pp. 415–31.

22. Quoted in Hadden, *Slave Patrols*, p. 151.

23. Henry Clay Bruce, *The New Man: Twenty-Nine Years a Slave. Twenty-Nine Years a Free Man* (York, Penn.: P. Ansadt & Sons, 1895), pp. 96–99.

24. Ibid.

25. Hadden, *Slave Patrols*, p. 112.

26. Octavia V. Rogers Albert, *The House of Bondage* (New York: Hunt & Eaton; Cincinnati: Cranston & Stowe, 1890), p. 109.

27. William J. Anderson, *Life and Narrative of William J. Anderson, Twenty-four Years a Slave* (Chicago: Daily Tribune Book and Job Printing Office, 1857), p. 20.

28. Frederick Douglass, *My Bondage and My Freedom* (New York: Miller, Orton & Mulligan, 1855), pp. 286–87.

29. Mullin, *Flight and Rebellion*, p. 128.

30. *Virginia Gazette* (Rind), Williamsburg, June 2, 1774.

31. *Virginia Gazette* (Rind), Williamsburg, December 22, 1768.

32. *Virginia Gazette* (Purdie & Dixon), Williamsburg, March 26, 1767.

33. *Virginia Gazette* (Purdie), Williamsburg, March 22, 1776.

34. *Virginia Gazette* (Purdie), Williamsburg, July 12, 1776.

35. *Virginia Gazette* (Rind), Williamsburg, April 23, 1772.

36. Janet Duitsman Cornelius, *When I Can Read My Title Clear: Literacy, Slavery, and Religion in the Antebellum South* (Columbia, S.C.: University of South Carolina Press, 1992). Former slaves left some interesting commentary on the religiosity of slave masters. Alexander Hemsley wrote: "I was in bondage in Queen Anne County, Maryland, from birth until twenty-three years of age. My name in slavery was Nathan Mead. My master was a professor of religion, and used to instruct me in a hypocritical way in the duties of religion. I used to go to church on Sunday to hear him talk, and experience the contrary on Monday" (pp. 32–33).

37. Frederick Douglass, *Life and Times of Frederick Douglass* (Hartford, Conn.: Park Publishing, 1881), pp. 70–72. Almost the same discourses can be found in Frederick Douglass, *My Bondage and My Freedom* (New York: Miller, Orton & Mulligan, 1855).

38. Mrs. Emma J. Ray, *Twice Sold, Twice Ransomed* (Chicago: Free Methodist Publishing House, 1926), p. 16.

39. Elijah P. Marrs, *Life and History of the Rev. Elijah P. Marrs* (Louisville, Ky.: Bradley & Gilbert, 1885), p. 12.

40. David R. Toussaint, *Western & Eastern Treasures*, November, 1997. There are no known genuine slave tags from any jurisdiction except Charleston and Charleston Neck.

41. John Andrew Jackson, *The Experience of a Slave in South Carolina* (London: Passmore & Alabaster, 1862), p. 25.

42. Mullin, *Flight and Rebellion*, p. 119.

43. Ibid., pp. 106, 120.

44. Ibid., p. 106.

45. Ibid., p. 118.

46. J.G. Clinkscales, *On the Old Plantation* (Band & White Publishers, 1916), pp. 18–19.

47. *Virginia Gazette* (Rind), Williamsburg, May 30, 1766.

48. *Virginia Gazette* (Rind), Williamsburg, June 15, 1769.

49. Albert, *House of Bondage*, pp. 109–10.

50. John Jones's certificate of freedom, filed in Alton, Illinois, in 1844. Also cited in Langston Hughes, Milton Meltzer, and C. Eric Lincoln, eds., *A Pictorial History of Black Americans* (New York: Crown Publishers, 1956), p. 53.

51. Rev. William Troy, *Hair-breadth Escapes from Slavery to Freedom* (Manchester: W. Bremner, 1865), p. 29.

52. For example, see mention of Mrs. H. from Caroline Co., Maryland, and her parents in Benjamin Drew, *The Refugee: A North-Side View of Slavery; or, The Narratives of Fugitive Slaves in Canada Related by Themselves, with an Account of the History and Condition of the Colored Population of Upper Canada* (Cleveland, Ohio: Jewett, Proctor and Worthington, 1856), p. 34n.

53. Quoted in Drew, *The Refugee: A North-Side View of Slavery*, p. 35.

54. Olive Gilbert and Frances W. Olive Titus, *Sojourner Truth's Narrative . . . and Book of Life* (Boston: n.p., 1875), p. 53.

55. Broadside for runaways, August 23, 1852. Broadsides—Rewards file, Missouri Historical Society, St. Louis, Mo.

56. Military Pass, September 27, 1861, Meeker, Joseph R. Meeker Papers, Missouri Historical Society, St. Louis, Mo.

57. John Torpey, *The Invention of the Passport: Surveillance, Citizenship and the State* (Cambridge: Cambridge University Press, 2000), p. 10.

58. Passport no. 992, 1826, Passports Collection, Missouri Historical Society, St. Louis, Mo.

CHAPTER 3: THE ACCUMULATION OF BODIES, PART I— IDENTIFICATION AND PHOTOGRAPHY

1. The best political analysis of the class origins of American policing is still *The Iron Fist and the Velvet Glove* (Berkeley, Calif.: Center for Research on Criminal Justice, 1975). For a discussion of the politics of public health in the nineteenth century, see Andrew R. Aisenberg, *Contagion: Disease, Government, and the "Social Question" in Nineteenth-Century France* (Stanford, Calif.: Stanford University Press, 1999).

2. Benjamin Miller, *Fat of the Land: Garbage of New York—The Last Two Hundred Years* (New York: Four Walls Eight Windows, 2000), p. 19.

3. The US started keeping records on disease only in 1878 with the passage of the US National Quarantine Act. For an examination of the politics of epidemics

after that date, see Andrew Cliff, Peter Hogget, and Matthew Smallman-Raynor, *Deciphering Global Epidemics: Analytical Approaches to the Disease Records of World Cities, 1888–1912* (New York: Cambridge University Press, 1998).

4. See chapter 7 of Anthony Giddens, *The Nation-State and Violence: Volume Two of a Contemporary Critique of Historical Materialism* (Berkeley, Calif.: University of California Press, 1987).

5. Foucault, *Discipline and Punish*, pp. 220–21.

6. "From 1828 to 1861 there were, by Grimsted's count, at least 1,218 riots," David Grimsted, *American Mobbing 1828–1861: Toward Civil War* (New York: Oxford University Press, 1998). Grimsted notes that rioting in the North was often antislavery in motivation (even when it was anti-Black), while in the South mob violence tended to be less of a challenge to the prevailing order. In fact, mob violence often involved authorities in the South and meshed well with formal law and coexisted harmoniously with racial/labor discipline on and off the plantation. On Southern mob violence, see Christopher Waldrep, *Roots of Disorder: Race and Criminal Justice in the American South,1817–1880* (Urbana, Ill.: University of Illinois Press, 1998); also Paul A. Gilje, *Rioting in America* (Bloomington, Ind.: Indiana University Press, 1996). On the class race politics of that era, see David R. Roediger, *The Wages of Whiteness: Race and the Making of the American Working Class* (London: Verso, 1991).

7. Williams, James, *Life and Adventures of James Williams, a Fugitive Slave, with a Full Description of the Underground Railroad* (San Francisco: Women's Union, 1873), p. 16.

8. Dennis C. Rousey, *Policing the Southern City: New Orleans, 1805–1889* (Baton Rouge, La.: Louisiana State University Press, 1997); Thomas Reppetto and James Lardner, *NYPD: A City and Its Police* (New York: Henry Holt, 2000); James Richardson, *The New York Police: Colonial Times to 1901* (New York: Oxford University Press, 1970); "The Police Uniform," *New York Times*, June 1854, cited in Bryan Vila and Cynthia Morris, *The Role of Police in American Society: A Documentary History* (Westport, Conn.: Greenwood, 1999).

9. On the pollution, crime, and chaos of the early industrial city, see Otto L Bettmann, *The Good Old Days— They Were Terrible!* (New York: Random House, 1974); and Luc Santé, *Low Life: Lures and Snares of Old New York* (New York: Farrar Straus Giroux, 1991).

10. Harry A. Groesbeck, Jr., *The Process and Practice of Photo-Engraving* (Garden City, N.J.: Doubleday, 1924), pp. 5–7; and Helmut Gernsheim, *Creative Photography: Aesthetic Trends, 1839–1960* (New York: Bonanza Books, 1962), pp. 235–42. The ingredients of this new art—the camera obscura and photo-sensitive chloride of silver and other light-sensitive chemicals—had been known to science for decades, and the first temporary "drawing with light" had been

achieved possibly as early as the second decade of the nineteenth century, but definitely by 1827.

11. John Tagg, *The Burden of Representation: Essays on Photographies and Histories* (Minneapolis: University of Minnesota, 1988), p. 43.

12. For good discussion of Lombroso, see Stephen Jay Gould, *The Mismeasure of Man* (New York: W.W. Norton, 1993).

13. See John Tagg, *The Burden of Representation: Essays on Photographies and Histories*, (Minneapolis: University of Minnesota Press, 1988); Alan Trachtenberg, *Reading American Photographs: Images as History, Matthew Brady to Walker Evans* (New York: Hill & Wang, 1989); Alan Sekula, "The Body and the Archive," October 39 (1986): pp. 3–64. Another early politico-demographic use of the photography was a study of African-born American slaves produced by J.T. Zealy in March 1850 at the behest of professor Louis Agassiz. A prominent Harvard scientist, Agassiz was in search of proof for the once-popular "separate creation" thesis that humankind had no common evolutionary origin and thus justified racism and slavery on "scientific" grounds. Zealy's plates were full-frontal nudes in which the subjects trapped within a matrix of dehumanizing forces stare out at the viewer with piercing rage. For Allan Trachtenberg, one of the most astute interrogators of photography, these portraits embodied the best and the worst of photography—some of the most "extraordinary daguerreotypes." As crass and brutal forms of subjugation the plates sting the eye. On the one hand the plates "subjugate" and objectify the people "captured" in the image. Yet the photos, in presenting the subjects' eyes directly (something rarely done in daguerreotypes), convey a subversive humanity brimming with hatred, humiliation, and dignity. The Zealy plates were in many ways bound up with nineteenth-century obsessions with body types that would lead to phrenology and eugenics. The use of scientific and documentary photographs to examine/construct the other through the collection and distribution of physical, mental, moral, and racial types would carry on well into the twentieth century. But photography had a more direct and practical role in the construction of surveillance when the medium served to create identification and evidence within the institution of the law.

14. Simon A. Cole, *Suspect Identities: A History of Fingerprinting and Criminal Identification* (Cambridge, Mass.: Harvard University Press, 2001), p. 16.

15. Harris B. Tuttle, Sr., "History of Photography in Law Enforcement," *Finger Print and Identification Magazine* (October 1961).

16. Thomas Byrnes, *1886 Professional Criminals of America* (New York: Chelsea House, 1969 [1886]); Reppetto and Lardner, *NYPD*, pp. 81–82; Cole, *Suspect Identities*, p. 21.

17. Chinese Mug Book, California Historical Society, North Baker Research Library, San Francisco; short biography of Delos Woodruff from *San Francisco Alta*,

December 7, 1874, Biographical Collection, California Historical Society, North Baker Research Library, San Francisco. Unfortunately, in most cities the majority of such photo records have been destroyed or lost.

18. San Francisco Historical Collection, San Francisco Public Library, Mug Book Collection, Vol. No. 5, Box No. 1, "Criminal Photography Key, Dec 22, 1871 to Nov 22, 1872," p. 1,882.

19. San Francisco Historical Collection, San Francisco Public Library, Mug Book Collection, Vol. No. 5, Box No. 1, "Criminal Photography Key, Dec 22, 1871 to Nov 22, 1872," p. 1,544.

20. Ibid., p. 1,542.

21. Of course, Max Weber made these points long ago in numerous essays; see Gerth and Mills, eds., *From Max Weber: Essays in Sociology*; Michel Foucault, *Power-Knowledge: Selected Interviews and Other Writings, 1972–1977* (New York: Pantheon 1980).

22. This description based on photo illustration in Edward Marshall, "Everybody's Fingerprint Should Be Kept on File," *New York Times Magazine*, May 26, 1912.

23. Quoted in Cole, *Suspect Identities*, p. 26.

24. Ibid., p. 27.

CHAPTER 4: THE ACCUMULATION OF BODIES, PART II— EARLY BIOMETRICS

1. It was "1,525 grammes—anaemic and shrunken by illness." See "Bertillon's Brain Weighed," *New York Times*, Feburary 16, 1914.

2. Jon Wiener, "Paris Commune Photos at the New York Gallery: An Interview with Linad Nochlin," *Radical History Review* no. 32 (1985), p. 61; Andy Grundberg, "Review of Photos by August B. Braquehais," *New York Times*, September 14, 1984.

3. Quotes from Karl Marx and V.I. Lenin, *The Civil War in France: The Paris Commune* (New York: International Publishers, 1985), pp. 106, 109; Allan Sekula, "The Body and the Archive," *October* 39 (1986): pp. 3–64.

4. Sekula, "Body and Archive"; Henry T.F. Rhodes, *Alphonse Bertillon: Father of Scientific Detection* (New York: Able-Schuman, 1956).

5. Coles, *Suspect Identities*, p. 48.

6. Along with measuring body parts like "head length" or "left foot length," the meticulous French bureaucrat created a detailed and standardized "morphological vocabulary." Thus, lips could be "pouting," "thick," or "thin," while the irises

were variegated into fifty different colors. To organize and retrieve this mass of statistical information Bertillon devised a indexing scheme that slowly refined into smaller and smaller categories, each more precise than the last. Thus all files were organized in a descending order, first by "sex" (which even then was not always such a clearly delineated category). From there the files proceeded first by "head length" (small, medium, or large); then by "head breadth"; then "middle finger length"; then "foot size," "fore arm" and "little finger." Below that level came division by eye color (all fifty) and finally by ear length. This "method of classification broke a file of 120,000 cards down into groups of around twelve cards each" Alphonse Bertillon, *Signaletic Instructions: Including the Theory and Practice of Anthropometrical Identification*, trans. R.W. McClaughrty (Chigaco, 1896), p. 20; Coles, *Suspect Identities*, p. 45.

7. "Identifying Criminals Around the World," *New York Times Magazine*, May 30, 1909; "An Interview with Emma Goldman," *New York Times Magazine*, May 30, 1909. This last article noted kindly that despite her origins there was "so little of the Russian or the Jewess about [Goldman's] looks."

8. Alphonse Bertillon, *Instructions for Taking Descriptions for the Identification of Criminals and Others by the Means of Anthropometric Indications*, trans. Gallus Muller (Chicago, 1889).

9. Berthold Laufer, *Annual Report Smithsonian Institution*, 1912; Other evidence of ancient uses of fingerprinting comes from ancient Assyrian and Babylonian clay tablets.

10. Francis Galton, *Memories of My Life* (New York: AMS Press, 1974), p. 37.

11. Coles, *Suspect Identities*.

12. Henry Faulds, "On the Skin Furrows of the Hand," *Nature*, October 28, 1880.

13. Harris Hawthorn Wilder, "Palms and Soles," *American Journal of Anatomy*, no. 1 (1902): p. 440.

14. Coles, *Suspect Identities*. In the US dactyloscopy was long left to the fiction of Mark Twain. His 1894 novella *Pudd'n Head Wilson* told the tale of a bookish lawyer solving a baby-swapping case thanks to his collection of "fingermarks."

15. Delancy M. Ellis, ed., *New York at the Worlds Louisiana Purchase Exposition: St. Louis, 1904* (Albany, N.Y.: J. B. Lyon, 1907); "Policeman's Finger Prints," *New York Times*, February 14, 1909; "Civil Service Thumb Prints," *New York Times*, December 20, 1909; "Latest Development of Thumb Prints in Detecting Crime," *New York Times*, February 7, 1909; "Extension of Finger Printing," *New York Times*, February 2, 1912.

16. Charles B. Brewer, "Finger-Prints: Their Use in the United States Navy and Else Where," *Century*, September 1909. On the Dawes Act, see Peter Matthiessen, *In the Spirit of Crazy Horse* (New York: Penguin, 1992).

17. "Fresh Paint Traps Slayer," *New York Times*, November 11, 1910; "Convicted on an Assumption," editorial, *New York Times*, November 12, 1910; *People v. Jennings*, 252 Ill. 534, 96 N.E. 1077 (1911).

18. Nikolas Rose, "Governing 'Advanced' Liberal Democracies," in Andrew Barry, Thomas Osborne, and Nikolas Rose, eds., *Foucault and Political Reason* (Chicago: University of Chicago Press, 1996), p. 44.

19. "For a World-wide Fingerprint Plan," *New York Times*, June 6, 1913; "Argentina Leads America," *New York Times*, June 7, 1913.

20. "Exaggerated a Small Grievance," *New York Times*, May 23, 1916.

21. Quote in "Finger Print Record Is No Crime Stamp," *New York Times*, June 19, 1916; also see "Take Finger Prints of Boys," *New York Times*, June 13, 1916.

22. Aaron M. Blattman, "Finger Print Records," letter, *New York Times*, June 20, 1916.

23. Quotes from "Modify Finger Printing," *New York Times*, December 30, 1916.

24. On "plant protection," see chapter 7 in Joan M. Jensen, *Army Security in America, 1775–1980* (New Haven, Ct.: Yale University Press, 1991).

25. William Preston, *Aliens and Dissenters: Federal Suppression of Radicals, 1903–1933* (Cambridge, Mass.: Harvard University Press, 1963); Robert K. Murray, *Red Scare: A Study in National Hysteria, 1919–1920* (Minneapolis: University of Minnesota Press, 1955); James Weinstein, *The Decline of Socialism in America: 1912–1925* (New Brunswick, N.J.: Rutgers University Press, 1984); "Red Ark with 250 All Ready to Sail," *New York Times*, December 20, 1919.

26. For example, regarding a "stolen child," see "Children and Their Identification," *New York Times*, September 7, 1920; this editorial is opposite a piece about an unauthorized strike.

27. "Finger-Prints for Everybody," *Literary Digest*, July 19, 1919.

28. "All Fingers Should Be Printed," *New York Times*, December 20, 1919.

29. "Law to Fingerprint Babies Proposed," *New York Times*, July 15, 1920; "Proposes National Fingerprint Bureau," *New York Times*, July 18, 1920; "A Suggestion Worth Considering," *New York Times*, July 16, 1920; "Finger-Printing All Children," *Literary Digest*, July 25, 1931.

30. "To Exchange Fingerprints," *New York Times*, August 15, 1919.

31. "Fingerprints in Business," *New York Times*, August 24, 1919; "Finger Prints Aid War on Criminals," *New York Times*, May 6, 1917.

32. Ibid.

33. "Expect Taxi Strike Settlement Today," *Cleveland Plain Dealer*, May 25, 1920.

34. "Striking Taxi Men Firm in Demands," *Cleveland Plain Dealer*, May 24, 1920; "Fingerprints Cause Strike," *New York Times*, May 24, 1920.

35. "Finger-Printing Everybody," *Literary Digest* April 20, 1929; "Hotel Workers Here Being Fingerprinted," *New York Times*, January 15, 1936. On the attempt to register prints in public schools, see "Fingerprinting in Schools," letter to the editor, *New York Times*, November 26, 1936.

36. "J.E. Hoover Talks to DAR on Crime," *New York Times*, April 24, 1936; "Boy Scouts Vote to File Fingerprints of 1,000,000 in Department of Justice," *New York Times*, May 23, 1936; Vera Connolly, "Uncle Sam Wants Your Mark," *Good Housekeeping*, December 1935; Grace Phelps, "Has Your Child Been Fingerprinted?" *Parents Magazine*, February 1936; Sterling Gleason, "Protect Your Family by Recording Their Fingerprints," *Popular Science Monthly*, October 1932; "Finger-Prints to Protect Checks from Forgery," *Literary Digest*, May 13, 1933.

37. "Fingerprints of Fascism," *New Republic*, June 10, 1936; *Thumbs Down! The Fingerprint Menace to Civil Liberties* (New York: American Civil Liberties Union, 1938).

38. "Fingerprints of Fascism," p. 118.

39. *Why Fingerprinting?* (Berkeley, Calif.: Citizens' Committee on Universal Registration, 1937), p. 11.

40. Cited in *Thumbs Down!* p. 11.

41. Ibid., p. 18.

42. "Fingerprints of Fascism," p. 118.

CHAPTER 5: CRUEL GAM SAAN

1. For rates of entry, see Lucy E. Salyer, *Laws Harsh as Tigers: Chinese Immigrants and the Shaping of Modern Immigration Law* (Chapel Hill, N.C.: University of North Carolina Press, 1995), p. 67; Him Mark Lai, Genny Lim, and Judy Yung, *Island: Poetry and History of Chinese Immigrants on Angel Island, 1910–1940* (San Francisco: Hoc Doi, Chinese Cultural Foundation, 1980, 1986), p. 8. These numbers are all the more impressive if one considers the intensive system of identification, surveillance, and policing established by the United States Customs Bureau and then, after 1903, by the Labor Department's Bureau of Immigration.

2. Statement from R.T. Fergusson, November 17, 1917, National Archives Pacific Sierra Region, Record Group 85, INS, Densmore Investigation, Box 2, Folder 2; Case of Tom Quon Poy and Tom Quon Sook (time line) [1917]; National Archives Pacific Sierra Region, Record Group 85, INS, Densmore Investigation, Box 2, Folder 3.

3. Quoted in Ronald Takaki, *Strangers from a Different Shore: A History of Asian Americans* (Boston: Little, Brown 1989), p. 80.

4. Carry McWilliams, *Factories in the Fields* (Berkeley, Calif.: University of California Press, 1999); Takaki, ibid., Alexander Saxton, *The Indispensable Enemy: Labor and the Anti-Chinese Movement in California* (Berkeley, Calif.: University of California Press, 1971).

5. Andrew Gyory, *Closing the Gate: Race, Politics, and the Chinese Exclusion Act* (Chapel Hill, N.C.: University of North Carolina Press, 1998).

6. See Philip S. Foner, *The Great Labor Uprising of 1877* (New York: Pathfinder, 1978).

7. Gyory, *Closing the Gate*, pp. 70–71.

8. *Tenth Census of the United States*, I, 382, 399.

9. Interestingly, no photographs were required at first on either Chinese- or US-issued certificates; instead, identification was determined only by a rough physical description and the traveler's signature. As early as 1884, federal Judge Hoffman, one of four who heard Chinese immigration cases, suggested using photo IDs, but that technological innovation wasn't adopted until the turn of the century. So too in New York City was photography dismissed because of obfuscating optics of racism: "If Chinamen cannot be told apart in the flesh still less can they be distinguished by photographs," wrote the *New York Times*. "The Caucasian mind has been unable to grapple successfully with the problem of making distinctions without differences"; see "The Similarity of Chinamen," *New York Times*, August 26, 1885. For the exact language, see Chinese Restriction Act, May 6, 1882, United States Statute 58, Sec. 4. The full section is as follows: SEC. 4. That for the purpose of properly identifying Chinese laborers who were in the United States on the seventeenth day of November, eighteen hundred and eighty, or who shall have come into the same before the expiration of ninety days next after the passage of this act, and in order to furnish them with the proper evidence of their right to go from and come to the United States of their free will and accord, as provided by the treaty between the United States and China dated November seventeenth, eighteen hundred and eighty, the collector of customs of the district from which any such Chinese laborer shall depart from the United States shall, in person or by deputy, go on board each vessel having on board any such Chinese laborer and cleared or about to sail from his district for a foreign port, and on such vessel make a list of all such Chinese laborers, which shall be entered in registry-books to be kept for that purpose, in which shall be stated the name, age, occupation, last place of residence, physical marks or peculiarities, and all facts necessary for the identification of each of such Chinese laborers, which books shall be safely kept in the custom-house; and every such Chinese laborer so departing from the United States shall be entitled to, and shall receive, free of any charge or cost upon application therefor, from the collector or his deputy, at the time such list is taken, a certificate, signed by the collector or his deputy and attested by his seal of

office, in such form as the Secretary of the Treasury shall prescribe, which certificate shall contain a statement of the name, age, occupation, last place of residence, personal description, and fact of identification of the Chinese laborer to whom the certificate is issued, corresponding with the said list and registry in all particulars. In case any Chinese laborer after having received such certificate shall leave such vessel before her departure he shall deliver his certificate to the master of the vessel, and if such Chinese laborer shall fail to return to such vessel before her departure from port the certificate shall be delivered by the master to the collector of customs for cancellation. The certificate herein provided for shall entitle the Chinese laborer to whom the same is issued to return to and re-enter the United States upon producing and delivering the same to the collector of customs of the district at which such Chinese laborer shall seek to re-enter; and upon delivery of such certificate by such Chinese laborer to the collector of customs at the time of re-entry in the United States, said collector shall cause the same to be filed in the custom house and duly canceled.

10. *The City of New York v. Miln*, 36 US (11 Pet.) 102 (1837).

11. If a Chinese person attempted to disembark without the proper documentation or if the collector thought the person's documents were bogus, the traveler could be detained until a departing ship could take him or her back to China. For the first thirty years these captives were housed at the expense of the shipping firms; in San Francisco detainees were locked in a shed on the dock of the Pacific Mail Steamship Company. By all accounts this was a grim place—dark, cold and unsanitary. "Here you are cramped and doomed never to stretch," wrote one anonymous deportee. A government office described the "accommodations" as a "fire trap." As for exercise, the prisoners were allowed to stand on an outdoor stairwell for fifteen minutes every several days and breathe fresh air; otherwise they were locked in the dark. Quoted in Salyer, p. 63.

12. Hudson N. Janisch, "The Chinese, the Courts, and the Constitution: A Study of the Legal Issues Raised by Chinese Immigration, 1850–1902," J.S.D. diss., University of Chicago Law School, 1971, pp. 495–96.

13. "Statement of Robert T. Fergusson," October 9, 1917, Record Group 85, INS, Densmore, Box 2, Folder 2.

14. "Partnership Book in Chinese, Captured by Customs Inspectors on the Premises of the Fictitious Firm Operating under the Name of Quong Fat Cheung, at No. 30 Waverly Place, San Francisco, Cal." 1914, RG 85, cited in Angel Island, Part II, National Archives and Records Administration web page.

15. Correspondence, "Wong Ock Gar to Wong Som Gar," October 5, 1914, Record Group 85, INS, Densmore: Coaching letters, Box 1, Folder 7.

16. Correspondence, "Wong Bing Foon to Wong Som Gar," October 6, 1914, Record Group 85, INS, Densmore: Coaching letters, Box 1, Folder 7.

17. Translation of Chinese letter intended for Tom Quon Sook and Tom Quon Poy, May 15, 1917 (file no. 54184/138// 10126/1076), RG 85, INS, Box 1, Folder 5.

18. "Statement of Robert T. Fergusson," October 9, 1917, Record Group 85, INS, Densmore, Box 2, Folder 2.

19. "Statement of Richard Rankin," April 18, 1917, Record Group 85, INS, Densmore, Box 4, Folder 2.

20. "Statement Made by Lee Tin Yat," April 20, 1917, Record Group 85, INS, Densmore, Box 2, Folder 3: p. 2.

21. "Statement of Robert T. Fergusson," October 9, 1917, Record Group 85, INS, Densmore, Box 2, Folder 2.

22. "Statement of Robert T. Fergusson," October 9, 1917, Record Group 85, INS, Densmore, Box 2, Folder 2.

23. "Statement of Fong Get," September 12, 1917, Record Group 85, INS, Densmore, Box 4, Folder 4.

24. "Memorandum for the Commissioner," June 11, 1918, Record Group 85, INS, Densmore: Coaching Letters, Box 1, Folder 5.

25. "Exhibit 10: Yip Wo's Testimony Made in CR2 (1913)" 1913, Record Group 85, INS, Densmore: Coaching Letters, Box 1, Folder 6.

26. "'O' exhibit 10, translated by H.K. Tang," December 8, 1924; Record Group 85, INS, Densmore: Coaching Letters, Box 1, Folder 6.

27. "My father wrote . . ." Coaching Note, translated by H.K. Tang," May 30, 1918; Record Group 85, INS, Densmore: Coaching Letters, Box 1, Folder 5.

28. "Statement of Richard Rankin," April 18, 1917, Record Group 85, INS, Densmore, Box 4, Folder 2.

29. "Administrative History," no date, Record Group 85, INS, Densmore, Box 1, Folder 1; "Second Conspiracy," no date, no name, Record Group 85, INS, Densmore, Box 3, Folder 5. On the postinvestigation riot, see Lai, Lim, and Yung, *Island*, p. 19.

30. Cited in Salyer, *Laws Harsh as Tigers.*

31. Salyer, *Laws Harsh as Tigers*, p. 47; "Bars Are Down," *San Francisco Call*, April 9, 1893.

32. "It May Lead to War," *San Francisco Call*, Sept 20, 1892; "A Pagan Problem," *San Francisco Call*, March 28, 1893.

33. *Fong Yue Ting v. the United States*, 149 U.S 698, 713 (1893); "Now the Chinese Must Go," *San Francisco Call*, May 16, 1893.

34. See Stanford M. Lyman, "Conflict and the Web of Group Affiliation in San Francisco's Chinatown, 1850–1910," *Pacific Historical Review*, no. 43 (November 1974); Richard Dillon, *The Hatchet Men: The Story of the Tong Wars in San*

Francisco's Chinatown (New York: Coward-McCann, 1962); C.Y. Lee, *Days of the Tong Wars: California 1847–1896* (New York: Ballantine Books, 1974).

35. Yong Chen, *Chinese San Francisco, 1850–1943: A Trans-Pacific Community* (Stanford, Calif.: Stanford University Press, 2000), p. 152.

36. Wong Kai Kah, "A Menace to America's Oriental Trade," *North American Review* 178, no. 568 (March 1904): pp. 414–24.

37. Quoted in Chen, *Chinese San Francisco*, p. 153.

38. US Code Sec. 298 Title 8, Chapter 7.

CHAPTER 6: OF ONES AND ZEROS

1. The point here is that the state, even if viewed as necessary, is an institution based on the monopolization of the legitimate use of violence. From this fact can flow an almost natural, teleological drive toward despotism.

2. I am deeply indebted to the excellent work of David Lyon. His book is undoubtedly the best yet on computer surveillance and my analysis below extends from his work. See David Lyon, *The Electronic Eye: The Rise of Surveillance Society* (Minneapolis: University of Minnesota University Press, 1994).

3. Mike Davis, *City of Quartz: Excavating the Future in Los Angeles* (London: Verso, 1990).

4. Two of these mechanical calculators are displayed in the *Muséee du Ranquet* (Clermont-Ferrand).

5. Quoted in, Jerry M Rosenberg, *The Death of Privacy: Do Governments and Industrial Computers Threaten Our Personal Freedom?* (New York: Random House, 1969), p. 82.

6. Charles Babbage, cited in Karl Marx, *Capital*, Vol. 1 (London: Penguin, 1976), p. 469.

7. Nick Dyer-Witheford, *Cyber-Marx: Cycles and Circuits of Struggle in High-Technology Capitalism* (Champaign, Ill.: University of Illinois Press: Chicago, 1999), p. 2; Simon Shaffer, "Babbage's Intelligence: Calculating Engines and the Factory System," *Critical Inquiry* 21 (1994): pp. 203–27.

8. There is no better source on these matters than chapter 15, section 5 in Karl Marx, *Capital*, Vol. 1 (London: Penguin, 1976).

9. Robert Sobel, *IBM: Colossus in Transition* (New York: Bantam Books, 1983), pp. 14–16; Geoffrey Austrian, *Herman Hollerith: Forgotten Giant of Information Processing* (New York: Columbia University Press, 1982). Conductors tell me that a different, more informal version of the same system still exists today,

but now it uses random number patterns on tickets rather than actual descriptions.

10. Austrian, *Herman Hollerith*, p. 58.

11. Anthony Giddens, *The Nation-State and Violence: Volume Two of a Contemporary Critique of Historical Materialism* (Berkeley, Calif.: University of California Press, 1987).

12. Edwin Black, *IBM and the Holocaust: The Strategic Alliance Between Nazi Germany and America's Most Powerful Corporation* (New York: Crown Publishers: 2001), p. 55.

13. "Similarly, census records created for general statistical purposes were used during World War II to round up innocent Japanese Americans and to place them in internment camps." See congressional testimony of Barry Steinhardt, associate director, American Civil Liberties Union, National Commission on the Future of DNA Evidence, Monday, March 1, 1999.

14. Black, *IBM and the Holocaust*, p. 104.

15. Margaret Carlson, "The Case for a National ID Card: Big Brother Already Knows Where You Live; Why Not Let Him Make You Safer?" *Time Magazine*, January 21, 2002; Alan M Dershowitz, "Why Fear National ID Cards?" *New York Times*, October 13, 2001.

16. When the Social Security Act (P.L. 74–271) was enacted, it did not expressly mention the use of SSNs, but it authorized the creation of some type of record-keeping scheme. Treasury Decision 4704, a Treasury regulation enacted in 1936, required the issuance of an account number to each employee covered by the Social Security program. The Social Security Board considered various numbering systems and ways (such as metal tags, etc.) by which employees could indicate that they had been issued a number (*New York Times*, November 1, 1936).

17. Robert Ellis Smith, "Social Security Numbers: Uses and Abuses," *Privacy Journal* (2001), p. 2.

18. Ibid.

19. Social Security Administration, "Privacy and Customer Service in the Electronic Age" (Washington, D.C.: November 1997).

20. Arthur J. Altmeyer, *The Formative Years in Social Security* (Madison, Wis.: University of Wisconsin Press, 1966), p. 70.

21. Ibid., pp. 68–71.

22. Social Security Administration, "Privacy and Customer Service in the Electronic Age"; Alan F. Westin and Michael A. Baker, *Databanks in a Free Society: Computers, Record-Keeping and Privacy* (New York: Quadrangle, 1972), pp. 33–34.

23. "Invasion of Privacy: Our Right to Be Left Alone Has Disappeared, Bit by Bit in Little Brotherly Steps," *Time*, August 25, 1997.

24. Robert N. Anthony and Marian V. Sears, "Who's That," *Harvard Business Review*, May 1961, p. 66.

25. Ibid., p. 70.

26. Public Law 87–397, 26 US Code 6109.

27. Sobel, p. 159.

28. US Department of Health, Education and Welfare, "Records, Computers and the Rights of Citizens," Report of the Secretary's Advisory Committee on Automated Personal Data Systems, (Washington, D.C.: US Government Printing Office, 1973). This report also created the concept of "fair information practices" regarding use of personal information. As one expert explained it, "Collecting information for one purpose (Social Security) and using it for another (government sector matching, private sector locator services, etc.) without the individual data subject's consent violates those Fair Information Practices." See Edmund Mierzwinski, "Misuse of Social Security Numbers," congressional testimony by Federal Document Clearing House, Tuesday, May 22, 2001; Westin and Baker, *Databanks*, p. 37.

CHAPTER 7: SURVEILLANCE AND THE SINEWS OF COMMERCE

1. Unknown nineteenth-century author quoted in Roy A. Foulke, *The Sinews of American Commerce* (Brooklyn, N.Y.: Dunn & Bradstreet Inc., 1941), p. 287.

2. Ibid., pp. 288–89; *Dun & Bradstreet: A Company History* (n.p.: n.d.).

3. Ohio, Vol. 52, p. 489, R.G. Dun & Co. Collection, Baker Library, Harvard Business School.

4. Vermont, Vol. 6., p. 276j, R.G. Dun & Co. Collection, Baker Library, Harvard Business School.

5. Ohio, Vol. 52., p. 472, R.G. Dun & Co. Collection, Baker Library, Harvard Business School.

6. John B. Rule, *Private Lives, Public Surveillance: Social Control in the Age of Computers* (New York: Schocken Books, 1974), p. 180.

7. Ibid.

8. Ibid.; Lewis Mandell, *The Credit Card Industry: A History* (New York: Twayne Publishers, 1990); Robert D. Manning, *Credit Card Nation: The Consequences of America's Addiction to Credit* (New York: Basic Books, 2001); Matty Simmons, *The Credit Card Catastrophe: The 20th-Century Phenomenon That Changed the World* (Fort Lee, N.J.: Barricade Books, 1995).

9. Alan Axelrod, and Charles Phillips, *What Everyone Should Know about the 20th Century: 200 Events That Shaped the World* (Avon, Mass.: Adams Media Corporation, 1995), p. 182.

10. "The History of the Bankcard Industry," (Philadelphia: Merchant Services, n.d.); Jerry M. Rosenberg, *The Death of Privacy* (New York: Random House, 1969), p. 45.

11. David Evans and Richard Schmalensee, *Paying with Plastic: The Digital Revolution in Buying and Borrowing* (Cambridge, Mass.: MIT Press, 1999), p. 73.

12. Pete Earley, "Government to Share Deadbeat List with Private Credit-Rating Bureaus," *Washington Post*, April 25, 1984.

13. Evans and Schmalensee, *Paying with Plastic*, p. 64.

14. "Visa Computer Pinpoints Use of Lost, Stolen Cards," *Wall Street Journal*, August 3, 1984; Richard A. Shaffer, "Firms Ready to Escalate War on Counterfeit Credit Cards," *Wall Street Journal*, September 14, 1984.

15. Alison Taylor, "US Household Wealth Shrinks by 4.5%" *World Markets Research Centre Daily Analysis*, December 6, 2002.

16. Brad Reagan "Mortgage Debt Spurs Bankruptcies," *Wall Street Journal*, November 6, 2002; "Markets Personal Bankruptcy Filings at Record Pace," *Los Angeles Times*, November 26, 2002.

17. "American Express Moves Toward Interstate Banking," Dow Jones News Service, November 25, 1980; Alan F. Westin and Michael A. Baker, *Databanks in a Free Society: Computers, Record-Keeping and Privacy* (New York: Quadrangle, 1972), p. 303.

18. "Bank Group Forms Nationwide Automated Teller Network," Dow Jones News Service, April 7, 1982.

19. "IntelliStripe 50 Manual-Insertion Reader Added to Mag-Tek's Card Reader Options," *Business Wire*, May 19, 1997.

20. "Service Industries Following Banks' Lead in Automation," Dow Jones News Service, July 21, 1983; Rudolph A. Pyatt Jr., "MOST, Network Exchange Create Region's Largest ATM System," *Washington Post*, March 26, 1984.

21. "Prepayment Cards Management Report," *Business and Management Reports*, December 31, 1991.

22. "2nd Suspect Arrested in NW Killings," *Washington Post*, June 26, 1984.

23. Rudolph A. Pyatt Jr., "MOST, Network Exchange Create Region's Largest ATM System.," *Washington Post*, March 26, 1984.

24. Michele Foucault, *Power/Knowledge: Selected Interviews and Other Writings, 1972–1977* (New York: Pantheon, 1980), p. 73.

25. James Woundhuysen, "Chequelless, Cashless, Clueless in the Smart Card Society," *Management Today*, November 1, 1990.

26. David Harvey, *The Condition of Postmodernity* (Oxford: Blackwell, 1989).

27. "Hand-Held Scanners Invade Industrial Market," Dow Jones News Service, April 4, 1983.

28. Linda M. Watkins, "Bar Codes Are Black-and-White Stripes and Soon They Will Be Read All Over," *Wall Street Journal*, January 8, 1985 ; "Bar Codes: Reading between the Lines" *Smithsonian* 29, no. 11 (February 1999); Ben Nelson, *Punched Cards to Bar Codes: A Complete History of Automated Data Collection* (Peterborough, N.H.: Helmers Publishing, 1997).

29. Mark Vernon, "Network: Smart Cards Get Smarter," *Independent*, February 18, 1997.

30. Lorna Doubet, "Built-in Intelligence: Impact of Smart Cards Debated," *San Francisco Chronicle*, September 24, 1987.

31. Ibid.

32. William Shaw, "If You Stepped into the Future, It Would Look Like Finland," *The Independent* (London), July 9, 2000.

33. Jeff Howe, "The Data Game: P-Track Was Only the Beginning," *Village Voice*, November 12, 1996.

34. Keely Harrison, "The Naked Ape: Electronic Surveillance of Consumer's Choices," *Super Marketing*, March 24, 1995.

35. Personal communication to author, May 2002.

36. This from an Electronic Privacy Information Center (EPIC) study sited in Galen Svanas, "Our Own Business," *Brandweek*, July 14, 1997.

37. Noel C. Paul, "How Marketers See You: They Go High Tech to Get Inside Your head," *Christian Science Monitor*, December 11, 2000; "The Internet Wants Your Personal Info: What's in It for You?" *Business Week*, April 5, 1999.

38. Judge Buchwald, "Court Decisions Second Judicial Department U.S. District Court: S.D.N.Y." *New York Law Journal* 225, no. 63 (April 3, 2001).

39. Noel C. Paul, "How Marketers See You," *Christian Science Monitor*, December 11, 2000.

40. "NetZero's CyberTarget Division Announces Strategic Alliance with NFO Worldwide and InsightExpress," *Business Wire*, December 6, 2000.

41. Peter Kruger, "Identify Yourself," *Communications International*, October 1, 1996; Steve Higgins, "Computers & Technology Web Interests Consider Rules on Collecting Surfer Profiles," *Investor's Business Daily*, November 19, 1996.

42. Dianne Klein, "You Are Where You Live," *Los Angeles Times*, April 16, 1989; Michael J. Weiss, *The Clustering of America* (New York: Tilden Press Book/Harper & Row, 1988).

43. http://cluster1.claritas.com/claritas/Default.jsp?main=3&submenu=seg&subcat=segprizm#groupU3. (Accessed in 2003).

44. John Goss, "'We Know Who You Are and We Know Where You Live': The Instrumental Rationality of Geodemographic Systems," *Economic Geography* 71, no. 2 (April 1, 1995).

45. L. Scott Tillett, "Software Helps Insurers Analyze Data," *Internet Week*, January 8, 2001.

46. Liz Kowalczyk, "With Costs Up, HMOS HMOs to Monitor Patients Blue Cross-Blue Shield, Tufts OK Claim Analysis," *Boston Globe*, April 8, 2001; "Managed Care Monitor Disease Management: Employers Want More 'Managed' Care," *American Health Line* 6, no. 9 (April 10, 2001); Diane E. Lewis, "Devices Keep Close Watch on Workplace," *Boston Globe*, June 24, 2001.

47. Nancy Pekala, "High-Tech, High-Touch Screening Sifts Out Quality Applicants," *Journal of Property Management* 66, no. 2 (March 1, 2001).

48. Jacqueline Emigh, "Conquering the Mountain of Data," *Smart Partner/ZDWire* May 14, 2001; Walter Hatch, "When Privacy Goes Public," *Seattle Times*, February 8, 1987.

49. Ibid.

50. Robert O'Harrow Jr., "Data Firms Getting Too Personal?" *Washington Post*, March 8, 1998.

CHAPTER 8: CAMERA LAND

1. Spencer S. Hsu, "D.C. Forms Network of Surveillance, Police Video Links Raise Rights Issues," *Washington Post*, February 17, 2002; Spencer S. Hsu, "D.C. Police Cameras Raise Privacy Issues," *Washington Post*, February 15, 2002; Jess Bravin, "Washington Police to Play 'I Spy' Camera Network Will Monitor People All over District; Civil Libertarians Worry," *Wall Street Journal*, February 13, 2002; Polly Hanson, deputy chief of the D.C. Metro Police, phone interview, March 18, 2002; Kevin Morrison, Communications Director for the MPD, phone interview, March 14, 2002; William Schwabe, Lois M. Davis, and Brian A. Jackson, MR–1349-OSTP/NIJ, 2001 Rand and International Association of Chiefs of Police.

2. Interviews and conversations with former anti-CCTV and former prisoner activist Tom Cahill, 1998. One of the founders of Stop Prison Rape, activist Tom Cahill was jailed and brutally assaulted for smashing the CCTV in a San Antonio, Texas, woodworking factory's rest rooms.

3. Cahill, interview; Oscar Newman, *Defensible Space* (New York: Macmillan, 1972); Oscar Newman, *Architectural Design for Crime Prevention* (Washington, D.C.: Department of Justice, 1973).

4. For a detailed discussion of aesthetics and security and redevelopment, see Neil Smith, *The New Urban Frontier: Gentrification and the Revanchist City* (New York: Routledge, 1996).

5. Caroline Wilson, "Securing America's New Town Centers," *Security Management* (publication of the American Society for Industrial Security), June 1, 1992.

6. Ann Longmore-Etheridge, "Bagging Profits Instead of Thieves," *Security Management* 45, no. 10 (October 1, 2001).

7. Kelly Norton, "Cashing in on CCTV Technology," *Security Management*, March 1, 1992.

8. Wendy Cole, "Police to Monitor Bus Station via TV," *The Record* (Northern New Jersey), March 20, 1985.

9. Johnny Barnes, executive director of the ACLU of Washington, D.C., phone interview, March 14, 2002; Jay Stanley and Barry Steinhardt, "Drawing a Blank: The Failure of Facial Recognition Technology in Tampa, Florida," ACLU Special Report, January 3, 2002. This same report documents the technical failures of the FaceIt technology in Tampa; such shortcomings may soon be resolved.

10. Mara Verheyden-Hilliard, executive director, Project on Civil Justice, phone interview, March 14, 2002.

11. Mark Liiv, Whispered Media, phone interview, March 19, 2002.

12. Steven Martin, spokesperson for SBR production, phone interview, March 19, 2002.

13. Dean Starkman and Dagmar Aalund, "High-Tech Security Gadgets Prove Major Selling Point," *Wall Street Journal Europe*, August 14, 1998.

14. Nicholas Watt, "Police Put 'Ring of Steel' Round City to Halt Bombers," *Times* (London), July 2, 1993.

15. "Bombs Strike Three Areas of London; IRA Is Suspected in Fatal Explosion," *Washington Post*, April 25, 1993; Tim Rayment, John Davison, and James Dalrymple, "IRA Devastates Heart of the City," *Times* (London), April 25, 1993.

16. "Peeping 'Bobbies' Creating U.K. Opportunities for Surveillance Equipment Vendors," *Security Technology News*, August 26, 1994; "Home Office—Winners Switch on CCTV to Stamp Out Crime," *M2 Presswire*, April 4, 1995.

17. Clive Norris and Gary Armstrong, "CCTV and the Social Structure of Surveillance," *Crime Prevention Studies* 10, pp. 157–78, 168.

18. William Schwabe, Lois M. Davis, and Brian A. Jackson, *Challenges and Choices for Crime-Fighting Technology: Federal Support of State and Local Law Enforcement* (Santa Monica, Calif.: RAND, 2001) p. 15; Laura J. Nichols "Cutting Edge of Technology," IACP Executive Brief, International Association of Chiefs of Police, in collaboration with the National Institute of Justice, Office of Science & Technology, March 2001; Bill Zalud, "CCTV Deters Lawsuits, Reduces Officers' Court Time," *Security*, October 1, 2001.

19. "High-Tech Security on Tampa Streets," Associated Press, July 1, 2001; Amy Herdy, "Eye on Ybor: Police Cameras Go Spy-Tech," *St. Petersburg (Fla.)*

Times, June 30, 2001; Interestingly, it is the right wing that leads opposition to surveillance; see David McGuire, "Rep. Armey Blasts Tampa over Face-Recognition System," *Newsbytes News Network*, July 2, 2001. S.A. Mathieson, "Online: In Sight of the Law," *Guardian* (London), March 1, 2001; "FaceIt creates a unique 'faceprint' by analyzing facial structure. While the system measures about 80 different points, it can make a positive identification based on as few as 14"; Andy Sullivan, "U.S. Urged to Regulate Face-Scan Technology Security Industry Reacts to Backlash," *San Diego Union-Tribune*, August 9, 2001.

20. Carol Power, "Big Brother Is Watching and Analyzing," *Irish Times*, September 7, 2001.

21. William Schwabe, Lois M. Davis, and Brian A. Jackson, *Challenges and Choices for Crime-Fighting Technology: Federal Support of State and Local Law Enforcement* (Santa Monica, Calif.: RAND, 2001) p.15.

22. "SR's Offensive Spy System for Downtown," *Santa Rosa (Calif.) Press-Democrat*, October 3, 1996; Christy Scattarella, "Here's Looking at You—If You're Doing Drugs," *Seattle Times*, July 22, 1993; J.P. Ellery, "Warren's Watching You, Residents Warned of TV Surveillance in Parks," *Worcester (Mass.) Telegram & Gazette*, September 12, 1995; Agnes Blum, "Citizen Surveillance—You're Being Watched: Technology Helps Big Brother Keep a Constant Eye on the Public," *Norfolk (Va.) Virginian-Pilot/Ledger-Star*, August 27, 2001.

23. Liz Kay, "Los Angeles Camera Becomes New Weapon in War on Graffiti Vandalism," *Los Angeles Times*, December 24, 2001.

24. Richard Stehr, "Intelligent Vehicle Highway Systems Director of Planning, Development, and Traffic, Metro Division, Minnesota Department of Transportation," congressional testimony before the Subcommittee on Investigations and Oversight Committee on Public Works and Transportation, July 21, 1994.

25. "TV Surveillance of Freeway to Expand," *Seattle Times*, April 9, 1986; Jim O'Brien "CCTV Watches the World Go By," *Security Management*, June 1, 1992; Stehr, testimony.

26. Brian DeBose, "Millions Spent to Develop Cameras; Budgets on Rise for Surveillance," *Washington Times*, April 17, 2002.

27. "Use of Cameras to Deter Drugs Termed Success," *Houston Chronicle*, April 24, 1985.

28. Courtenay Thompson, "Looking for Trouble," *Portland Oregonian*, July 15, 1994.

29. Tim Doulin, "Cameras to Watch Students," *Columbus Dispatch*, September 3, 1994.

30. Susan Baldrige, "Cameras, 2-Way Mirrors, Guards and Your Kids; Super-Tight Security Now Top Priority in Local Schools," *Lancaster (Pa.) New Era*, January 25, 2002.

31. Jennifer Bjorhus, "Cameras on Campus: Big Brother at School?" *Seattle Times*, January 14, 1995.

32. Barbara Dority, "A Brave New World—or a Technological Nightmare? Big Brother Is Watching," *The Humanist* 61, no. 3 (May 1, 2001)..

33. Katie Hafner, "Where the Hall Monitor Is a Webcam," *New York Times*, February 27, 2003.

34. Kim Brooks, Vincent Shiraldi, and Jason Ziedenberg, "School House Hype: Two Years Later," (Washington, D.C.: Justice Policy Institute/Children's Law Center, 2002).

35. Jason Williams, "Officials: Cameras Help Schools," *Greensboro (N.C.) News & Record*, October 24, 1994; "School Leaders Will Endorse Use of Surveillance Cameras," *Greensboro (N.C.) News & Record*, October 24, 1994.

36. "Cameras to Be Installed at School Receiving Threats," Associated Press, September 12, 2001.

37. David Bradvica, "Skaters Run into Speed Bump," *Riverside (Calif.) Press-Enterprise*, May 31, 1995.

38. Kristina Marlow, "Sit Down, Be Quiet: The Camera Is Watching," *Chicago Tribune*, December 24, 1994.

39. Roger Stuart, "The Right to Remain Unsnooped Upon," *Pittsburgh Post-Gazette*, January 8, 1995.

CHAPTER 9: THE DIGITAL LEASH

1. Mark Timms, "The Pros and Cons of Proximity," *Security Management*, November 1, 1990.

2. "Ramtron Forms RF Identification Systems Joint Venture," *Business Wire*, October 28, 1991.

3. "UNOVA Signs Letter of Intent to Buy Amtech Corporation's Transportation Systems Group," *Business Wire*, April 9, 1998.

4. "Dallas Will Test a Windshield Scanner System for Road Tolls," *Chicago Sun-Times*, February 14, 1988; "Ration Roads? Or Charge for Them?" *Washington Post*, February 21, 1988; "Basix Corp. Units Get Orders," *Wall Street Journal*, May 27, 1986.

5. "Ration Roads?"; Andrew Herrmann "Tollway Scanners May Mean No Small Change for Drivers," *Chicago Sun-Times*, February 29, 1988.

6. Nancy J. Perry, "Good News About Infrastructure," *Fortune*, April 10, 1989; Janet Pearson, "'Toll Tags' Eyed for Creek 'Pike Cars," *Tulsa (Okla.) World*, April 20, 1989; William Trombley, "Congestion Fuels a Renaissance:

New Toll Roads May Fill Gap in Highway Finances," *Los Angeles Times*, April 17, 1988.

7. "Lockheed and AT&T Form Development and Marketing Alliance for Intelligent Transportation Systems," PR Newswire, April 13, 1992; John P. Keith, "High Tech Can Reduce Traffic," *Newsday*, February 23, 1987; John Lancaster, "Va. to Inaugurate Flash Passes on Dulles Toll Road," *Washington Post*, September 18, 1987.

8. Marjorie Anders, "Authorities to Experiment with Radio Wave Toll Collection," Associated Press, November 15, 1988.

9. Joseph D. McCaffery, "Delaware River Agency Joins in Effort to Devise Automatic Toll Collection ," *Newark (N.J.) Star-Ledger*, November 25, 1994.

10. Allan Johnson, "Intelligent Vehicle Highway System," Congressional Testimony, Wednesday, June 29, 1994.

11. Thomas C. Palmer, "Cooperation to Begin Sunday Between Fastlane, E-ZPass," *Boston Globe*, November 17, 1999; Elizabeth Doran, "E-ZPass: Filling Up the Fast Lane," *Syracuse (N.Y.) Post-Standard*, September 22, 1998; "Road Charging System That Takes the Toll out of Driving," *Irish Times*, June 22, 2001.

12. Doug Most, "E-ZPass Privacy Rules Proposed Bill Would Prevent Access to Data," *The Record* (Northern New Jersey), January 30, 1998.

13. Thomas C. Palmer Jr., "State Cracks Down on Fast Lane Violators Threatens to Withhold Vehicle Registrations," *Boston Globe*, February 14, 2001; Thomas C. Palmer Jr., "Complaints About Fast Lane Mistakes Are Pilling Up," *Boston Globe*, June 10, 2001; Joe Malinconico, "State Slices E-ZPass Truck Surveillance," *Newark (N.J.) Star-Ledger*, August 1, 2000.

14. Cerisse Anderson, "'E-ZPass' Records Held Subject to Police Subpoena," *New York Law Journal* 218, no. 3 (July 3, 1997). Interestingly, the court decisions portrayed the Triborough Bridge and Tunnel Authority's resistance to the police (not court) subpoena as "somewhat nebulous" because the TBAT "cited no cases or statutes to support its position." In short, the E-ZPass authorities showed little inclination to protect their customers' privacy. See "Court Decisions: Police Commissioner, *City of New York v. Triborough Bridge and Tunnel Authority*," *New York Law Journal* 218, no. 4 (July 7, 1997); Ross Kerber, "MTA Gives Court Toll-Use Data Spurs Privacy Fears About Fast Lane," *Boston Globe*, August 13, 2001; Todd Wallack, "They Know Where You've Been," *San Francisco Chronicle*, February 12, 2001.

15. Simson Garfinkel, "Someday Smart Roads May Watch Us Too Closely," *Cleveland Plain Dealer*, May 8, 1995; Chet Bridger, "Nowhere to Hide Now: Computer Monitoring of Your Daily Life Is Making Privacy a Thing of the Past," *Buffalo News*, February 7, 2000; Ross Kerber, "MTA Lives Court Toll-Use Data Spurs Privacy Fears About Fast Lane," *Boston Globe*, August 13, 2001; Ross Kerber, "The

Privacy Tradeoff," *Boston Globe*, January 8, 2001; "N.J. Prepares for High-Tech Road Toll System" *Baltimore Sun*, April 20, 1997.

16. Television broadcast, New York-WABC, August 6, 2001.

17. Alan Sipress, "'Big Brother' Could Soon Ride Along in Back Seat; Traffic Monitoring Stirs Privacy Fears," *Washington Post*, October 8, 2000.

18. "Traffic Command, Texas Style," *Geo Info Systems*, April 1, 1996.

19. Adam Clymer, "Bay Area Traffic Tracking Creates Concern for Privacy," *New York Times*, August 26, 2002.

20. "Cutting Edge" *Peoria (Ill.) Journal-Star*, July 24, 2001.

21. Matthew L. Wald, "Car 'Black Box' Reveals Details from Accidents," *New York Times*, May 30, 1999.

22. G. Chambers Williams III, "'Black Boxes' Stir Auto Controversy," *San Antonio Express-News*, May 21, 2000.

23. "Vehicle Tracker to Help Sort Insurance Claims," *Times of India*, February 6, 2002.

24. "Elite and Independent Witness Seek to Reduce Fraudulent Claims," Business Wire, July 23, 2001; Patrick Ponticel, "Everything Should Be Connected," *Automotive Engineering International*, December 1, 2000.

25. Simson Garfinkel, "Privacy and the New Technology: What They Do Know Can Hurt You," *The Nation*, February 28, 2000; Williams Cole, "Metrocard Meddling?" *Village Voice*, December 23, 1997.

26. "Chicago's CTA to Sell Transit Cards from Bank ATMs," *Bank Network News*, July 10, 2000.

27. Kurt Streeter, "Los Angeles: It's Decision Time for MTA in the Battle over Bus Service Transit," *Los Angeles Times*, January 9, 2002; John Mcquaid, "Unwelcome Neighbors: How the Poor Bear the Burdens of America's Pollution," *New Orleans Times-Picayune*, May 22, 2000; David R. Baker, "Bus Riders Blast Fare Hike Proposal During Hearing," *Los Angeles Daily News*, July 11, 1999; Eric Moses, "Fare Boycott Reaches Valley," *Los Angeles Daily News*, September 2, 1998.

28. "Cerebral Cortex Coaches Coming! Masterminds of Motorola Creating Brainy Metro Buses," PR Newswire, January 28, 2002.

29. Charles Russo, "Bugged on the Bus: Surveillance in the Aftermath of Terrorism," *San Francisco Bay Guardian*, September 19, 2001.

30. Jonah Cushman Jr., "Identification Cards Linked to Biometrics Considered," *Houston Chronicle*, January 20, 2002.

31. "NATA Working on Biometric ID Card for Travelers, Aviation Workers," *Weekly of Business Aviation*, November 19, 2001; "NATA to Adopt Private Approach to Passenger ID," *Aviation Daily*, November 13, 2001.

32. Robert O'Harrow Jr., "Air Security Network Advances; Lockheed to Develop Surveillance System to Check Travelers' Backgrounds," *Washington Post*,

March 1, 2003; "Paging Big Brother; Airline Security Plan Assaults Constitution," *Syracuse (N.Y.) Post-Standard*, March 4, 2003.

33. Alan Gathright, "No-Fly Blacklist Snares Political Activists," *San Francisco Chronicle*, September 27, 2002.

34. Ann Davis, "Far Afield: FBI's Post-Sept. 11 'Watch List' Mutates, Acquires Life of Its Own," *Wall Street Journal*, November 19, 2002; *Electronic Privacy Information Center v. Transportation Security Administration*, Complaint for Injunctive Relief, Filed in United States District Court for The District of Columbia.

CHAPTER 10: THE NEW TAYLORISM

1. This information is based on three interviews with a computer technician at Charles Schwab's headquarters in San Francisco, November 2000. All quotes from "Winston" are from these interviews.

2. *2001 Workplace Monitoring and Surveillance: Policies and Practices* (New York: American Management Association, 2001).

3. Pearl Washington, "Watching the Work Place," *Washington Post*, September 2, 1984.

4. Ibid.

5. Sidney Pollard, *The Genesis of Modern Management: A Study of the Industrial Revolution in Great Britain* (Cambridge, Mass.: Harvard University Press, 1965).

6. *Taylor's Testimony Before the Special House Committee*, in Frederick Winslow Taylor, *Scientific Management* (New York: Harper, 1947), p. 79. This book compiles Taylor's major works; all are paginated separately, and several are cited below.

7. Ibid., pp. 84–85.

8. Ibid., p. 83.

9. Harry Braverman, *Labor and Monopoly Capital: The Degradation of Work in the Twentieth Century* (New York: Monthly Review Press, 1974), p. 99.

10. Taylor, *Scientific Management*, p. 85.

11. Frederick Winslow Taylor, *The Principles of Scientific Management* (1911), reprinted in *Scientific Management*, pp. 48–49, 53.

12. Braverman, *Labor and Monopoly Capital*, p. 107.

13. Taylor, quoted in Braverman, *Labor and Monopoly Capital*, pp. 112, 113, 119.

14. Ibid., p. 107.

15. Aspect Communications Website: http://www.aspect.com/solutions/index.cfm, accessed July 1, 2002.

16. "The architect Tom Markus (1993) points out that work buildings are structures of control, encompassing physical control over raw materials and capital and social control over the utilization of labor power. Writers on the labour process have seen the factory or the mill as originating in the necessity to house and control the emergent social relations of the capitalist labor market": Christopher Baldry, "The Social Construction of Office Space," *International Labour Review* 136, no. 3 (October 11, 1997).

17. International Data Corporation, Framingham, Mass.; John Wagley, "Human Resources: I Spy," *Institutional Investor,* April 1, 2002.

18. Doug Hanchett, "Computer Goof-offs Beware: The Boss May Be Watching," *Boston Herald,* August 6, 2000.

19. Ibid.; "Victoria's Secret Attempts to Seduce Employees," *Business Wire,* May 16, 2000; "SurfCONTROL Helps Prevent Upcoming Webcast from Paralyzing Corporate Networks," Dow Jones News Service, February 4, 1999.

20. "Study Looks at Internet-Use Surveillance by Employers," Dow Jones Business News, July 9, 2001; "Web Study Raises Privacy Issue," *Milwaukee Journal Sentinel,* July 10, 2001.

21. Patti Ryan, "Daycare Goes Live to Air Digital Technology and the Internet Let Working Parents Peek in on Their Kids," *Toronto Globe and Mail,* May 25, 2001; Cindi Katz, "The State Goes Home: Local Hyper-Vigilance of Children and the Global Retreat from Social Reproduction," *Social Justice* 28, no. 3 (September 22, 2001); Tyler Hamilton, "Candid Cameras: Child Care Centres Are Experimenting with Web Cams That Let Parents Look in on Their Kids' Activities Via Internet—It May Be Fun But Is It Right?" *Toronto Star,* March 4, 2002.

22. Tammy Joyner, "Big Boss Is Watching," *Atlanta Constitution*, July 25, 2001.

23. Neil Irwin, "Security Software Spies on Workers; SilentRunner Finds Unusual Traffic,"*Washington Post*, August 17, 2001; William Jackson, "Security Pros Warned of Enemy Within," *Government Computer News*, November 19, 2001; http://www.silentrunner.com/default.asp (accessed July 1, 2002); http://www.raytheon.com/c3i/c3iproducts/c3i021/c3i021.htm (accessed July 1, 2002).

24. "Editors Pick," *PC Magazine*, July 1, 2002.

25. Jackson, "Security Pros Warned."

26. Greg Miller, "Hard Drive 'Truth Serum' Checks on Staff," *Winnipeg Free Press*, November 10, 2000.

27. Ibid.

28. *Intel Corporation v. Kourosh Kenneth Hamidi and Face-Intel*, Civ. A. No. 98AS05067 (Superior Court of the State of California, County of Sacramento).

29. Memorandum in support of appeal of defendants Griffin and Reeves from order requiring them to submit to a search of their personal computer equipment,

Northwest Airlines, Inc., Plaintives v. Teamsters Local 2000, et al., Defendants, Civil Action No. 00–08DWF/AJB, United States District Court for the District of Minnesota (March 8, 2000); and Memorandum in support of motion to dissolve temporary restraining order against individual defendants Ted Griffin and Kevin Reeves from order requiring them to submit to a search of their personal computer equipment, *Northwest Airlines, Inc., Plaintives v. Teamsters Local 2000, et al., Defendants*, Civil Action No. 00–08DWF/AJB, United States District Court for the District of Minnesota; Marica Stepanek,, "If Subpoenaed, Your PC's Hard Drive Is an Open Book," *Business Week Online*, May 11,2000.

30. For a description, see: http://pokky.net/ (accessed July1, 2002); interview with David Grubs, Pokky Systems technician and rep/dealer, November 2000.

31. Interview, Andre Ostabie, November, 2000.

32. Interview, Julia (pseudonym), waitress, October, 2000.

33. Mitch Irsfeld, New Foodservice Tools Could Flow from Microsoft's Expanded PDA Initiative, *Nation's Restaurant News*, May 29, 2000.

34. "Systech Delivers Solution for National Wholesale Liquidators," *Business Wire*, November 15, 2000.

35. Interview, Mary Hart, director of marketing, Loronix, November 2000; "Loronix Information Systems," *Advanced Imaging*, January 1, 2002; "Comverse Infosys' Loronix Division Expands Digital Video Surveillance and Security Coverage for Calgary Airport," *Business Wire*, November 30, 2001; "Visionics and Loronix Team to Add Facial Recognition Capability to Digital Video Platform," *Telecomworldwire*, October 18, 2001.

36. Amy Zuber, "Sandwich Chains Upgrade, Revamp Menus, Grow Portfolios to Tap into New Markets," *Nation's Restaurant News*, June 24, 2002; Alan J. Liddle, "Hand-Holding Increasingly in Vogue Among Operators Looking to Technology for an Edge," *Nation's Restaurant News*, October 30, 2000.

37. Dina Berta, "It's No Mystery: Secret Shoppers Can Improve Service," *Nation's Restaurant News*, November 6, 2000.

38. Richard Newman, "New Jersey Bank Wages a Battle to Regain Consumer Confidence," *Hackensack (N.J.) Record*, November 19, 2000.

39. Kathryn Rem, "Managers Send in Secret Shoppers to Report Back on Customer Service," *St. Louis Post-Dispatch*, April 7, 2002.

40. Interview, Mary Alice Martinez, RN, November 2000; interview, Bob Lee, director of nursing, Mid-Peninsula Medical Center, November 2000; John Borsos, director of organizing, SEIU Local 250, November 2000; Hill-rom website: www.hill-rom.com (accessed, November 13, 2000).

41. Carol Birkland, "When Every Mile Counts," *Fleet Equipment*, May 1, 2002. It is worth noting that in Victoria, Australia, this sort of monitoring is illegal: "The Surveillance Devices Act, introduced by the former government of

Jeff Kennett in 1999, makes such practices unlawful without the consent of each driver or the union that represents them." See "GPS Truck Bosses Risk Jail, " ABIX—Australasian Business Intelligence: *The Daily Telegraph*, March 23, 2002.

42. John Mesenbrink, "Biometrics Keeps on Truckin'," *Security*, June 1, 2002.

43. ADPRO, "Security and Surveillance for the Trucking Industry," n.d.

44. Christian Parenti, "Atlas Finally Shrugged: Us Against Them in the Me Decade," *The Baffler*, no. 13 (Winter 1999).

45. Interview, Charles Richardson, director, Labor Extension, Technology & Work Programs, University of Massachusetts, Lowell, October 2000.

46. See http://www.ups.com/about/story.html.

47. Jeremy Schlosberg, "Hell on Wheels: Help Wanted, Truck Drivers. Great Pay, Spectacular Benefits, Abusive Bosses. Apply to UPS, Greenwich, Connecticut," *New England Monthly*, January 1988.

48. Ibid.

49. Ibid.

50. This and following sections based on interviews with Ken Sternad, United Parcel Service, vice president for public relations, October 2000; Joan Schnorburt, United Parcel Service, Public Relations Dept., October/November 2000; Ken Shapir, United Parcel Service, Aviation Technologies, October, 2000; Pat Canavan, UPS vice president for package project management, November, 2000.

51. Interview, Charles Richardson.

52. Interview, Steve Henderson, a UPS driver, November, 2000.

53. Interview, Steve Early, Communication Workers of America representative and journalist, November 2000; John Miceli, Communication Workers of America, vice president, Local 1298, November 2000.

54. Joyner, "Big Boss Is Watching."

55. Dyer-Witheford, *Cyber-Marx*, p. 85.

CHAPTER 11: THE BENEVOLENT GAZE

1. James C. Scott, *Seeing Like a State: How Certain Schemes to Improve the Human Condition Have Failed* (New Haven, Conn.: Yale University Press, 1999); John Gilliom, *Overseers of the Poor: Surveillance, Resistance, and the Limits of Privacy* (Chicago: University of Chicago Press, 2001); Leslie Margolin, *Under the Cover of Kindness: The Invention of Social Work* (Charlottesville, Va.: University Press of Virginia, 1997.

2. For a full account of this history, see David J. Rothman, *The Discovery of the Asylum: Social Order and Disorder in the New Republic* (New York: Walter de Gruyter, 2002); Michel Foucault, *Madness and Civilization: A History of Insanity in the Age of Reason* (New York: Vintage, 1973), and *Discipline and Punish: The Birth of the Prison* (New York: Vintage, 1979).

3. Michael B. Katz, *In the Shadow of the Poorhouse: A Social History of Welfare in America* (New York: Basic Books, 1986), p. 11.

4. Frances Fox Piven and Richard A. Cloward, *Regulating the Poor: The Functions of Public Welfare* (New York: Vintage, 1971), p. 47.

5. Katz, *Poorhouse*, p. 18. As Piven and Cloward point out, taxonomies of the poor are very old in the west: "Even before the sixteenth century, the magistrates of Basel had defined twenty-five different categories of beggars together with appropriate punishments for each" (Piven and Cloward, *Regulating the Poor*, p. 8).

6. *Fifth Annual Report, Constitution and By-Laws of the Baltimore Association for the Improvement of the Condition of the Poor, November 1854* (Baltimore: John Woods, Printer), p. 7. This document is held in the open stacks of Social Work Library of Columbia University.

7. Katz, *Poorhouse*.

8. On this transformation, see Katz, *Poorhouse*; Karen W. Tice, *Tales of Wayward Girls and Immoral Women: Case Records and the Professionalization of Social Work* (Chicago: University of Illinois, 1998); John Ehrenreich, *The Altruistic Imagination: A History of Social Work and Social Policy in the United States* (Ithaca, N.Y.: Cornell University Press, 1985).

9. Baltimore Association for the Improvement of the Condition of the Poor, *Report*, p. 7.

10. "Hand-Book for Friendly Visitors Among the Poor," Charity Organization Society, 1883, Community Service Society Collection, Box 99, casework—friendly visitor folder, Rare Books and Manuscripts Library, Columbia University.

11. The best article on this cultural transformation is still the classic one: E.P. Thompson, "Time, Work Discipline, and Industrial Capitalism," *Past and Present* 38 (December 1967); for another angle of the culture of industrialism, see Max Weber, *The Protestant Ethic and the Spirit of Capitalism* (New York: Routledge, 2001); R.H. Tawney, *Religion and the Rise of Capitalism* (New York: Mentor, 1948).

12. "Charities Reference Card," Charity Organization Society of Baltimore City, 1899. This document is held in the open stacks of Social Work Library of Columbia University.

13. "Some Facts About the Child-Beggars," Charity Organization Society of Baltimore City, 1894. This document is held in the open stacks of Social Work Library of Columbia University.

14. Katz, *Poorhouse*, p. 58.

15. Tice, *Tales of Wayward Girls*, p. 20.

16. Ibid., p. 38

17. Ibid., p. 46.

18. The emergence of social work as a formal field dates from 1898 with the opening of the first professional social work training school as an annual summer course run by the New York Charity Organization Society. As for the interconnection between social work and corrections: in 1879 the Conference of Boards of Public Charities was renamed the National Conference of Charities and Corrections.

19. Quoted in Tice, *Tales of Wayward Girls*, p. 49.

20. "Report of Committee on Case Record Writing and Written Reports," n.d. (circa 1924), Community Service Society Collection, Box 98, casework committee folder, Rare Books and Manuscripts Library, Columbia University.

21. Ibid.

22. "The Mayos," Social Case Histories, series II, Group A no. 1, October 1920, Community Service Society Collection, Box 98, casework committee on methods folder, Rare Books and Manuscripts Library, Columbia University.

23. "Report of Committee," op. cit.

24. "Memorandum," notes on case #126241, November 17, 1916, Community Service Society Collection, Box 99, casework difficult-cases committee folder, Rare Books and Manuscripts Library, Columbia University.

25. "The Mayos."

26. "A Belated Analysis," Social Case Histories, series II, Group B no. 1, October 1920, Community Service Society Collection, Box 98, casework committee on methods folder, Rare Books and Manuscripts Library, Columbia University.

27. "A Musician's Family," Social Case Histories, series II, Group A no. 2, October 1920, Community Service Society Collection, Box 98, case work committee on methods folder, Rare Books and Manuscripts Library, Columbia University.

28. Cited in Tice, *Tales of Wayward Girls*, p. 31.

29. Ibid., p. 32.

30. Ibid.

31. Alexander Johnson, *Adventures in Social Welfare* (Fort Wayne, Ind.: Fort Wayne Printing, 1923), p. 289; Tice, *Tales of Wayward Girls*, p. 32.

32. Tice, *Tales of Wayward Girls*.

33. Linda Gordon, *Pitied But Not Entitled: Single Mothers and the History of Welfare* (New York: Free Press, 1994).

34. Margolin, *Under the Cover of Kindness*, p. 97.

35. Frances Fox Piven and Richard A. Cloward, *Regulating the Poor: The Functions of Public Welfare* (New York: Random House, 1971); *Poor People's Move-*

ments: Why They Succeed, How They Fail (New York: Random House, 1979); *The New Class War* (New York: Random House, 1982).

36. Piven and Cloward, *Regulating the Poor*, pp. 164–65.

37. Quoted in ibid.

38. Lawrence Mead, *Beyond Entitlement: The Social Obligations of Citizenship* (New York: Free Press, 1986), p. ix.

39. Ibid., pp. 13, 84–85.

40. Ibid., pp. 7, 9, 10.

41. Judy Wiessler, "INS Wants to Deny Welfare to Illegal Aliens," *Houston Chronicle*, March 10, 1985.

42. Pete Earley, "Watching Me, Watching You: A Growing Government Computer Network That Makes a Mockery of Privacy," *Washington Post Magazine*, May 11, 1986.

43. Ibid.

44.Eric Conrad, "Welfare to Use Photo Cards for Paying Clients in Philly," *Harrisburg Patriot*, March 12, 1987.

45. GAO/OSI–95–20 "Use of Biometrics in Proposed EBT Program," p. 2.

46. Kelly Richmond, "Reshaping the Welfare State," *The Record* (Northern New Jersey), June 19, 1994; William Claiborne, "Federal, State Benefits Systems Move Toward Cashless Automation," *Washington Post*, June 1, 1994.

47. Gilliom, *Overseers of the Poor*, p. 78.

48. Christopher D. Cook, "Swiping Benefits," *The Progressive*, March, 1999; Christopher D. Cook, "To Combat Welfare Fraud, States Reach for Debit Cards," *Christian Science Monitor*, May 25, 1999.

49. "Aid-Recipient Fingerprinting Condemned," *San Francisco Chronicle*, May 22, 2000; Katti Gray, "Fingerprinting Welfare Clients: Suffolk Lawmakers Move to Decrease Fraud," *Newsday*, September 15, 1993; Katti Gray, "Lazio Plan on Welfare Fraud," *Newsday*, January 12, 1994.

50. Joseph P. Fried, "Prosecuting Welfare Fraud Ineffective, Judge Says," *New York Times*, June 24, 1993.

51. Gilliom, *Overseers of the Poor*, p. 95.

CHAPTER 12: THE EYE OF JUSTICE

1. Interview with Russ Heimrich, California Department of Corrections, March 12, 2001.

2. "According to the Bureau of Justice Statistics (BJS), on Dec. 31, 2000, there were 3.8 million offenders on probation, approximately 725,000 offenders on parole,

and more than 2 million offenders incarcerated in either prisons or jails." Larry Solomon and Cranston Mitchell, "From Prison to the Community," *Corrections Today*, August 1, 2002; Jonathan D. Salant,"1 in 32 Behind Bars or on Probation," *Wisconsin State Journal*, August 26, 2002; For a snapshot of a big- city probation department, see the Los Angeles County Probation Department's website. In LA during fall 2002 approximately 46,000 adults were under its supervision, as were approximately 12,000 minors. Approximately 65 percent of these adult probationers were also subject to some type of computer-based monitoring.

3. "Trends in State Parole," Special Report, Bureau of Justice Statistics, October 2001, NCJ 184735; Atiya Hussain, "From Crowded U.S. Prisons Comes Unwieldy Problem," Reuters News, August 21, 2002;. It's true that the system contains many violent offenders, but 51 percent of all state and federal prisoners are serving time not for violence but for drug, property, and public order offences (Bureau of Justice Statistics, US Department of Justice, summary findings, December 31, 2001, at http://www.ojp.usdoj.gov/bjs/prisons.htm).

4. "Prisoner Releases: Trends and Information on Reintegration Programs," GAO–01–483, June 18, 2001, p. 3.

5. Ralph Frammolino, "Tally of Cons Paroled to County Up 20% in Year," *Los Angeles Times*, February 15, 1990.

6. Interview with Russ Heimrich, California Department of Corrections, March 12, 2001.

7. Bureau of Justice Statistics, "Trends in State Parole."

8. Melanie Lefkowitz, "Helping Ex-Convicts Shift from Prison to Society," *Newsday*, July 14, 2002.

9. "Preventing Parolee Failure Program: An Evaluation." (Sacramento, Calif.: California Department of Corrections, 1997).

10. Brian Kates, "Shelters Besieged by Ex-Cons, Crisis of Drugs, Crime," *New York Daily News*, April 7, 2002.

11. See Christian Parenti, *Lockdown America: Police and Prisons in the Age of Crisis* (London: Verso, 2000).

12. George M. Anderson, "Parole Revisited," *America*, March 4, 2002.

13. Jerome Skolnick, *Search and Destroy: African American Males in the Criminal Justice System* (New York: Cambridge University Press, 1996), p. 131.

14. Solomon Moore, "Hard Time," *Los Angeles Times Magazine*, February 4, 2001.

15. Leif B. Strickland, "Tighter Reins: Tough Parole Program Keeps Tabs on Offenders," *Dallas Morning News*, August 8, 1999. There are times when it's really hard not to enjoy such sentences. For example: "A Beverly Hills neurosurgeon, convicted of being a slumlord, was ordered to spend 30 days in one of his rundown, rat-infested buildings, with an electric device strapped to his ankle to assure

authorities he had not left" (Joseph R. Tybor "Unusually Creative Judges Now Believe Some Punishments Can Fit the Times," *Chicago Tribune*, July 3, 1988).

16. Michael C. Coleman, "No Jail Space for Offenders," *Houston Chronicle*, March 17, 1990; Amy Pyle, "Teens 'Jailed' But Don't Go Behind Bars: Surveillance Device Keeps Youths Home," *Los Angeles Times*, October 4, 1989; "Punishment Without Imprisonment," *Boston Globe*, May 15, 1991; Sheryl Nance "Corrections Group Urges Alternatives to Jail," *New York Law Journal*, April 20, 1990.

17. John Making, "'Star Wars' Meets 'Police Story,'" *Houston Chronicle*, August 14, 1987.

18. Matthew P. Blanchard, "Satellite Monitoring Network Creates Virtual Jail for Suspects," *Pittsburgh Post-Gazette*, September 9, 2001; Stuart Pfeifer, "O.C. to Track Sex Criminals with GPS Probation," *Los Angeles Times*, December 23, 2001.

19. Quote from, Blanchard, "Satellite Monitoring"; for other details, see the newscast "Law Enforcement Agents Using GPS to Keep Track of Parolees," *CBS News: Morning News*, March 4, 2002. Some of the latest technology seems to come from the repertoire of wildlife management, as *Corrections* magazine explained: "Field monitoring devices, or 'drive-by' units, are another type of continuous signaling technology. Probation or parole officers or other authorities use a portable device that can be hand-held or used in a vehicle with a roof-mounted antenna. When within 200 to 800 feet of an offender's ankle or wrist transmitter, the portable device can detect the radio signals of the offender's transmitter." See Ann H Crowe, "Electronic Supervision: From Decision-Making to Implementation Offender," *Corrections Today*, August 1, 2002. For a comprehensive overview, see Ann Crowe et al., *Supervision with Electronic Technology* (Lexington, Ky.: American Probation and Parole Association, 2002).

20. Blanchard, "Satellite Monitoring"; For the current number from the Florida Department of Corrections, which had 900 people under electronic supervision in 2002, see http://www.dc.state.fl.us/pub/annual/0001/stats/stat_cs.html.

21. "New York to Receive Federal Funds for Offender Reentry Efforts," press release, Department of Justice, Office of Justice Programs July 15, 2002; Blanchard, "Satellite Monitoring."

22. Jean Rimbach, "N.J. Tests Satellites to Monitor Juvenile Parolees," *The Record* (Northern New Jersey), April 1, 1998.

23. Julia C. Martinez, "Satellites May Shed Light on Parolees," *Denver Post*, July 17, 2001.

24. Del Quentin Wilber, "Teens Slip Monitors, Are Held in Killings," *Baltimore Sun*, July 31, 2002; "Teens Accused of Killings After Removing Monitors," Associated Press Newswire, July 31, 2002.

25. "Caught Red-Ankled," *Houston Chronicle*, November 17, 1989.

26. On the LEAA, see, Christian Parenti, *Lockdown America: Police and Prisons in the Age of Crisis* (Verso: London, 1999).

27. "The Region," *Los Angeles Times*, June 4, 1986.

28. Denise Hamilton, "Shooting of Youth Marks Escalation of Gang Violence to a Deadlier Level," *Los Angeles Times*, April 6, 1989; "Supervisors Approve $404,000 for Anti-Gang Unit in DA's Office," *Orange County Register*, March 23, 1988.

29. "Guardsman Will Take on Gangs with Computer," *Portland Oregonian*, July 13, 1989.

30. Terry Hyland, "Phoenix Officer to Omaha: You Can Beat Gangs," *Omaha World-Herald*, Saturday, April 21, 1990.

31. James Tortolano, "Countywide Anti-Gang Agency Would Cover 3 Cities," *Los Angeles Times*, December 11, 1989.

32. Leslie Berger, "Gang Statistics Compiled in Vast Database," *Los Angeles Times*, May 22, 1992; "Half of Young L.A. Blacks Tied to Gangs," *St. Petersburg Times*, May 22, 1992.

33. Keith M. Jajko, "Computer System to Aid Simi Police Track Gangs," *Los Angeles Daily News*, July 28, 1992.

34. *Orange County Weekly*, July 11—17, 1997, p. 10.

35. Ray Dussault, "CAL/GANG Brings Dividends," *Government Technology*, December, 1998.

36. Interview, Lt. Marin Rivera, MAGEC, October 26, 1998.

37. For the California law, see California Penal Code, Street Terrorism Enforcement and Prevention Act, chapter 11, section 186.20–186.27. A growing number of states also have "gang enhancement status"; for example, Utah, Arizona, Tennessee, and Florida have laws similar to California's ("Governor OKs Laws to Fight Drugs, Gangs," *Orange County Register*, September 25, 1988).

38. "National Threat Warning System Update: Continued Use of NCIC after 2002 Winter Olympic Games," *Police Chief*, April 1, 2002.

39. Cited in congressional testimony for fiscal year 1998, submitted by Gerald P. Lynch, Esq., executive director, Middle Atlantic–Great Lakes Organized Crime Law Enforcement Network on behalf of the Regional Information Sharing Systems (RISS) program, April 17, 1997; David Garland, *The Culture of Control: Crime and Social Order in Contemporary Society* (Chicago: University of Chicago Press, 2001); David Garland, *Punishment and Modern Society: A Study in Social Theory* (Chicago: University of Chicago Press, 1993); David Garland ed., *Mass Imprisonment: Social Causes and Consequences* (New York: Sage, 2001).

40. "Cincinnati Prepares for More Unrest," *Washington Post*, April 12, 2001; Cincinnati Suffers More Rioting over Police Shooting," *St. Louis Post-Dispatch*, April 11, 2001; Amy DePaul and Peter Slevin, "Cincinnati Officials Impose Curfew; Mayor Acknowledges Race Woes as City Acts to Quell Violence," *Washington*

Post, April 13, 2001; Liz Sidoti, "Cincinnati Violence Festered," *Tulsa (Okla.) World*, April 14, 2001. The Ohio State Attorney General's Office was using Cincinnati's gang intelligence database as the template for a new statewide system to be called Project GUARD (Gang Unit Access and Research Database). See Jennifer Edwards, "City a Model for Gangbusters," *Cincinnati Post*, March 2, 2001. Numerous other states that are already linked to the Feds are expanding and upgrading their internal local and regional networks. See "Today's News Update," *New York Law Journal*, April 24, 2002; "National Threat Warning System Update"; Don Thompson, "Consultant Capitalizes on Ties to U.S. Homeland Security Chief," Associated Press Newswire, December 17, 2001. As this article pointed out, "The nearly $3 billion-a-year company hasn't asked Ridge's permission to use his image now that he's in his new job, but it wasn't a problem before, said Jeannette Gang, a KPMG managing director"; Mark Perbix, "Automating Arrest Warrants Between Courts and Law Enforcement," *Police Chief*, October 1, 2001.

41. Adam Taylor, "Police Photo Squads Under Fire," *News Journal*, August 25, 2002; Oliver Burkeman, "U.S. City Where You Can Be Guilty Until Proven Innocent," *The Guardian* (London), August 27, 2002; "Wilmington Police Photograph Future Suspects," Associated Press Newswire, August 25, 2002.

42. Burkeman, "U.S. City."

43. Taylor, "Police Photo Squads."

44. Statement of Nancy Kingsbury, managing director, Applied Research and Methods, congressional testimony, March 12, 2003; Jane Black, "At Justice, NSEERS Spells Data Chaos," *Business Week*, May 2, 2003

45. Richard Benke, "Database Files Faces, Fingerprints of Illegal Immigrants," *Denver Post*, June 21, 1998; INS press office statistics; congressional testimony of Glenn A. Fine, inspector general, US Department of Justice, Technology and Immigration Enforcement, Friday, October 12, 2001.

46. Ann Davis, "Plan to Fingerprint Visitors to U.S. Raises Many Doubts," *Wall Street Journal*, July 31, 2002. On the turf battles between agencies, see Shane Harris, "Bureaucratic Battles Bog Down Biometrics," *Government Executive*, January 1, 2002.

47. Marjorie Valbrun, "INS Gains Ground as Turf Wars Ease Agencies' Increased Cooperation Helps Nab Criminal Immigrants," *Wall Street Journal*, April 24, 2002.

48. David Lyon, *The Electronic Eye: The Rise of Surveillance Society* (Minneapolis: University of Minnesota Press: 1994).

49. Joseph R. Greene, assistant commissioner for investigations, US Immigration and Naturalization Service "INS Interior Enforcement," congressional testimony, June 19, 2002; interview, Michael Flynn, assistant director for investigations in the INS's Western Region, February 1998.

50. Michael Flynn, interview.

51. Parenti, *Lockdown America*, p. 149.

52. Robin Herman, "British Police Embrace 'DNA Fingerprints'; But These Gene Scans Worry Civil Libertarians," *Washington Post*, November 24, 1987; David Perlman, "Police Advised on Using DNA to Solve Crimes," *San Francisco Chronicle*, January 8, 1988.

53. Susan Moffat, "Plan for DNA Database Assailed," *Los Angeles Times*, January 16, 1992.

54. Selwyn Raab, "Cuomo Seeks Genetic Data of Offenders," *New York Times*, May 10, 1992.

55. Public Law 103–322; Karen Young Kreeger, "Dramatic Growth in DNA-Based Forensics Doesn't Translate into Job Opportunities," *The Scientist*, April. 17, 1995.

56. Pierre Thomas and Mike Mills, "FBI Crime Laboratory Being Probed; Scientist Alleges Conclusions Were Altered to Help Prosecute Cases," *Washington Post*, September 14, 1995; Pierre Thomas "Justice Dept. Probe Casts Shadow on FBI Lab Data," *Washington Post*, January 31, 1997; Damian Whitworth, "Why My Son Should Not Have Died," *The Times* (London), Wednesday, July 11, 2001.

57. Karen F. Donovan, "Florida Court Receptive to DNA Evidence," *National Law Journal*, 13, no. 34, (April 29, 1991).

58. "110 Wrongful Convictions, and Counting," *New York Times*, August 27, 2002.

59. Randolph E. Schmid, "DNA's No Minuscule Molecule; Gene Code Called upon to Solve Major Mysteries," *Denver Post*, August 8, 1998.

60. Congressional testimony of Barry Steinhardt, associate director, American Civil Liberties Union, National Commission on the Future of DNA Evidence, Monday, March 1, 1999.

61. Michael Moss and Ford Fessenden, "New Tools for Domestic Spying, and Qualms," *New York Times*, December 10, 2002; Chisun Lee, "Nation's Largest Law Enforcement Agency Vies for Total Spying Power: The NYPD Wants to Watch You," *Village Voice*, December 18, 2002.

CHAPTER 13: VOYEURISM AND SECURITY CULTURE

1. Phil Fisher, "Lost Innocence," *Cincinnati Enquirer*, September 8, 2002.

2. John Hanchette, "Terrorism Portents for Future: American Culture Faces Huge Change," *Gannett News Service*, September 11, 2001.

3. Chris Coursey, "Another Day That Will Live in Infamy," *Santa Rosa (Calif.) Press Democrat*, September 12, 2001.

4. Slavoj Zizek, "The Desert of the Real," *In These Times*, October 29, 2001. For a longer, but not necessarily better, version of the same arguments, see Slavoj Zizek, *Welcome to the Desert of the Real: Five Essays on September 11 and Related Dates* (London: Verso, 2002).

5. Pew Research Center for the People & the Press, "Survey Report: Americans Favor Force in Iraq, Somalia, Sudan and Other Important Findings," January 22, 2002; quoted from the web page http://people-press.org/reports/display.php3?PageID=186. Interestingly the survey found that "more educated, higher income, and middle-aged (30–64 year old) people are the most likely to believe sacrifices will be necessary."

6. Pew Research Center for the People & the Press, "Survey Report: Domestic Concerns Will Vie with Terrorism in Fall Criticisms of Bush and Congress as Job Worries Increase," June 27, 2002. Available at http://people-press.org/reports/display.php3?PageID=621.

7. Mark Crispin Miller, *Boxed In: The Culture of TV* (Evanston, Ill.: Northwestern University Press, 1988), p. 19.

8. Anyone familiar with Volume One of *Capital* will recognize the arguments here.

9. Umberto Eco, *Travels in Hyperreality* (New York: Harcourt Brace Jovanovich, 1986), pp. 7, 9.

10. J. Clay, "Show Makes Springer Look Like Playdays," *Leicester Mercury*, August 9, 2001; Ross Warneke, "High Infidelity Lowers the Tone," *The Age* (Australia), January 17, 2002.

11. Caryn James, "Taking a Chance When There's Nothing at Stake, *New York Times*, July 28, 2002; Bill Mann, "Reality TV Turns to Torture," *Santa Rosa (Calif.) Press Democrat*, March 3, 2002. See also www.cheater.com.

12. "Children's Center to Aid Missing and Exploited," *Washington Post*, April 20, 1984; *Omaha World-Herald*, January 25, 1984.

13. "WFLD to Premiere 'America's Most Wanted,'" PR Newswire, January 29, 1988.

14. Jeffrey Yorke, "Landover Neighbors Relive Night of Horror When 5 Were Slain," *Washington Post*, March 11, 1988.

15. Ibid.

16. "New TV Show Helps Capture Some of Nation's Most-Wanted Fugitives," *St. Petersburg Times*, March 30, 1988.

17. Simon Firth, "Live! From My Bedroom," *Salon*, January 8, 1998; http://archive.salon.com /21st/feature/1998/01/cov_08feature.html.

18. Mary Beth Oliver, "Influences of Authoritarianism and Portrayals of Race on Caucasian Viewers' Responses to Reality-Based Crime Dramas," *Communication Reports* 9 (1996); Mary Beth Oliver and G. Blake Armstrong, "The Color of

Crime: Perceptions of Caucasians' and African Americans' Involvement in Crime," in Mark Fishman and Gray Cavender, eds., *Entertaining Crime: Television Reality Programs*, (New York: Aldine de Gruyter, 1998).

19. "Cable TV Industry Sells Home Security Services," Dow Jones News Service–Edited *Wall Street Journal* Stories, September 15, 1981.

20. "Alarm Systems That Pay Off in Peace of Mind," *Business Week*, April 10, 1989; David Colker, "Weird and Wonderful Are on Display at Vegas Expo," *Los Angeles Times*, January 10, 2002.

21. It's worth noting that 90+ percent of private home security alarms are false. Michael Cohen, "Home Secure Home Crime Is Down, But Demand for Security Systems Is Way Up," *Boston Globe*, April 26, 1999; Kenneth Lelen, "Security Blankets for the Home; Pace of Installations Rises Despite Drop in Burglary Rate," *Washington Post*, December 26, 1998.

22. Steven D. Levitt, "The Changing Relationship Between Income and Crime Victimization," *Economic Policy Review* 5, no. 3 (September 1999).

23. Cara Nissman, "Turning Your Castle into a Fortress with Updated Security Systems," *Boston Herald*, November 8, 2001.

24.http://www.wherifywireless.com/prod_watches.htm (October 2002).

25. Colker, "Weird and Wonderful."

26. http://whereify.com/flash.htm (October 2002).

27. Average prices based on data from various websites and an interview with Kevin Wolf, public relations spokesperson for @Road, October 27, 2002.

28. See http://www.intellicamspy.com/vehicle_tracker.htm (October 2002).

29. Cindi Katz, "The State Goes Home: Local Hyper-Vigilance of Children and the Global Retreat from Social Reproduction," *Social Justice* 28, no. 3 (2001), pp. 51, 54.

30. Communication to author, March 2003.

31. Denise Abbott, "Sense of Security: High-Tech Defense Measures Can Help Home Owners Sleep Easy in Uncertain Times," *Hollywood Reporter*, June 21, 2002; Peter Hartlaub, "Safe House, High-end 'Panic Room' Hideouts Becoming More Common," *San Francisco Chronicle*, April 8, 2002.

32. Interview with Gary Paster of the American Safe Room Door Corporation, October 2002.

33. Robert K. Merton, *Social Theory and Social Structure*, rev. edn. (New York: The Free Press, 1968).

34. Peter Worsley, *The Trumpet Shall Sound: A Study of Cargo Cults in Melanesia* (New York: Schocken, 1958,1990); Dana Calvo, "Opening a Door to Panic Rooms," *Los Angeles Times*, March 27, 2002; Bobbie Leigh, "An Alarming Trend: Bulletproof Living," *Wall Street Journal*, November 29, 1996.

35. Christy Gutowski, "Foster Parents Accused of Horrific Abuse; Prosecutors Say Videotape Shows Beating of Mentally Disabled Boy," *Chicago Daily Herald*, October 2, 2002; Christy Gutowski, "State Exploring Why Abuse Wasn't Detected," *Chicago Daily Herald*, October 3, 2002; Stacy St. Clair, "More Details of Beating Revealed at Hearing," *Chicago Daily Herald*, October 10, 2002.

CHAPTER 14: FEAR AS INSTITUTION

1. Ted Bridis, "FBI Memo Details Surveillance Lapses in Terror, Spy Cases," Associated Press, October 10, 2002; "One Year Later," *Nation*, September 23, 2002.

2. Dan Eggen, "FBI Misused Secret Wiretaps, According to Memo," *Washington Post*, October 10, 2002.

3. "USA Patriot Act Boosts Government Powers While Cutting Back on Traditional Checks and Balances," ACLU Legislative Analysis on USA PATRIOT Act, November 1, 2001; USA PATRIOT Act—An Analysis by the ACLU, January 12, 2002; *Civil Liberties After 9–11: The ACLU Defends Freedom*, September 20, 2002

4. See http://www.eff.org/Privacy/Surveillance/Terrorism_militias/20011031_eff_usa_patriot_analysis.html.

5. Ibid.

6. See http://www.darpa.mil/iao/.

7. Jeffery Rosen "Total Information Awareness," in "The Year in Ideas," *New York Times Magazine*, December 15,2002.

8. The real total for TIA funding comes from the EPIC (http://www.epic.org/events/tia_briefing). In many ways TIA is the worst-case scenario, the end result of proliferating digital everyday surveillance. When I began this book, the attacks of 9/11 had not yet happened, TIA did not exist, and my argument called on readers to *imagine* the digitalized informational landscape that could be centrally monitored with a something like TIA. Much has changed since then and one need not try and imagine anything since the critical imagination has once again been overtaken by the implementation of actual policies.

9. Peter Lewis, "At Last," *Fortune*, December 30, 2002; William Safire," You are a Suspect," *New York Times*, November 14, 2002; William New, "Back to the Future," *National Journal*, June 14, 2002; William New, "The Poindexter Plan," *National Journal*, September 7, 2002. For one of the earliest mentions, see "Statement by Dr. Tony Tether, Director, Defense Advanced Research Projects Agency, Submitted to the Subcommittee on Emerging Threats and Capabilities, Committee

on Armed Services United States Senate," "Fiscal 2003 Defense Request: Combating Terrorism," April 10, 2002.

10. "Total Information Awareness," *Washington Post*, November 16, 2002.

11 For discussion of this point, see William Safire, "You are a Suspect"; Matthew Engel, "This Perfect System," *Guardian* (London), November 19, 2002.

12. John Markoff and John Swartz, "Bush Administration to Propose System for Wide Monitoring of Internet," *New York Times*, Friday December 20, 2002.

13. Christine Chinlund, "Getting the Rest of the Story," (op-ed) *Boston Globe*, September 23, 2002; Clarence Page "The Failings of Arab Profiling," *Chicago Tribune*, September 22, 2002; Democracy Now, September 24, 2002; see http://www.webactive.com/pacifica/demnow/dn20020924.html.

14. Daniel Levitas, "The Radical Right After 9/11," *Nation*, July 22, 2002.

15. John Giuffo and Joshua Lipton, "Reverberations," *Columbia Journalism Review*, January 1, 2002.

16. *Chicago Tribune*, December 20, 2002.

17. Henry Weinstein and Greg Krikorian, "Caught Between Dueling Policies," *Los Angeles Times*, December 21, 2002.

18. *Los Angeles Daily News*, December 19, 2002.

19. State Department press releases and documents, Federal Information & News Dispatch, Inc., December 13, 2002. According to this press release, "SEVIS implements section 641 of the Illegal Immigration Reform and Immigrant Responsibility Act (IIRIRA) of 1996. IIRIRA requires the INS to collect current information on an ongoing basis from schools and exchange programs relating to non-immigrant foreign students and exchange visitors during the course of their stay in the United States. In addition, the USA PATRIOT Act amended section 641 to require full implementation of SEVIS prior to January 1, 2003. In addition, the Enhanced Border Security and Visa Entry Reform Act of 2002 adds to and clarifies the requirement to collect information, as well as requires an educational institution to report any failure of an alien to enroll no later than 30 days after registration deadline."

20. Ann Davis, "Some Colleges Balk at FBI Request for Data on Foreigners," *Wall Street Journal*, November 25, 2002.

21. *Olmstead v. United States*, 277 U.S. 438 (1928).

22. Neil Howe and William Strauss, "Through Prism of Tragedy, Generations Are Defined," *Christian Science Monitor*, September 23, 2002.

23. Milton Mayer, *They Thought They Were Free: The Germans 1933–1945* (Chicago: University of Chicago Press, 1955), pp. 166 –72.

24. Sophocles, cited in Charles Grove Haines, *The Revival of Natural Law Concepts: A Study of the Establishment and of the Interpretation of Limits on Legislatures with Special Reference to the Development of Certain Phases of American Constitutional Law* (Cambridge, Mass.: Harvard University Press, 1930), p. 5.

25. Sec. 228. See online at http://www.constitution.org/jl/2ndtreat.htm.

26. Among its fans were Ho Chi Minh and Fidel Castro.

27. Elizabeth Cady Stanton, "The Seneca Falls Declaration, Adopted in Convention, 1848." See online at http://www.constitution.org/woll/seneca.htm.

28. Henry David Thoreau, *On the Duty of Civil Disobedience* [1849, original title: *Resistance to Civil Government*] quote from electronic version, no page numbers. See: http://www.constitution.org/civ/civildis.htm.

INDEX

INDEX

Lightning Source UK Ltd.
Milton Keynes UK
UKOW050426181011

180483UK00002B/80/A